Contents

W9-ADT-532

Illustrations

Plates

Acknowledgments

I would like to recognize several colleagues whose insights have been helpful in developing this project: John V. Murra, to whom my greatest debt is owed, and also Lucille Kerr, Roberto González Echevarría, Walter Mignolo, Ciriaco Morón Arroyo, Frank Salomon, and David I. Grossvogel. To others whose scholarly interest in Hispanic and Andean cultures has enhanced my own I am also grateful: Sara Castro-Klarén, Raquel Chang-Rodríguez, Pierre Duviols, Regina Harrison, Mercedes López-Baralt, Julio Ortega, Juan Ossio, Franklin Pease, and Jorge Urioste. To my Syracuse colleague JoAnn Cannon go special thanks for reading an earlier version of the manuscript.

For permission to reprint portions of the 1980 edition of the *Nueva corónica y buen gobierno*, which John Murra and I coedited, I am indebted to Siglo Veintiuno Editores, Mexico City. An earlier version of chapter 4 previously appeared in *Studies in the Anthropology of Visual Communication* (vol. 5, no. 2: 78–96), and sections of chapters 3 and 5 were first published in *Dispositio, Revista Hispánica de Semiótica Literaria* (vol. 4, no. 10: 27–47). I wish to thank the editors of those journals for permission to use these materials.

I am grateful to Syracuse University, and especially to Louis W. Roberts, for the encouragement and support I received for the preparation of this book.

This book is dedicated to my husband, David S. Adorno, who has accompanied me on the long journey from European royal libraries to Peruvian colonial mining towns in search of "el autor Ayala."

Guaman Poma

Introduction

In the pages that follow I have attempted to perform an act of decolonization in the forum of historical literary scholarship. My work began as a response to the writers and commentators of Spanish American literary history who summarily dismissed the writings of the small handful of ethnic Americans who were, in effect, members of the first generation of Latin American writers. This dismissal had everything to do with the fact that these early authors were native Americans whose ethnic roots reached deep into the pre-Columbian soil of the New World. Marginalized politically and socially in their own lifetimes, they occasionally took up the pen to launch a counteroffensive. Their traditional native oral cultures did not prepare them for written expression in European tongues, and their political self-interest often distorted their accounts of ancient history. As a result, these native voices were marginalized for a second time by the world of literary scholarship.[1] Yet these proud and desperate individuals had lived through the first, critical moments of Spanish American cultural and political history and they had engaged in a process of decolonization in which the territories to be recovered were not only geographical but also spiritual and historical.[2] What they had to say—and especially how they went about saying it—constitutes a fascinating chapter in the history of the confrontation of the Western world with the rest of the world.

The story I want to tell concerns one person's engagement with the European language of the foreign conqueror, and particularly with the many discursive formations that made up the European world of letters at the time. My project is to reconstruct the ways in which a native American (in this case, Andean) author of the late sixteenth and early seventeenth centuries, Felipe Guaman Poma de Ayala,[3] translated his experience into the language of the other. What I want to know is how the literary subject took up the challenge of cross-cultural communication in the first hundred years after the Spanish invasion and conquests in the New World.

A consideration fundamental to Guaman Poma's efforts, and to my own in this study, is the fact that he wrote his *Nueva corónica y buen gobierno* [1615] explicitly for King Philip III of Spain.[4] The Peruvian author was painfully aware of the difficulties of communicating across barriers linguistic and cultural. Shaping the rhetoric of his discourse were his experiences with the juridical, historical, and religious literature of the Spanish Golden Age and his expectations about his designated reader or *destinataire*.

History Writing and Polemic

Before turning to the ethnic Andean's writing, a few words are in order about the historical and historiographical context in which his work appeared. At the time of the production of the second wave of *Crónicas de Indias* in the seventeenth century, historiography, like history itself, had changed its orientation. Conquest efforts had subsided, leaving fantastic and historical events to intermingle in the popular imagination. As a result, the chronicles of New World history then being produced were reworkings, even plagiarisms, of previous chronicles, or oblique remembrances of deeds long past (Esteve Barba 1964:19). Nevertheless, the aspiration—or pretense—of discovering and communicating objective truths in history prevailed. The Renaissance norm of historical truth, the *res gestae* to which the *Crónicas de Indias* claimed to subscribe, consisted of the "unadorned reporting of things that had happened, free of distortion, addition, or omission, as though it were possible to record human actions in words as faithfully as a musical performance might be recorded by an infallible phonograph" (Nelson 1973:40).

Although adhering to this illusion, most New World chronicle literature can be called allegorical, in Hayden White's terms (1973b:261), insofar as such works were written in the service of "compulsive powers" such as religion or specific ideologies and typically drew moral implications from historical facts or reduced historical events to the status of manifestations of moral forces presumed to direct the universe. The New World chronicles were "allegorical" in this sense because they elaborated typically providentialist, imperialist versions of Spanish conquest history based on philosophies of the just war. Woven into the narrations were the greatest philosophical and practical problems generated by the discovery and colonization of the New World: first, the legal claims by which to justify the European conquest of indigenous American peoples; and, second, the methods by which to control and govern the newfound populations (Zavala [1947] 1972:19).

Within the historiographic treatise, the justifications of conquest and colonization sometimes appeared as points of contention but most often represented the distillation of particular ideological positions, which the authors attempted to impose on their readers. As a result of their pragmatic motives, the sixteenth-century chronicles of Peru can be divided into two categories: those that defended the private interests of the conquistadores and their descendants (as *relaciones* or petitions of individuals for imperial favors), and those that served the political interest of administrators concerned with governing the native populations and establishing the rights and strategies for doing so (Ossio 1976–77:193). The most well-known authors of the second group were Pedro Sarmiento de Gamboa and his mentor, Francisco de Toledo. Among the many writers of the period that has come to be identified with the tenure of Viceroy Toledo (1569–1581), Sarmiento and Toledo himself are the ones most remembered for using historiographic and documentary literature as the battleground on which to press their political suits against native autonomy (Means 1928:519; see also pp. 462–497).

In like manner, the Amerindian writers presented their arguments in the guise of unadorned reporting. Their recovery of history was as fraught with personal motives and collective self-interest as were the historiographic works produced by European chroniclers—soldiers, clerks, and priests—of the generations before them.

Guaman Poma stands out as one who entered vigorously into the debate.[5] His particular viewpoint on political matters can easily be summarized: opposing the direct rule of the foreigners, Guaman Poma lobbied for the restitution of lands and the return of traditional Andean governance. Because he was of matrilineal descent from Inca nobility, he made his claim to aristocracy on the basis of his paternal Yarovilca Allauca Huanoco lineage, which predated the "usurper" Incas of more recent times (see Tello 1942; Varallanos 1959:59–68). Rabidly anticlerical, he decried the greed of all holders of colonial office, civil as well as ecclesiastical. He defended the Andeans as civilized Christians and attacked the Spaniards as lost sinners. At the same time, he promoted the institutionalization to the Christian religion and the creation of a sovereign Andean state that would form part of a universal Christian empire presided over by the Spanish king. In short, his stance was complex but coherent and always unequivocal: in favor of native rule and opposed to colonialism, Guaman Poma was anti-Inca but pro-Andean, anticlerical but pro-Catholic.

In the articulation of his views, Guaman Poma employed a type of speech act that prevails throughout his work and has the character of a hidden polemic. In this type of discourse, as defined by Bakhtin, the speaker implies or alludes to another person's words—without referring specifically to that prior speech act—for the expression of his or her own intention. Hidden polemic is like any single line in a dialogue insofar as it responds to a previous speech act without explicitly referring to it.[6] Guaman Poma's engagement in hidden polemic had two consequences: on an immediate level, it allowed him to integrate into his own discourse countless attacks against contentions that he never specified and commentaries on authors whom he never named. When disentangled from his own remarks, the identification of these alien speech acts makes his own speech more intelligible. Second, the presence of hidden polemic informs and explains the compositional principles of his discourse; it is responsible for the respective roles that history writing, oratory, and fiction play in structuring his work.

The polemical thrust of Guaman Poma's book—and even its specific methods of articulation—have their precedent in earlier sixteenth-century writings, such as those of José de Acosta and Bartolomé de las Casas, with which Guaman Poma was acquainted. Both Acosta and Las Casas employed compositional strategies in which the description of phenomena and the narration of events became the proofs of the dialectical demonstration (Mignolo 1982:86). Whereas Acosta in his *Historia natural y moral de las Indias* limited his argumentative structure to the examination of the works of nature, Las Casas in the *Historia apologética* offered persuasive and rhetorical as well as demonstrative, dialectical arguments in studying the works of humanity's free will (ibid.:87). Although Guaman Poma did not follow the pattern of demonstrating causes and describing effects in the learned manner of Acosta and Las Casas, he quickly discovered the potential of the apparently neutral discourse of history for embracing rhetorical arguments of persuasion.

Guaman Poma masked his intent by presenting his persuasive assertions as though they were statements of fact; he hid and disguised as simple historiographic narration his engagement in polemic. His explanation of the appearance of the first Andeans in the Indies, for example, as well as the provenance of their racial and ethnic stock and the origin of the imperial Inca, were all taken up as historical events simply recounted. Seldom did the author acknowledge that such issues were involved in a passionate debate. He nowhere gave an explanation of why he called his book the "first of the new chronicles," yet, like Acosta, he attempted what the Jesuit considered a novel enterprise: to explain the Andean presence in the old "New World" and to write the moral history of civilized humanity in America.[7] Bolder than Acosta, who ventured to call his own work "new" only in his prologue, Guaman Poma proclaimed the novelty of his work in its very title.

For Guaman Poma, the concept of history included its being preserved in some form; thus he lamented that the record of ancient Andean civilization consisted of "unas historias cin escriptura nenguna" ("some narrations, which were never written down") ([1615] 1980:8).[8] His task, he suggested, was one of translation from the oral to the written mode; his job was to pass the record from one medium to another, to transpose, not to invent or even to interpret. By calling himself a chronicler,[9] Guaman Poma claimed a prerogative that was concerned with the public good and stood above self-interest. He qualified himself for the historian's task by proclaiming his Christian religious devotion and by asserting that his history would perform the services of all good history: namely, to provide doctrine and example by which all mortals should live. His protestations about the usefulness ("utilidad y provecho") of his book conformed in a general way to the ethical, public goal of the writing of history.

Like his narrative stance as guardian of the public good, Guaman Poma's efforts as private petitioner relied on the illusion of historical truth that he created to disguise his polemical contentions. The idea of a *probanza de méritos*, or personal petition to the king, to seek recompense for services rendered, was explicit in Guaman Poma's appeal to King Philip III: "Agradéscame este seruicio de treinta años y de andar tan pobre, dejando mi casa y hijos y haziendas para seruir a vuestra Magestad" ("Reward me for this service of thirty years, for going about in poverty, abandoning my home and children and domestic labors in order to serve your Majesty") (ibid.:976). It is at this level and in this context as a *carta relatoria* that Guaman Poma's work might properly be called a letter to the king ("carta al rey"), which is the epithet that has been used so often to describe it.[10]

Also in the general category of the *relación*, he cast the chapter of his book called "Pregunta su Magestad" ("His Majesty Inquires")—an imaginary dialogue with the king of Spain—as the formal, official type of report presumably solicited by the monarch:

Pregunta Sacra Católica Real Magestad al autor Ayala para sauer todo lo que ay en el rreyno de las Yndias del Pirú para el buen gobierno y justicia y rremediallo de los trauajos y mala uentura y que multiprique los pobres yndios del dicho rreyno. . . . A la pregunta de su Magestad rresponde el autor y habla con su Magestad. (ibid.: 974)

(His Holy Catholic Royal Majesty inquires of Ayala, the author, in order to know about everything that exists in the kingdom of the Peruvian Indies, for the sake of good government and justice and to relieve the Indians from their travails and mis-

fortunes so that the poor Indians of the aforementioned kingdom may multiply. . . .
To his Majesty's questions, the author will respond and speak to his Majesty.)

Here Guaman Poma mimics the formula of the *relación* typified in the
Relaciones geográficas de Indias (1586) (see Jiménez de la Espada 1965).
Such reports fulfilled an official obligatory function insofar as they com-
plied with government requests for information. Often taking the form of
responses to questionnaires, this type of *relación* did not subscribe to any
traditional literary model but rather to the exigencies of providing data
about the newly discovered lands and their peoples in an orderly fashion
(Mignolo 1982:70–71).

Inventing not only his own compliance but also the official request,
Guaman Poma elaborated his responses and inverted the conventional
character of the *relación*. In the novel and the chronicle, forensic oratory
normally served to legitimize the status of the witness as worthy and re-
liable (see González Echevarría 1976:28–29); as the witness created a relationship with an external authority, that authority's fictional presence in
turn authorized the witness. But Guaman Poma subverted the formula
when he created the king's fictional persona as an uninformed and naïve
inquirer. Thus, although Guaman Poma created the figure of the sovereign, he bled it of the prestige that he transferred instead to himself; he
made the character "el autor Ayala" the source of knowledge and, therefore, authority.

The *carta relatoria* and the *relación*, on the one hand, and the *crónica*
and *historia* on the other, constituted two opposing, though complementary, categories within historiographic discourse. Authorial purpose
differed considerably between them: the *carta* and *relación* were written
out of a sense of obligation to testify and inform, whereas history and
chronicle aspired to elaborate, from such data as *relaciones* could provide,
the complex relationships among historical events. It is only from the
perspective of the reception of all such works in this century, not from that
of their original production in the sixteenth, that they may be viewed as
pertaining to a single category (Mignolo 1982:59). In spite of Guaman
Poma's avowal that he intended only to inform, not to interpret, he contradicted himself with the statements that reveal that he considered his
work a *crónica,* not a *carta*. Although he once referred to his work as a
letter ([1615] 1980:975), he commonly called it a "libro y corónica," and
twice requested its publication:

Y la dicha merced pide y suplica para cienpre de la dicha ynpreción a su Magestad,
del dicho libro conpuesto por el dicho autor, don Felipe Guaman Poma de Ayala,

señor y *capac apo*, ques préncipes, pues que lo merese de la dicha auilidad y trauajo. (Ibid.:11; see also p. 7)

(And he requests and petitions the aforementioned favor of his Majesty, of the said impression, forever, of the said book composed by the aforementioned author, Don Felipe Guaman Poma de Ayala, lord and powerful *Apu*, which means prince, because he deserves it for his aforementioned talents and labors.)

Thus Guaman Poma moved one step farther away from the notion of responsive, externally motivated testimony (*carta relatoria*) and one step closer to that of assertive, formally executed discourse (*crónica*).

Although Guaman Poma obviously had aspirations for his work as a formal treatise, it is difficult to place his book definitively in the field of either the public, historiographic enterprise or the informal, private citizen's *relación*. This is the case because his work is organized as a succession of three distinct parts. His *Nueva corónica* consists of the story of ancient Peru from the biblical Creation to the reign of the Inca Huayna Capac (ibid.:1–369). Subsequently, the chapter called "Conquista," which begins with the arrival of the first Spaniards to Peru and ends with the conclusion of the Spaniards' civil wars after the conquest, is a separate unit (ibid.: 370–437); see his table of contents, p. 1182). The remaining two-thirds of the book, the *Buen gobierno*, is a synchronic and exhaustive description of life in the Peruvian viceroyalty (ibid.:438–1189). This portion of the work consists not of the recording of great and memorable deeds, but rather of the account of everyday occurrences to which Guaman Poma claimed eyewitness testimony.

It is in the *Buen gobierno* that Guaman Poma appealed to the conventional notion of historical truth as a literal account of events that actually happened. The notion of historical truth pertained to "the kind of correspondence that should obtain between the testimony of a witness in a courtroom and the events he describes" (Nelson 1973:1). In such a manner, Guaman Poma materialized the spirit of the courtroom and the spectacle of the witness presenting himself to a presiding authority. This occurs not only in the dialogue with the king but throughout the detailed descriptions of the colonizers' exploitation of the native population. In the same attitude, the Andean author copied out letters and legal documents and inserted them into his work. Applicable here is the juridical definition of the *relación* as that "brief and succinct report made publicly to a judge, orally or in writing, about the facts of a particular case" (see *Diccionario de autoridades* [1726–37] 1964:3:556).

On the other hand, neither the *Nueva corónica* ([1615] 1980:1–369) nor the chapter called "Conquista" (ibid.:370–437) can qualify as a *relación*. Guaman Poma could not vouch personally for the experience of his people from the time of the legendary arrival in the Indies of one of the sons of Noah, nor did he have firsthand experience of the Spanish invasion and conquest of Tawantinsuyu.[11] Furthermore, he did not adhere to the established criteria for determining historical truth. What happened instead, as I shall demonstrate later, is that the events of history became the unstable elements in both the narrations of the *Nueva corónica* and "Conquista." Factual accounts dissolved as Guaman Poma abandoned the exegesis of history to move in another direction. Calling into question the teleological and ethical dimensions of historical events, he examined meaning and morality and framed his own literary response.

Challenging the Canon

Guaman Poma's claim to the generic definition of his work as a chronicle is significant in light of his political intent. Yet the issue of genre raises questions that extend beyond his own immediate literary experience to focus on the creative acts that constituted and attended the birth of the Spanish American literary consciousness. Stated in the most comprehensive terms, the question that I seek to answer is what aspects of literary canon and convention became the conditions that made possible the debut of the literary subject that was uniquely and self-consciously both Hispanic and American.

The implications of my study of Guaman Poma's book concern literature, but literature in its relationship to society. His encounter with the world of letters, which he first viewed as an avenue of political intervention in colonial affairs when all traditional channels for social participation were closed to him, ultimately became a lost cause. This is evidenced in his dizzying and desperate movement from one generic formula to another to recount history and argue for colonial reform. The result is an exposition that turns inside out the discourses of the *Siglo de Oro*, deemphasizing their esthetic qualities and drawing attention to their social implications as instruments of political power. It should be evident by the end of my examination that Guaman Poma implicitly offered a critique of European discursive formations insofar as he revealed their inability to represent fully social reality or serve the cause of justice.

The study that follows begins with the problem of Guaman Poma's version of the Spanish conquest of Peru in the light of the written histories with which he was familiar. He contradicted his documentary sources and elaborated a fictionalized narration of events that had much more to do with his own political arguments than with the rigorous demands of writing history. My investigation of Guaman Poma's chronicle in comparison with the juridical treatises on the rights of conquest leads me to argue that his rewriting of history was based on the primarily Dominican expression of the philosophy of the just war.

Chapter 2 further explores Guaman Poma's approach to historiographic issues by examining his use of the literary biography to narrate the lives of the Incas. Instead of writing a chronicle of Andean history, he wove, through the biographies of the Incas and his version of the conquest, an epic tale of Andean experience. Inasmuch as the *Nueva corónica* followed the epic formula as an "imitación de historia," this first part of his work may be considered among the first attempts to create the epic saga of Spanish America. Yet the distance from the exemplary biography to moralist literature was but one short step, and a consideration of the nineteen "prologues" that conclude many of the chapters of the book brings up the issue of religious literature.

In chapter 3, I approach what I consider to be the major result of this investigation, namely, the discovery of how prominent a role the literature of religious conversion played in Guaman Poma's work and, by analogy, how largely such catechisms and sermons published in Amerindian languages must have loomed on the literary horizon of the entire social class of *indios ladinos*, or ethnic Americans literate in Castilian. By exploring the extent to which ecclesiastical rhetoric entered into the articulation of the new American voice, I hope to have illuminated that moment when the native elite encountered for the first time the literature of the conquerors. I am convinced that those religious writings—not the juridical or the historiographic treatises—provoked Guaman Poma's entrance into the polemic on the nature of the New World natives and the rights by which to govern them; the catechisms and *sermonarios* were the immediate sources of the contentions against which he found it necessary to defend his race.

As I pursued the problem of the generic identification of his work, it became apparent that the principal issue was not history versus fiction, but rather, ecclesiastical rhetoric versus poetics. Tracing the way the inner teleology that animates the *Nueva corónica* as an epic construct breaks down, I argue that the sermon intrudes on, and finally overwhelms, Guaman Poma's efforts to create an epic story.

Chapters 4 and 5 examine the varying degrees to which Guaman Poma's drawings corroborate and contradict the written texts they accompany. The question I seek to answer is whether visual representation frees the author/artist from the European historiographic and literary conventions that he manipulates in writing. Analyzing spatial composition on the pictorial field, and examining certain codes of iconographic representation as carriers of allegorical pictorial meaning, I contend that these drawings corroborate the ultimate implications of the written text. Through pictures and prose, Guaman Poma declares that there is no point of productive contact between European and Andean cultures; each remains hopelessly separate from the other, and understanding between the two is impossible. The examination of narrational point of view that closes this study serves as a summary of Guaman Poma's position: standing proud but isolated within his own cultural sphere, the author quixotically presents himself as the hero of an encounter in which his opponent does not understand the terms of the engagement or the stakes of the challenge.

The present challenge is to describe Guaman Poma's mostly unexamined excursion into the world of letters, all the while remembering that it is only a part, although a significant one, of his story.

1. Contradicting the Chronicles of Conquest

Guaman Poma claimed that one of his principal objectives in writing the *Nueva corónica y buen gobierno* was to retell the history of the Spanish invasion and conquest of Peru. He knew that period of history from two sources: the oral traditions of his own people, and the written accounts of Spanish historians, which had already been published abroad. His own rewriting of the events in question was informed not only by his ethnic Andean perspective, but also, and significantly, by a European philosophy of conquest that allowed him to express his views in a way that was intelligible and acceptable to outsiders. To evaluate Guaman Poma's key assertions about the Spanish conquest of Peru in the light of the political polemic on which they drew, one must reinsert his claims about Peruvian history into the stream of historiographic dialogue into which they originally fed. Although I have situated Guaman Poma's discussions in the context of Spanish political philosophy, I am concerned less with his contributions to the polemic of his time—for these are in themselves predictable—than with setting the stage for a subsequent discussion about the teleological formulation of his work. Guaman Poma fictionalizes Peruvian conquest history in a verbal structure more hypothetical than historiographic; through his literary enterprise, he attempts to make sense of a past long gone and a present that seems to deny the very existence of that lost era.

Guaman Poma's Exploitation of Written Histories

"A writer's desire to write can only come from previous experience with literature," says Northrop Frye, and the novice will "start by imitating whatever he's read, which usually means what the people around him are writing" (1964:40). It should be added that, in spite of a lack of experience on the part of the would-be author—or perhaps because of it—he or she will also look around to size up the potential audience or designated readers. If imitating what's being written around them provides authors with literary conventions, assessing their potential audience helps them choose among those possible models. Guaman Poma looked for the literary codes through which he could best communicate with his intended reader, King Philip III, and the most serious of the works available to him, notably historiography, and the literature of religious devotion, provided the models.

The contradictory models Guaman Poma used aid in producing the contradictory effects. The historical datum generates his concern for the precision of facts, whereas the biblical injunction, emphasizing not the particular or specific event but rather the "typical, recurring, or what Aristotle calls universal event," inspires the ahistorical quality of the exemplary figure (ibid.:64). In the first instance, Guaman Poma's models are, for example, Agustín de Zárate's *Historia del descubrimiento y conquista del Perú* [1555], which gives him the precise number of "gente de a caballo y de enfantería y arcabuseros" to put into his account of Gonzalo Pizarro's uprising; in the second, such models include Fray Luis de Granada's *Memorial de la vida cristiana* [1566], which offers biblical heroes and prophets whose timeless and exemplary tales represent not the history but the quintessence of moral human experience.

At the outset, Guaman Poma's claim that his work is historical meets with skepticism. Certain events in his history of the conquest of Peru, for example, are invented: his father's reception of Pizarro and Almagro and their band at Tumbes and the willing welcome of the authority of Charles V over the land; the Andeans' failure to resist the Spaniards in attempted battles; and the termination of the civil wars among the Spaniards with the defeat and capture of Hernández Girón by the Andean lords. The Peruvian *coronesta* embroiders these episodes into a narration taken in part from the Spanish chronicles of the Peruvian conquest, thereby creating a kind of patchwork effect. By dividing these accounts into the categories of fact and fancy, one might conclude, with Porras Barrenechea (1948) and others, that Guaman Poma is a historian who lies.[1]

Looking at the connection between historical truth and fiction as it was understood in Guaman Poma's time, however, suggests another way to examine the implications of the "Conquista" chapter. Historiography then was associated with the poetic and rhetorical arts and its "fictive" nature was commonly recognized (White 1976:23–24). "'Truth' was equated not with 'fact' but with a combination of fact and the conceptual matrix within which it was appropriately located in the discourse;" many kinds of truth played a role in history, and these truths were presented to the reader through fictional techniques of representation (ibid.:24). To open the discussion of Guaman Poma's discourse, one might well ask: What "facts" are presented and what are the assumptions or conceptual matrix on which their exposition is based?

In the *Nueva corónica*, the facts concern the social, political, and economic administration of an enormous pre-Columbian empire.[2] The assumption on which their exposition is based is that the organization of that society was superior to that brought by the conquering invaders from Spain ([1615] 1980:890). In "Conquista," the facts are that the Andean state was invaded and conquered by the Spaniards around 1532; the conceptual matrix is constituted by the conviction that the Spaniards had no right to do so. In the *Buen gobierno*, Guaman Poma presents facts about the forced labor imposed on the native population, especially in the mines, and the loss of lives and confiscation of property produced by the witch-hunts at the turn of the seventeenth century. Behind these accounts is the assumption that the Spaniards did all this without justification in violation of every precept of justice and of their own laws.

For Guaman Poma, first angry and ultimately defeated by all that he sees around him, the world of ideas comes to occupy at least as much importance as the world of facts. His "new chronicle" of Peruvian history and his story of the conquest are less a litany of historical detail than the dramatization of an intricate hypothesis. What appears to be the narration of historical events is merely the raw material out of which he constructs his argument in defense of the rights of the Andean people. When he pretends to inform, he is engaging in debate; when he purports to explain, he is attempting to persuade. His integration of historical and fictional elements can best be elucidated in light of the chronicle literature that he reads and contradicts as well as of the Scholastic political philosophy of conquest that he exploits.

Well versed as he is on the published *Crónicas de Indias*, Guaman Poma uses the philosophical treatises on the just war to shape his "history." Although he copies from the works of Zárate and Fernández as chroniclers, his inspiration comes from Vitoria and Soto as political theorists and Las Casas as polemicist. The epigraph of Guaman Poma's conquest "history" might well be "y no ubo conquista," for he insistently declares that there had been no military conquest of Peru: "Y ancí fue conquistado y no se defendió" ("And thus they were conquered and did not defend themselves") (ibid.:388; see also pp. 164, 377, 564, 573, 971, 972). Isolating his story of the Peruvian conquest from both the *Nueva corónica* and the *Buen gobierno*, he makes a distinction that bears directly on the role of "Conquista" in the work's overall teleological design.

In his history of the Spanish conquest, Guaman Poma blends published historiographic sources of European origin with accounts from oral tradition that were no doubt recalled by his informants who had "dined with the Inca" (ibid.:1088-1089). His description of the first Spanish conquistadores, and the sense of wonderment that he conveys about their appearance and behavior, could only come from his own heritage of oral traditions. He tells how the Spaniards "talked to" their books and papers, how their garb covered them like shrouds, and how they seemed to be of identical social rank because of their undifferentiated attire.[3] At the same time, and in spite of accusing Agustín de Zárate and Diego Fernández el Palentino of lacking verified information "about events for which there remained living eyewitnesses" (p. 1088), Guaman Poma copies and paraphrases the preceding citation about them from the *Symbolo catholico indiano* of the Franciscan author Luis Jerónimo de Oré (cf. Oré 1598:f37v, and Guaman Poma [1615] 1980:1088).

Most notable among such borrowings are Guaman Poma's accounts of the events that took place from the arrival of President de la Gasca to Peru to his victory over the rebellion of Gonzalo Pizarro.[4] In comparison to his narration of preceding events, Guaman Poma gives prominence (four pictures and four pages of prose) to the uprisings of both Gonzalo and Hernández Girón. Following Zárate's text on the de la Gasca/Pizarro confrontation, Guaman Poma uses Fernández's work to orient his account of the Hernández uprising.[5] Although he follows both of these sources on particulars, he abandons them at crucial points in the narration in order to showcase the alleged heroic role his father and other Andean *curacas* (ethnic lords) played.

Specifically, Guaman Poma echoes Zárate's *Historia del descubrimiento y conquista del Perú* ([1555] 1947) with regard to the encounters between Gonzalo and de la Gasca, found in the sixth and seventh books of Zárate's chronicle.[6] When he departs from Zárate's text, as in the account of Pizarro's effort to burn the settlement of Huánuco, he does so for the purpose of celebrating the Andeans' valor. While paraphrasing Zárate, he nevertheless inserts the name of his father as the hero of the defense of Huánuco. In addition, he highlights the bravery of the Andean warriors in battle by increasing the number of Spaniards who attacked the city (thirty in Zárate; three hundred in Guaman Poma) and subsequently reducing the number of Spanish survivors from forty to four (cf. Zárate [1555] 1947, book 6, chap. 12:555-556, and Guaman Poma [1615] 1980:423).

After the narration of this event, Guaman Poma returns to the same chapter 12 of the Zárate text to narrate Diego Centeno's successful takeover of Cuzco[7] and Gonzalo's definitive defeat and execution.[8] Guaman

Poma's additions to the Spaniard's narration again reflect indigenous Andean concerns and his desire to promote the importance of the Spanish captain Luis de Avalos de Ayala, to whom he attributes the donation of his own Spanish surname. For example, Guaman Poma characterizes the bloody battle at Huarina Pampa as "la gran batalla que fue mayor en este rreyno entre cristianos, *que no con los yndios*" ("the greatest battle in this kingdom, which was fought among Christians, *not with the Indians*") ([1615] 1980:425; emphasis mine). On describing de la Gasca's battle preparations in the Valley of Jauja, he comments that the president "yua haziendo más gente y maltratando a los yndios" ("went about gathering more troops and ill-treating the Indians") (ibid.:427).[9] As he narrates de la Gasca's organization of the royal forces, he again paraphrases Zárate, except that he adds the name of Avalos de Ayala to Zárate's list of officers.[10]

Guaman Poma concludes his narration of the conquistadores' civil wars, which dominated Peru from 1538 to 1550, with an account of the rebellion and defeat of Francisco Hernández Girón. He takes as his source the *Segunda parte* of Diego Fernández's *Historia del Perú* ([1571] 1963). Unlike the care with which he copied and paraphrased Zárate's book, Guaman Poma follows El Palentino's account only in broadest outline. His most important departure from Fernández's text concerns the role that he attributes to the Andean *caciques* in opposing and vanquishing the rebel; this issue is crucial to his polemical argument.

According to Porras Barrenechea (1948:16–17), El Palentino and other documentary sources indicate that the native troops attacked not only the rebel forces of Hernández Girón but also the army of the crown. Only Guaman Poma, says Porras, turns these acts of indigenous reprisal against all foreigners into an act of loyalty and service to the Spanish king. In effect, Guaman Poma abandons El Palentino's text as the latter relates how the followers of Hernández Girón were captured and punished in Cuzco ([1571] 1963), *Segunda parte*, book 2, chap. 56: v. 165:56–57) and how Hernández Girón himself was captured by Miguel de la Serna and Juan Tello and taken to Lima for execution (ibid.: chap. 58: v. 165:59–62). Instead, from the battle of the king's forces against Hernández Girón onward, Guaman Poma claims that his father, "don Martín de Ayala," and Don León Apo Guasca and Don Juan Guaman Uachaca, *caciques* of Changa, were among "the aforementioned illustrious Indian captains" ("los dichos prencipales yndios capitanes") who participated in the struggle against the rebel ([1615] 1980:433). According to Guaman Poma, they were responsible for Hernández's defeat and flight, despite being gravely outnumbered by the Spaniards and their native allies (ibid.:435). The event is introduced into the narration by a drawing that shows "*Capac*

Apo don Martín Guaman Malqui" and other ethnic lords pursuing the fleeing Spaniards (plate 1). Seeing only the rumps of the galloping horses as they disappear (ibid.:434; see also p. 426), one appreciates Guaman Poma's apparent visual satire.

In these accounts, the Andean author ignores the battle at Pucara in which the rebel was definitively undone, according to El Palentino (Porras Barrenechea 1948:17). Instead, he proclaims the truthfulness of his own account of the Don Martín de Ayala/Apo Alanya victory over Hernández Girón and visually confirms the latter's capture by Andean lords (ibid.:436; plate 2).

Throughout the "Conquista" chapter, Guaman Poma weaves together the data of the printed histories with accounts either alive in the oral traditions or devised by his own invention. Whatever the variety of his sources, whatever the veracity of events narrated, the focus of the entire chapter is the loyalty and valor of the Andean lords in serving the Spanish king. Overall, the written histories play an important role. They provide the sequence of events and pertinent details, such as the names of Spanish officers, as the background against which Guaman Poma narrates a story of the postconquest civil wars in which the only heroes are Andean.

Respect for History

In spite of his use of written and oral accounts blended with episodes of his own invention, Guaman Poma uses his sources with discrimination. His respect for the factual truth of history can be demonstrated through his treatment of miraculous events, such as the visions of the Virgin Mary and St. James (patron saint of Spain), which were reported during the conquest of Peru. Although he attributes to these events a political meaning, his reporting of them concurs with standard historiographic practice.

As a historian, Guaman Poma would not be permitted to invent characters or events, the "mentiras" and "imitación" of poetry, as the theoretician of historiography Luis Cabrera de Córdoba called them (1611: f 11 r). However, he could "invent" the formal relationships that obtained among those elements (White 1973b:262). The historian's job would be to describe and verify events; his would be the burden of accountability to the facts (Krieger 1974:56). In the case of miraculous visions and visits of the apostles to the Indies, Guaman Poma may be dealing with events that had been consecrated as historical by the force of oral tradition. By his framing of these accounts, it is clear that he deals with them in the manner of the serious historian.

In pictures and in writing, Guaman Poma narrates three miracles: the

CONQVISTA
BATALLA·Q̃·HIZO·E̅

seruicio desu mag̃d el ex.^{mo.r} capacapo don martin de ayala p̃.delante
chinchaysuyo y apo uasco-apoguamā uacha ca hanbuci chansa io cien sol
dados y frā hernandes trecientos sol da dosfue uencido yse huyo-

apoguasco

guama uacha

en uata coiga

don

Plate 1. "A battle waged in His Majesty's service by Don Martín Guaman
        Malqui de Ayala" ([1615] 1980:434)

Plate 2. "Apo Alanya and Chuqui Llanqui capture Francisco Hernández Girón" ([1615] 1980:436)

failure of Manco Inca to ignite an Inca palace already converted into a Christian house of worship, and visions of the Virgin Mary and St. James, which caused Inca warriors to prostrate themselves in wonderment and submit to the Spanish troops ([1615] 1980:402–407; plate 3). Guaman Poma carefully inserts the phrase "They say that . . ." ("dizen que . . . ") at critical moments in these accounts; that is, he brackets the most fantastic aspects of these events, denying personal responsibility for their truthfulness and thus protecting his own credibility as a historian.

In this regard, Guaman Poma adheres to sixteenth-century historiographic precepts. The highest authorities of the period, namely, the current interpreters of Aristotle, approved the use of those elements that were in accordance with popular belief; angels and saints were the supernatural agencies that had come to replace the old heathen deities (Riley 1962:191). The only stipulation was that such events be handled through the narration of a third party; thus, the author or narrator avoided making a personal judgment on the matter (ibid.:192–193). Guaman Poma's consistent use of the qualifier "dizen que" safeguards his own impartiality not only on the question of legendary miracles but also of his descriptions of traditional Andean rituals and belief systems.[11] The care with which he treats the narration of miracles and the exposition of Andean beliefs suggests that he is not indifferent to the search for factual truth in history, but rather possesses a deep respect for it. At the same time, he protects himself from accusations of adherence to indigenous beliefs.

On the other hand, in presenting those episodes of conquest history that explicitly contradict his written sources (the heroic role of the Andean lords, just examined), Guaman Poma neither qualifies his own or the other versions, nor identifies the accounts that he contradicts. He uses no historiographic device that would indicate that his purpose is to set the historical record straight. Yet his respect for history as a literary genre on one hand, and his indifference to its precepts on the other, leave many issues unresolved.

The Dominican Philosophy of Conquest

To support his argument that the Andeans should be exempt from paying tribute to the Spaniards, Guaman Poma recapitulates the principal points of his version of Andean history. He declares that the ancient Andeans were "white," that is, descendants of the sons of Adam, and that they followed in pre-Christian times the "ley de cristiano" ("Christian law"), although the Inca later forced all Andeans to become idolaters ([1615] 1980:80, 87, 119). In the sixteenth century, they submitted to the

Plate 3. "Miracle of St. Mary"
([1615] 1980:404)

authority of the Spanish king and the Roman Catholic pope, becoming baptized Christians and "servants" of God and the Spanish king. When he concludes his argument by stating that the Andeans are not slaves but free under God ("no son esclabos, cino libres por Dios" [ibid.:901]), he is, in effect, rejecting the Aristotelian theory of natural slavery, which was advocated by many of those who considered the wars of conquest to be just (see Hanke [1959] 1975).

Guaman Poma's praise for some members of the Dominican order, however, suggests his own particular allegiance:

Pero ellos algunos son grandes cristianos y grandes letrados y predicadores y lo fueron desde sus antepasados. Que por ellos muchos ereges se conuertieron a la fe en el mundo. (Ibid.:660)

(But some of them are great Christians and great learned men and preachers, and they were so since their predecessors. That because of them many heretics in the world converted to the [Christian] faith.)

He is probably referring to one or more of the following: the theologian and jurist Francisco de Vitoria; his disciple Domingo de Soto; the missionary Bartolomé de las Casas; and Las Casas's colleague in Peru—the author of the first Quechua grammar and dictionary—Domingo de Santo Tomás.

The Dominicans' arguments for Spanish restitution of Andean property greatly influenced Guaman Poma's articulation of his own views, and it is interesting to speculate on what his ties to the order might have been. According to his own account (ibid.:660), the Dominicans were active in the diocese of Huamanga ("en las dichas dotrinas de Xauxa, de los Yauyos, de Guamanga, Parinacocha") during his lifetime. In fact, his devotion to Santa María de la Peña de Francia is an indirect indication of the Dominican presence in Huamanga and Castrovirreina.[12]

On practical issues, Guaman Poma shares the mood and method of the Dominicans. For example, one of the *memoriales* authored by Domingo de Santo Tomás and Las Casas in 1560 and sent to Philip II in defense of the rights of the *caciques* of Peru is echoed in Guaman Poma's own assertions. He takes the Dominicans' central arguments for his own. First, *encomienda* should be abolished because there is no legal justification for it.[13] On this point, Guaman Poma will make his own creative defense. Second, the *encomenderos* and all other non-Andeans should be prohibited from entering the natives' settlements. Third, the king should reinstate and honor the traditional privileges of the ethnic lords of Peru.[14]

The important difference between Guaman Poma's arguments and those of the Dominicans is that the latter seek justice in a general way, whereas Guaman Poma struggles for the redress of personal and collective grievances. Whereas the European defenders of the Andeans warn the king about the decline of his fortunes (and fortune) in Peru if the natives are not protected (Las Casas [1560] 1958: v. 5:466), Guaman Poma puts it more bluntly: the Andean race will disappear—not merely decline in numbers—and the crown will be left destitute:

Desde aquí de ueynte años no abrá yndio en este rreyno de que se cirua su corona rreal y defensa de nuestra santa fe católica. Porque cin los yndios, vuestra Magestad no uale cosa porque se acuerde Castilla es Castilla por los yndios. ([1615] 1980: 982)

(From here until twenty years from now, there will be no Indian in this kingdom by which your royal crown and the defense of our holy Catholic faith might be served. Because without the Indians, your Majesty is not worth anything. Because one must remember that Castile is Castile because of the Indians.)

The only Dominican author to whom Guaman Poma expressly refers is Domingo de Santo Tomás. However, the Peruvian chronicler's acquaintance with the works of Las Casas can be deduced from textual comparisons.[15] To find Las Casas in Guaman Poma's book indicates that the Dominican's polemical works did reverberate among the native population of Peru in the decades following Las Casas's death. One of his formal treatises in the field of political polemics, the *Tratado de las doce dudas* ([1564] 1958), provided an important source of rhetorical argumentation for Guaman Poma. The *Tratado* circulated among the Dominicans in the Peruvian viceroyalty (Lohmann Villena 1966:67), and it is likely that the Andean author became acquainted with the work through the members of the order in Huamanga.

Never following blindly these other texts, Guaman Poma manipulates them according to his own purposes. Lacking the European's reflexive respect for the written word, he treats other writings—from those of Acosta to Zárate and including those of Las Casas—with a cool detachment. Just as he follows historians such as Fernández and Zárate to the letter, then contradicts them flatly, so he repeats Las Casas's argument about the injustice of the conquest, then rejects the latter's claim to evangelization as a just title for colonial domination. Guaman Poma decries the direct ecclesiastical rule over the natives that Las Casas so warmly advocates.

In addition, Guaman Poma does not favor the return to the dynastic rule of strictly Inca hegemony that Las Casas had in mind (see Adorno 1978a, 1978b). Las Casas wrote the *Doce dudas* several years before the last Inca princes, Titu Cusi Yupanqui and Tupac Amaru, had died; with them vanished the last hope for the neo-Inca state that they had attempted to establish and maintain at Vilcabamba. By the time that Guaman Poma was finishing his project, the stakes of the game had changed: Titu Cusi and Tupac Amaru had been gone for approximately forty years, and the situation of the Andean natives had deteriorated beyond all hope. As a result, Guaman Poma does not engage in a debate as to *which* Andean ethnic or political group ought to rule, but rather whether the entire Andean citizenry has been denied rights of the most fundamental kind. By 1615, the Peruvian chronicler is more pro- and pan-Andean than anti-Inca in outlook; in this spirit, he nominates his own son, representing the Yarovilca dynasty, as the new ruler of "las Yndias del Pirú" ([1615] 1980: 963). Thus, he gives a new and creative twist to the arguments that Las Casas had put forward on behalf of the Inca succession in his 1564 treatise.

In a chapter that mimics the rhetorical style of ecclesiastical prose ("Conzedera, ermanos míos" ["Consider, my brothers"]), one of Guaman Poma's meditations reiterates Las Casas's propositions; this text can be taken apart, statement by statement, to show that the *Doce dudas* is its source:

Que aués de conzederar que todo el mundo es de Dios y ancí Castilla es de los españoles y las Yndias es de los yndios y Guenea es de los negros. Que cada déstos son lexítimos propetarios, no tan solamente por la ley, como lo escriuió San Pablo, que de dies años estaua de poción y se llamaua rromano. (Ibid:929)

(That you must consider that all the world is God's, and thus Castile belongs to the Spaniards and the Indies belongs to the Indians, and Guinea, to the blacks. That each one of these is a legitimate proprietor, not only according to the law, as St. Paul wrote, who for ten years resided [in Rome] and called himself a Roman.)

This passage refers to the first principle (*Principio I*) of Las Casas's treatise: all infidels have sovereign jurisdiction over their own territories and possessions; this right to jurisdiction is mandated not only by human legislation (Guaman Poma's "no tan solamente por la ley"), but also by natural and divine law (Las Casas [1564] 1958:486). Guaman Poma's reference to St. Paul has its origin in the same *Principio I*. In that passage, Las Casas cites Augustine's reference to Paul's epistle to the Romans (chapter 13, verse 1), in which the apostle insists that the Christian community obey the monarch under whose jurisdiction it lives, even though that ruler be a pagan. Thus, says Guaman Poma, St. Paul "called himself a Roman." In the same manner, Guaman Poma implies, the Spaniards should obey the Andean authorities while in the sovereign kingdom of Peru.

In the passage that follows, Guaman Poma points out that natives of Castile, though they be Jews or Moors, are subject to the laws of the land. Analogously, and "in the language of the Indians," those Spaniards living in Peru are considered foreigners, *mitmaq*; that is, they are persons sent out from their own homeland to attend to interests abroad. As such, they must obey Andean, not Spanish, law ([1615] 1980:929). In this instance, Guaman Poma is reiterating the second principle (*Principio II*) of Las Casas's treatise. His statement refers to the proposition in which Las Casas discusses the four classes of infidels and their respective rights and jurisdictions. The first class consists of those, such as the Jews and Moors, who, by living in Castile, are subject to the rule of the Christian kings by right and in fact (*"de jure y de facto"*) and are thus obligated to obey the just laws of the Spanish realm (Las Casas [1564] 1958:487–488). Referring to this first category of infidels, Guaman Poma coordinates the Scholastic notion with the Andean concept of *mitmaq*; the foreign settler must obey the laws of his new land, not those of his country of origin.

Guaman Poma continues and sums up his argument with the following statement:

Cada uno en su rreyno son propetarios lexítimos, poseedores, no por el rrey cino por Dios y por justicia de Dios: Hizo el mundo y la tierra y plantó en ellas cada cimiente, el español en Castilla, el yndio en las Yndias, el negro en Guynea. . . . Y ancí, aunque [el rey español] le haga merced al padre, al español en las tierras que se conponga con el rrey, no es propetario. Y ací a de tener obedencia al señor prencipales y justicias, propetarios lexítimos de las tierras, que sea señor o señora. ([1615] 1980:929)

(Each one in his own kingdom is a legitimate proprietor, owner, not because of the king but by God and through God's justice: He made the world and the earth and established in them every foundation, the Spaniard in Castile, the Indian in the Indies, the black in Guinea. . . . And thus, although [the Spanish king] grants a favor to the priest, or to the Spaniard in the lands that are settled under the king's authority, they are not landowners. And thus there must be obedience to the chief lords and magistrates, the legitimate proprietors of the lands, whether they be male or female.)

Thus, Guaman Poma classifies the Andeans as belonging to the fourth category of infidels, that is, those who have never been, and are not at present, subject to a Christian ruler, either by right or in fact. The reasons he gives are those Las Casas articulated: namely, that the Andeans had never usurped Christian lands nor done Christians any harm nor intended to do so; they had never been subjugated by any Christian prince or any member of the church (Las Casas [1564] 1958:489). By emphasizing the rights of the legitimate landowners and declaring that such rights are mandated not by the king, but by God, Guaman Poma appeals to the notion of natural law, the Scholastic concept of the right of all peoples to sovereignty over their own lands, followed since Aquinas (Höffner [1947] 1957:331–342).[16] Furthermore, his reference to Genesis I ("Dios hizo el mundo y la tierra y plantó en ellas cada cimiente") reiterates Las Casas's own citation of the first chapter of Genesis, which he offers in *Principio I* as proof of all peoples' rights to sovereignty in their own lands under the precepts of natural law (Las Casas [1564] 1958:468).

The juridical works Guaman Poma skillfully exploits serve his own political objectives. Although he has limited success in imitating the language of the European legal treatise, he nevertheless elaborates his "history" of the Spanish conquest of Peru so as to uphold and dramatize the principles that the juridical treatises put forth. Overall, it is as if he rewrote Andean history backwards, starting not with the oral accounts of legendary times, but with the *Tratado de las doce dudas* as the platform from which to argue retrospectively for native autonomy in the Andes.

The Dramatization of a Hypothesis

Guaman Poma's principal strategy is to show that the Peruvians provided no cause whereby the Europeans could have waged a just war against them. At the very beginning of his chronological narration of Andean history, Guaman Poma denies the validity of the title concerning the right of the Spanish to spread the gospel. He invalidates it by attributing the presence of the historical Cross of Carabuco to the visit of St. Bartholomew in apostolic times (ibid.:92–94).[17] He makes the point that this visit explicitly established Christianity in Peru prior to the arrival of the Spaniards:

Y ací los yndios somos cristianos por la rredimción de Jesucristo y de su madre bendita Santa María, patrona de este rreyno y por los apóstoles de Jesucristo, San Bartolomé, Santiago Mayor y por la santa crus de Jesucristo que llegaron a este rreyno más primero que los españoles. De ello somos cristianos y creemos un solo Dios de la Santícima Trinidad. (Ibid.:1090)

(And thus we Indians are Christians, on account of the redemption of Jesus Christ and of his blessed mother, St. Mary, patroness of this kingdom and by the apostles

Plate 4. "Don Martín de Ayala, the first ambassador of Huascar Inca,
to Francisco Pizarro, ambassador of the emperor Charles V"
([1615] 1980:377)

of Jesus Christ, St. Bartholomew, St. James the Greater, and by the holy cross of Jesus Christ, all of which arrived in this kingdom before the Spaniards. Because of them we are Christian and we believe in only one God of the Holy Trinity.)

The greatest and most direct polemical attack that Guaman Poma makes in his conquest history, however, is his contradiction of the notion of a military conquest altogether; this is the "y-no-ubo-conquista" ("and-there-was-no-conquest") argument to which I have already referred. Guaman Poma bases this claim on two assertions: first, he insists that the keys to the kingdom were peaceably handed over to Francisco Pizarro as emissary of Charles V at Tumbes (plate 4); second, he claims that the miraculous intervention of the Virgin Mary and St. James prevented the Incas from ever resisting the Spaniards by force (see plate 3). On both counts, he attempts to undermine any notion that there had been a just war of conquest in Peru.

Guaman Poma disavows the occurrence of any armed resistance that might have been considered a justification to wage war against the Peruvians. He makes Tumbes not the prelude to later violent encounters, but rather the stage on which the terms of welcome and peace were firmly established:

Y los españoles, don Francisco Pizarro y don Diego Almagro, y don Martín de Ayala[18] se hincaron de rrodillas y se abrasaron y se dieron paz, amistad con el enperador. Y le honrró y comió en su mesa y hablaron y conuersaron y le dio presentes a los cristianos. Acimismo le dio al señor don Mar[tín] de Ayala que fue primer enbaxador que de Atagualpa en el puerto de Tunbes, adonde saltó primero. ([1615] 1980:378)

(And the Spaniards, Don Francisco Pizarro and Don Diego Almagro, and Don Martín de Ayala knelt down and embraced each other and offered signs of peace and friendship in the name of their emperors. And the Andean lords honored the Spaniards and ate at the same table and spoke and conversed and gave presents to the Christians. In like manner, the Spaniards reciprocated to Don Martín de Ayala, who was the first ambassador—before those of Atahualpa—at the port of Tumbes, where the Spaniards first landed.)

Guaman Poma insists still another time on the immediate and definitive establishment of Andean/Spanish peace, on which occasion his combative tone becomes apparent. In this version, he declares that not only his father, but in fact the principal lords of each of the four subdivisions of the Inca empire had appeared at Tumbes to welcome and embrace the Spanish emperor's representatives. He names all of these "primeros ynfantes y señores, príncipes y principales grandes" and concludes, "De manera los quatro partes destos rreynos se fueron a darse de pas y a bezar los pies y manos del rrey nuestro señor enperador don Carlos de la glorio-sa memoria" ("So that the lords of the divisions of this empire went to offer themselves in peace and kiss the feet and hands of the king, our lord, the emperor Don Carlos of glorious remembrance") (ibid.:564; see also p. 971).[19] Whether his source is oral tradition or, more likely, a hypo-thetical event of his own creation, he gives it a political interpretation: "Y ací no tenemos encomendero ni conquistador, sino que somos de la corona rreal de su Magestad, seruicio de Dios y de su corona" ("And thus we have neither *encomendero* nor conqueror, but rather we belong to the royal crown of his Majesty, in service to God and crown") (ibid.:564).

With this assertion, Guaman Poma replies to two polemical arguments. The first is directed to the chronicles of the Peruvian conquest, which portrayed the Spaniards' military action as a response to the Incas' violent resistance. In most of these works, the war of conquest was justified and the imposition of *encomienda* sanctioned. Long after the conquest, there is a second matter, which is more crucial to Amerindian authors like Guaman Poma. He aims not only to revise the historical record, but also to deny the Europeans' racist charges of Andean cultural inferiority.

Implicit in the colonialist outlook is the assumption that the ignorance of the Andeans would have prevented their enlightened and free acceptance of Spanish rule. This notion was commonly accepted in learned Spanish cir-cles. Vitoria, for example, maintained that the aborigines' voluntary sub-mission to Spanish authority would have been an act of fear and confusion; it could not, therefore, constitute a legitimate title of conquest.[20] In con-trast, Guaman Poma's assertion about the Incas' free acceptance of Spanish rule lends historical dignity to his people and defends the civilized image of the contemporary Andean that he strives to create. His insistence on this act of diplomatic submission is, in fact, a return to the argument regarding the rational capacity of the indigenous people. Whereas political theorists had challenged the value of such peaceful surrenders, Guaman Poma re-sponds by painting a picture of Andean submission that is a model of con-summate statesmanship on the part of the Inca's ambassadors.

Of critical importance to the dramatization of principles concerning the unjust conquest is the representation of miracles and visions (see plate 3). The Peruvian author contends that the effect of these miraculous visions was to curtail the potential Andean resistance to the Spanish invasion. He gives each of these events—the failure of the consecrated temple to burn, the appearances of the Virgin Mary and St. James—the prominence of pictorial representations (ibid.:402, 404, 406), and he refers to them again later in his book (ibid.:655, 1090). Through them, he responds to the commonly held opinion that the conquest of the New World kingdoms was not worthy of miracles, that the natural superiority of the Spaniard over the aborigine made supernatural intervention on behalf of the conquistadores or missionaries unnecessary.

Vitoria's assessment of the circumstances is typical of the European attitude. In the 1530s he writes that he is not persuaded that the faith is spreading among the indigenous populations, because he has heard of neither miracles nor extraordinary signs, nor religious examples of conduct, which would serve the purposes of evangelization: "Pues milagros y señales no veo ninguno, ni tan religiosos ejemplos de vida; y sí, en cambio, al contrario, muchos escándalos y crímenes atroces y muchas impiedades" (cited in Höffner [1947] 1957:355). Likewise, in *De procuranda indorum salute*, José de Acosta suggests that the apostolic mission that renounces all employment of force or military protection is not applicable to the New World.

Taking the example of the tragic fate of Dominican and Jesuit missionaries in Florida, Acosta argues that the American natives cannot be converted peacefully because of their primitive ways; indeed, to trust in their reason and free will is like making friends with wild boars and crocodiles ([1588] 1954, book 2, chap. 8:443). Furthermore, Acosta argues, the apostolic method works only if miracles are produced, and, in America, such occurrences are all too scarce (ibid.:443–446). Although he finds this lack of miracles most distressing, he argues, nevertheless, that the superiority of the priests and the inferiority of those to be converted make the situation salvageable: "Porque aquellos a quienes se anuncia la fe son en todo muy inferiores en razón, en cultura, en autoridad; y los que la anuncian, por la antigüedad y prestigio de la religión, por su muchedumbre, su ingenio, su erudición y demás cualidades, son muy superiores" ("Because those to whom the faith is announced are on the whole very inferior in reason, in culture, in authority; and those who announce it, because of the antiquity and prestige of the religion, because of their great numbers, their genius, their erudition and other qualities, are very superior") (ibid.: 446). According to Acosta, then, conventional methods suffice to effect conversion of these simple peoples.

Guaman Poma contradicts the views Acosta and others represent when he argues, "Cómo hizo Dios milagro para hazelle merced a su Madre bendita a los españoles cristianos, por mejor decir que más quizo hazer merced la Madre de Dios a los yndios porque fuesen cristianos y saluasen las ánimas de los yndios" ("How God and his Blessed Mother performed a miracle to grant favor to the Spanish Christians; more properly speaking, how the Mother of God rather meant to grant favor to the Indians in order that they might become Christian and that the souls of the Indians might be saved'') ([1615] 1980:405). Not only does he thus dignify Andean experience and deny the notion of Andean resistance to or aggression toward the Spaniards, he also attempts to show that Christianity was already established in Peru. For example, when the Inca troops find it impossible to ignite the former Inca palace (Cuyus Mango), newly consecrated as a Christian temple, Guaman Poma interprets the episode as a divine signal indicating that the Andeans had already converted to Christianity: "En ese tienpo era señal de Dios questaua ya fixa la Santa Yglecia en el rreyno" ("At that time, it was a sign of God that the Holy Church was already established in the kingdom'') (ibid.:403; see also p. 655).

The narration of these events dramatizes Guaman Poma's claims that there had been no military conquest of Peru, an assertion made explicit on several other occasions (see ibid.:164, 377, 388, 564, 573, 971, 972). In addition, he accuses the Spaniards of having acted illegally; they carried no decree that would allow them ruthlessly to kill the Inca or other ethnic lords:

No truxo zédula para matar al rrey Ynga ni a los excelentícimos señores ni a los capitanes deste rreyno. . . . Y ací aués de conzederar y acauar con esto: Que no ay comendero ni señor de la tierra cino son nosotros propetarios lexítimos de la tierra por derecho de Dios y de la justicia y leys. (Ibid.:972)[21]

(He did not carry a decree by which to slay the Inca king or the illustrious lords or the captains of this kingdom. . . . And thus you must consider and conclude this: That there is no *encomendero* nor lord over the land but rather we are the legitimate proprietors of the land, by the right of God and of justice and the laws.)

This denial of foreigners' rights in Peru provides the key to Guaman Poma's interpretation of conquest history. For all of his accusations and dramatizations, however, Guaman Poma's program is not simply a peevish reply to the European histories of the Peruvian conquest. His task is not merely that of making his own people the heroes of the drama and the Spaniards its villains and traitors. The battle of history had already been lost, and Guaman Poma has a more immediate polemical objective. His argument about the nature of the New World natives, their origins and pre-Columbian civilization, is part of a defensive strategy aimed not at the past but at the present. Understanding this move, one can better appreciate the role that the author assigns to the narration of history in his literary project.

The Present Overwhelms the Past

The chapters of the *Nueva corónica* devoted to pre-Columbian Andean society play a specific role within the telic design of Guaman Poma's Andean history. Ironically, these chapters concerned with the past reveal that the author's purpose is not historiographic. His interpretation of the past supports his claims about the present; these, in turn, are articulated in ways to ensure the redress of grievances in the future. The moral and political implications of the past for the present are written into every line of the text, and the consistency of his effort makes it possible to argue that a coherence of intention underlies the entire work.

In both the *Nueva corónica* and the *Buen gobierno*, the mutual cross-referencing of past to future and present to past is a constant of Guaman Poma's rhetoric. The intrusion of his contemporary concerns into the historical narration affects the neutral historiographic illusion that he seeks to create. Attempting to offer a "referential illusion" at the level of discourse, he tries to give the impression that the historical referent is speaking for itself (see Barthes [1967] 1970:149; Benveniste [1966] 1971:206–208). But Guaman Poma frequently intrudes into the apparently narrator-less narration of history to offer moralizing commentary in his own stern and passionate voice. He thus creates a two-layered time, braiding, as Barthes says ([1967] 1970:148), the chronology of the subject matter with that of the language-act that reports it. The reader is transported from the historical to the historiographic mode, that is, from the Incas' past to the narrator's present. The voice of the narrator, Guaman Poma, constantly intervenes, not only in the prologues but also in the chapters' narrations. The result is a continual movement between historical time and narrational time in which the passionate commentary of the narrator threatens to engulf the feigned neutrality of the historical narration.

Guaman Poma's treatment of the issues of barbarity and paganism shows how his concern for the present overwhelms his interest in the past. The temporal compression of the *Nueva corónica y buen gobierno* narration reveals the immediacy and urgency of his "historiographic" mission and brings to the foreground his preoccupation for the contemporary implications of historical issues.

"Paganism" and "barbarity" had been considered synonymous terms from medieval times; from Burgos in 1512 onward, the fusion of the two concepts was the pretext by which to elaborate the juridical titles of conquest (see Höffner [1947] 1957:61, 264). Whereas the popular European mind considered barbarity (a group's location outside the normal practices that define a given secular culture) and paganism (being outside Christian religious culture) as one, Guaman Poma clearly distinguishes between the two in his discussions of the ancient Andeans. In effect, his argument places Andean society outside the space of European secular culture but superior to it, and on the very boundary of its religious culture. For example, in each of the four pre-Incaic ages of Andean history, Guaman Poma performs two operations: he admits the terms *"bárbaro"* and *"infiel"* as separate epithets, and simultaneously attenuates them in the context of an exposition that all but contradicts them; at the same time, he offers the "barbarity" of the ancients as a model worthy of imitation by the contemporary Christian reader.

In his "prologue" at the end of his discussion of the first ancient age of Andeans, the Vari Vira Cocha Runa, he declares that the Christian reader could benefit spiritually by emulating the pious ways of these barbarous infidels:

¡O, que buena gente! aunque bárbaro, ynfiel, porque tenía una sonbrilla y lus de conosemiento del Criador y Hazedor del cielo y de la tierra y todo lo que ay en ella. Sólo en dezir *Runa Camac, Pacha Rurac* [creador del hombre, hacedor del universo] es la fe y es una de las más graue cosas, aunque no supo de lo demás ley y mandamiento, euangelio de Dios, que en aquel punto entra todo. Ued esto, cristianos letores, de esta gente nueba y prended de ellos para la fe uerdadera y serbicio de Dios, la Sanctícima Trinidad. ([1615] 1980:52)

(Oh, what good people!—although barbarous and pagan—because they had a little shadow and light of the knowledge of the Creator and Maker of heaven and earth and all that is within it, only by saying "Runa Camac, Pacha Rurac" [creator of man, maker of the universe], they gave proof of their faith—and it is one of the most ponderous things—although they did not know of the rest of the law and commandments or the gospel of God—for on that point everything rests. See this, Christian readers, about this new people and learn from them to achieve the true faith and service of God, the Holy Trinity.)

He similarly defuses the charges of barbarity and paganism in his accounts of the successive Andean eras. He describes the Vari Runa (constituting the second of his four pre-Incaic periods of Andean civilization) as being technically barbarous but virtually Christian: "Y con ello parese que tenía toda la ley de los mandamientos y la buena obra de misericordia de Dios, aunque bárbaro, no sauiendo nada" ("And, with that, it seems that they had all the law of the commandments and the good works of God's mercy, even though they were barbarous, knowing nothing") (ibid.:56). He likewise lauds the humanity of the third and fourth eras, the Purun Runa and the Auca Runa, respectively (ibid.:62, 73-74). Summing up the civilization of the fourth era, he erases from the image of these pagan barbarians any trace of sinfulness and vice:

De cómo en aquel tienpo no se matauan ni se rrobauan ni se echauan maldiciones ni auía adúlteras ni ofenza en seruicio de Dios ni auía luxuria, enbidia, auaricia, gula, soberuia, yra, acidia, pereza. . . . Y abía mandamiento de Dios y la buena obra de Dios y caridad y temor de Dios y limosna se hazían entre ellos. (Ibid.:73)

(How, during that time, they did not murder nor rob one another nor utter curses, nor was there adultery or offenses against God. Nor was there lust, envy, avarice, gluttony, pride, ire, indolence or sloth. . . . And they had the commandments of God and the good works of God and charity and the fear of the Lord, and they gave alms to one another.)

Guaman Poma's narration therefore serves as a contradiction of the labels he applies to the ancient Andeans insofar as his narrator's voice intervenes to condemn and praise, in the language of the Christian orator: though Gentiles, Guaman Poma argues, the ancients worshipped the true God by the light of their natural reason.[22] Christianity itself is anticipated by the reference to the one god in three persons: "Tenían los yndios antigos conocimiento de que abía un solo Dios, tres personas" ("The ancient Indians had knowledge of the fact that there was only one God, in three persons").[23] Barbarity, in all four accounts, is reduced to the lack of a writing system ("los que son inorantes sin letras," "those who are ignorant of letters," in Las Casas's words).[24] In short, as the ancient Andeans are described in such a way as to defend the spiritual purity and innocence of their contemporary successors, the historian's voice is overcome by that of the strident polemicist.

In surveying Guaman Poma's efforts as a historian, we discover that the narratorless historical description is overtaken by the polemicist's historical interpretation, which is always embedded in immediate, contemporary concerns.[25] The present flows out and washes over every recollection of the past. For Guaman Poma, to write history is to engage in polemic and to reconstitute the events of history as they should have happened. By claiming to appropriate the conventions of the historiographic treatise, he effectively usurps the right to speak in the privileged forum to which even the sympathetic Las Casas would have denied him entrance.[26] Although Guaman Poma proclaims his devotion to historical truth, he undercuts it at every turn. His strategy is complex, and the problem of his work's generic identification requires further exploration. In the discussion of the theory of sixteenth-century historiography that follows, I shall examine one type of history writing—the biography—for which Guaman Poma displays a special affinity. With the biography, the author's move away from political history becomes patently apparent.

2. Searching for a Heroic Conception

Historical Truth and Moral Vision

In Hispanic literature, the link between written history and novelistic fiction has been affirmed from Cervantes to Borges and Carpentier (González Echevarría 1976:67). In examining Guaman Poma's work, one of the fundamental questions to be raised is the relationship of the separate but complementary discourses of history and fiction.

Both history and fiction are subject to the truth of coherence as well as to that of correspondence; that is, both must be coherent, possessing a logical and orderly relationship among the various parts, a kind of inner logic. In this regard, the discourse of the historian and the imaginative writer often overlap (White 1976:21). At the same time, both must subscribe to the truth of correspondence: fiction as well as history must be "adequate" to an image of something beyond itself if it is to lay claim to presenting an insight into human experience (ibid.:22, 23). Considering Guaman Poma's polemical posture, it is not surprising that the truth of coherence, the weaving of an internal logic, takes precedence over the truth of correspondence. In any event, the overlapping boundaries of history and fiction make it a challenge to locate Guaman Poma's work on the field of discourse.

To help determine the degrees to which history and fiction operate in Guaman Poma's "new" chronicle, we need to ask about the kinds of truth that are there represented. Does Guaman Poma's account correspond, to a greater degree, to what Aristotle called the particular truth of history or the universal truth of poetry? To frame an answer to this question, we must first examine the sixteenth- and seventeenth-century conception of history and the degree to which Guaman Poma subscribes to it. Although his narration of the Spanish conquest of Peru does not belong to the category of historiography, some parts of his discourse reflect historiographic aims. To understand what they are, it will be helpful to examine the theory of history for its other than purely political historical focus.

At the outset, we are reminded that the issue of particular, historical truth versus universal, poetical truth was not a clear-cut distinction in Guaman Poma's time. Even though a theorist such as Luis Cabrera de Córdoba distinguishes between the two, he also admits that each possesses some aspects of the other. In *De historia, para entenderla y escrivirla*, he points out the common ground that history shares with rhetoric and poetry.[1] Modern studies tell us that the classical precepts governing the art of oratory were applied to all forms of literature; the process of merging rhetoric and literature within a generalized view of eloquence was initiated in late antiquity (Gray 1968:205). Together, poetics and rhetoric furnished the techniques for eloquence (Struever 1970:53), and the "fictive" nature of historiography as a branch of rhetoric was generally recognized (White 1976:23–24). Even if Aristotle's *Poetics* had provided the authority to distinguish poetry from history, the explanation was by no means so clear that it did not produce endless debate among theoreticians and confusion among readers (Riley 1962:163–165).

The notion that the sixteenth-century European conception of history embraced many types of truth is of critical importance to this discussion. Especially pertinent is the idea that, for the great Spanish humanist Juan Luis Vives and his successors, such as Páez de Castro, the factual truth of history includes the *res togatae*, that is, civil affairs. These theoreticians amplified the concept of history to embrace the description of a people's civilization and thought as well as the trajectory of their political and military fortunes (Montero Díaz 1948:xvii, xxiii). Guaman Poma subscribes to this historiographic value in the chapters of the *Nueva corónica* that have been highly praised for their documentary information about life in pre-Columbian Peru.[2] Even though he often tips the balance of authority and prestige in favor of his own ethnic and regional loyalties, as in his description of the federal Inca administration ([1615] 1980:342–343), he generally takes seriously the historiographic obligation of describing the institutions of Andean society with factual accuracy and in considerable detail.

Sixteenth-century historiography also purported to adhere to the classical prerogative of serving as *magister vitae*, teacher of individuals and nations; thus it bore the burden of communicating moral as well as empirical truths. Preceptists preached and historians practiced their belief in this value (Montero Díaz 1948:xxix). Cabrera de Córdoba defines written history as the narration of truths, put forward by a wise man, in order to

teach the precepts of the virtuous life (1611:f 11 r). The Aragonese humanist Juan Costa goes beyond the exemplary character of history to propose
a moral essence that is intrinsic to the historiographic enterprise: history is
nothing other than the evident and lucid demonstration of the virtues and
vices, the study of which is embraced by moral philosophy (cited in Montero Díaz 1948:xxxv). Here it would seem that history's logical connection
with rhetoric appears. Yet the preceptists agree that the purpose of history
is to demonstrate the truth and to inform, not to persuade. Cabrera de
Córdoba, for example, makes the point quite clear in his Discurso 18,
entitled "Del estilo y elegancia del historiador." He compares the style of
speech, and therefore the intent, of the philosopher, the Sophist, the
historian, the poet, and the orator.

In Cabrera de Córdoba's analysis, the historian stands between the
extremes of the philosopher, who proposes the naked truth and whose
sentences are without passion or strong terms (1611:f 83 r), and the orator,
who must be forceful in the course of his oration, in order to marshal
spirits and take them where he will, "to love, to despise, to condemn, or
absolve, to take or leave things" (ibid.:f 83 v). The historian is perhaps
closest to the Sophist, whose intent is not to persuade but to please through
the use of words and manners of speaking more agreeable than verifiable:
"entretexiendo fabulas, apartandose de la materia, y de las cosas, imi-
tando a los pintores en el colorir con la variedad, igualando los contrarios,
e iguales" (ibid.:f 83 r). Standing between the discursive formations of
Sophism and poetry, history is to serve its readers in a disinterested way.
Through a prose that implicitly inspires but never overtly persuades, the
historian strives to lead readers to truths of moral and ethical, as well as
empirical, dimensions: "porque su intento, ni es delectar, ni persuadir:
pero deleita con la elegancia y orden de palabras de su elocucion: y con
los accidentes que contiene, y casos notables, y persuade a seguir el bien, y
apartarse del mal" ("because his intent is neither to delight nor to persuade: but he delights with the elegance and order of his elocution: and
with the chance happenings and notable deeds he persuades [the reader] to
follow the good and abandon evil") (1611:f 83 r-v).

Cabrera de Córdoba's statement that the goal of history is to serve the
public good ("El fin de la Historia es la utilidad publica" [ibid.: f 19 r])
has a political implication also. The historian's mission is closely con-
nected to the task of governing, and it is the prince's responsibility to
choose the best historians possible; both the prince's reputation and that
of his nation will be at stake in the historian's work (ibid.: f 16 v). Cabrera
de Córdoba, in fact, begins his treatise by proclaiming the formative value
that written history holds for the prince:

Uno de los medios mas importantes para alcançar la prudencia tan necessaria al Principe en el arte del Reynar es el conocimiento de las historias. Dan noticia de las cosas hechas, por quien se ordenan las venideras, y assi para las consultas son vtilissimas. (Ibid.:f 1 r)

One of the most important means to acquire the prudence so necessary to the prince in the art of governing is the knowledge of histories. They offer information about things done, for the sake of him who will order future deeds, and thus, for consultation, they are very useful.)

According to the preceptists, history was to be of great instrumental value in developing the rules by which to govern.

We find that Guaman Poma's historiographic practice adheres to some of these guidelines for truth in written history. Although, as we saw in chapter 1, he fails to follow the empirical datum of historical truth as it pertains to the political events of conquest, he does comply with the norm on matters pertaining to the *res togatae*. At the same time, he attempts to keep the teaching of moral truth constantly in front of his readers. He applies the goal of "utilidad pública" equally to the prince and to the private citizen and shares enthusiastically the historian's conviction that written history should serve the art of governance. His treatise is directly concerned with how Peru should be governed, and the dedication of his book to the Spanish king is the explicit acknowledgment of this objective. To this extent, Guaman Poma is justified in placing his work under the rubric of history. Yet how he goes about teaching his "history lesson" is another matter.

History is to teach by serving as a source of contemplation, not as a battle call to action. Its objective is to appeal to the faculty of the understanding ("el entendimiento") not that of the will ("la voluntad"). Therefore, although history, for Guaman Poma (as for the Sophists), is charged with the responsibility of making things vivid, it is not supposed to falsify. If successful, history helps the reader to follow the path of right and avoid evil.

Yet here we are reminded that all these subtle generic differences are matters of degree: the persuasion of history is of a gentle and passive kind, inclining the reader only by the beauty and order of its words, not by the force of its argument. Although Guaman Poma takes up historical questions, he interprets them according to his own political needs. For him, therefore, history is not the story of "what happened," but rather the story of "what happened to *us*." The telling of the truth about the exploitation and ruin of Peru requires, in Guaman Poma's estimation, far more than the facts of the military (or nonmilitary) conquest. The nature of the truth that he tells is larger than the mere facts; facts together with hypothetical events and broad assertions are set up in logical chains to lead to conclusions that are themselves only hypotheses leading to new conclusions. In order to explicate and communicate his notion of the truth, which is that of a moral catastrophe, Guaman Poma constructs the entire edifice of his history not to teach the facts of empirical experience but rather to communicate a moral vision. That moral vision comes to light by first examining Guaman Poma's own classification of his prose and by studying his use of a particular literary genre—the biography—which seems to subscribe to a specifically historiographic purpose.

Biographies of Incas and Kings

Although Guaman Poma entitles his work "Corónica," he uses the terms "*historia*" and "*uida*" to describe its various aspects. In addition, he places the narration called "Conquista" (the conquest of Peru, the Spanish civil wars) in a third category, which he fails to designate with any historiographic label. But to what particular narrations does he apply the terms "life" and "history"? In the epistles to the king that preface his work, there is a distinction that indicates that he divides specific types of topics into specific discursive categories.

In the "carta del padre del autor" to Philip III, Guaman Poma informs his reader that he has written about the ancient Andeans, and he uses the term "*historia*" to describe the result (ibid.:6). As he continues, he says that he will narrate the "lives" of the *corregidores* and all other colonist groups as well as those of the Andean ethnic lords and commoners (ibid.). At this juncture, it seems that *historia* refers to the ancient past, and *uida* to the lives and activities of the members of contemporary colonial society.

In the "carta del autor," the same terms are used, but with some variation as to what material will go into the respective categories. He announces that he will write the history of the ancient kings and the "lives" of the Indians from the time of the ancients through that of the twelve Incas (ibid.:8–9). He continues the catalogue by stating that he will narrate the "uidas" of the colonist groups as well as those of the "caciques prencipales y los yndios particulares," as he did in the previous epistle (ibid.:9). With this second letter, we realize that, although "*historia*" refers exclusively to ancient times, "*uida*" is not confined to the description of the modern. Thus, for example, we are offered the "*historias*" of the Inca as well as their "*uidas*." At stake are two conceptions of the historiographic object from which can be inferred two distinct purposes; a closer reading of Guaman Poma's text, and an understanding of the terms as they were used in his time, reveal the difference.

In his dedication to Don Pedro Alvarez Ossorio, the marqués de Astorga, Francisco López de Gómara offers the critical distinction in his *Crónica de los barbarrojas*:

Dos maneras hay, muy ilustre Señor, de escrevir historias; la una es quando se escrive la vida, la otra quando se qüentan los hechos de un emperador, o valiente capitan. De la primera usaron Suetonio Tranquilo, Plutarcho, Sant Hieronimo y otros muchos. De aquella otra es el comun uso que todos tienen de escrevir, de la qual para satisfaçer al oyente bastará relatar solamente las hazañas, guerras, victorias y desastres del capitán: en la primera hanse de deçir todos los vicios de la persona de quien se escrive. ([1545] 1853:331–332)

(There are two ways, illustrious Sir, to write histories; one consists of writing the life, the other, the deeds of an emperor or valiant captain. Suetonius Tranquilus, Plutarch, St. Jerome and many others used the first. More common is writing of that other type, in which, to satisfy the reader, it is sufficient to narrate only the great deeds, wars, victories, and misfortunes of the captain; in the first category, all the vices of the person about whom one is writing are to be told.)

The "*vida*," then, is biographical, offering not only an interpretation of the subject's public life (victories and defeats), but also of his or her private life. The public life of an individual alone constitutes the material of "*historia*." The "*vida*" might likely offer a more comprehensive view of the subject's character but a limited glimpse at the currents of history that swirled around that subject. So it is not surprising that, as López de Gómara indicates, "*historia*"—the history of a people's great achievements—was a more urgent and prevalent historiographic enterprise.[3]

Of all the characteristics that López de Gómara might have mentioned, he singles out the subject's vices as being crucial to the biographical portrait. To be honest, the biography must reveal not only the positive, but also the negative aspects of the individual; that is, the writer must offer not merely the political errors of the person in question, but also moral shortcomings, which may or may not be manifest in public deeds. In his "*vidas*," Guaman Poma does not write biographies of all the individuals of all the groups that he discusses, but he does dwell on the traits of vice mentioned by López de Gómara. Thus, Guaman Poma will tell how the God-fearing, righteous people of the first Andean ages turned to war and destruction in the last, how the Andean people during the time of the Incas turned to idolatry while still observing "los diez mandamientos y la ley de misericordia," and how the modern *caciques prencipales* and *yndios particulares* are best known for "sus rretos que uzauan antiguamente y de su cristiandad y pulicía y otras curiucidades destos rreynos" ([1615] 1980: 6). Although these general moral portraits or *"uidas"* of the Andean world are varicolored, the "lives" of the colonists, from the *encomenderos* to the lowliest vagabond Spaniard, are painted in consistently more somber tones: Andean civilization is remembered for its vices and its virtues; colonial society only for its vices.

Guaman Poma also uses the term *"uida"* in the strict sense of biography. The book that will "celebrate and make immortal the memory and name of the great departed lords" in the manner of history will also narrate the biographies of the twelve Incas (ibid.: 7). With regard to the historical reign of the Incas, Guaman Poma folds *"historia"* and *"uida"* together. Taking the individual's great public deeds on the one hand, and his or her moral portrait on the other, Guaman Poma makes biography his preferred mode of historical discourse (see Adorno 1974b). He creates three series of biographies: the Incas, the Coyas (the Incas' royal consorts), and the first ten viceroys. Whereas the viceroys seem to be fitting subjects for these conventional literary biographies, Guaman Poma's placement of Incas and Coyas in the same mold is more interesting, for he creates an intriguing hybrid combination of autochthonous legend and foreign literary conventions.

Since the High Middle Ages, Spanish chroniclers had put aspects of the royal biography in historiographic works that adopted the format of the succession of dynasties (Ruano 1952:77). Even though these chronicles had as their subject the political process, their authors focused on the history of a single nation or empire by personalizing their subjects. They tended toward biography by presenting all deeds as though they had been carried out by the king; intermingling personal events from the life of the monarch—his illnesses, the quality of his character—with those of historical significance, biography emerged and made national history itself appear as a series of personalized events (ibid.: 82).

In the fifteenth century, the new Italian biography was brought to Spain, but the Spanish elaboration of the genre resulted in only external similarities to the Renaissance model. With Pérez de Guzmán and others, the Spanish biography retained its allegiance to the medieval prototypes of the *canción de gesta* and hagiography (Romero 1944:138). The rejection of the Italian celebration of freely manifested individuality consisted in the tendency to summarize, in categorical formulas, the moral value of each episode and offer a moralizing *excursus* on the meaning of the pertinent ethical principles (ibid.:122, 124). In this way, the individual episode was raised to the plane of ideas postulated; from the individual example emerged the moral archetype (ibid.:122). By the end of the fifteenth century, the Spanish biography remained fixed in the model that Pérez de Guzmán had set forth in his *Generaciones y semblanzas* and Hernando del Pulgar followed in his *Claros varones de Castilla*.

It is quite likely that Guaman Poma came to know this literary tradition. One of the most popular items in the colonial Peruvian book trade in the late sixteenth century was Rodríguez de Almela's *Valerio de las historias de la Sagrada Escritura y de los hechos en España* ([1487] 1793; Leonard 1942:23), and it may well have provided Guaman Poma with a model. Writing in imitation of Valerius Maximus, Rodríguez de Almela offers examples of noble deeds accomplished by well-known historical personages: he follows each anecdote with a moral reflection. His book was reprinted several times between 1511 and 1587 (Rodríguez de Almela [1487] 1793:4–5), and it was considered, from 1520 until the preparation of the 1793 edition, to be the work of Pérez de Guzmán (Domínguez Bordona 1924:xxv–xxvi). This error reveals, however, the homogeneity of the tradition of moralistic, biographical exempla from Pérez de Guzmán through Rodríguez de Almela. Whereas both emphasized the moral lesson to be learned, Pérez de Guzmán drew the portrait first and outlined the lesson afterward, organizing his exposition by the individual personages. In contrast, Rodríguez de Almela ordered his discourse according to moral topics and gave anecdotes about historical figures to illustrate the principle. Internal evidence in the *Nueva corónica* shows that Guaman Poma explicitly followed the procedure used by Pérez de Guzmán. In any event, the late medieval Spanish tendency to combine intimate and mundane details from the life of the monarch with those of historical transcendence constituted the general concept out of which Guaman Poma worked.[4] Examining his biographies in the light of the Hispanic literary tradition, one discovers not only how he highlights the moral implications of historical events but also how he domesticates the image of the Inca, making it less exotic (the latter effect was no doubt intended for the benefit of the European reader).

Guaman Poma's narrative outline is exactly like that of the fifteenth-century Spanish biography, which discusses the lineage of the subject, physical description and moral character, notable (and not so notable) deeds (Romero 1944:118–122). To these and by way of conclusion are added the details of the subject's death and the names and number of offspring. A comparison of the typical format of Castilian biography with that of Guaman Poma reveals the similarity.

Pérez de Guzmán's portrait of Enrique III of Castile provides an example. The biographer first offers the king's lineage and its antiquity:

Este rey don Enrique el terçero fue fijo del rey don Iohan y de la reyna doña Leonor, fija del rey don Pedro de Aragon, e descendio de la noble e muy antigua e clara generaçion de los reyes godos e, señaladamente, del glorioso y catolico prínçipe Recaredo, rey de los godos en España. E, segunt por las estorias de Castilla paresçe, la sangre de los reyes de Castilla e su suçesion de un rey en otro se ha continuado fasta oy, que son mas de ochoçientos años, sin auer en ella mudamiento de otra liña nin generaçion, lo cual creo que se fallará en pocas generaçiones de los reyes christianos que tan luengo tienpo durase. . . .

E este rey don Enrique començo a reynar de poco mas de onze años e reyno diez e seis, ansi que biuio mas de veinte e siete años. ([1450] 1924:11-12)

(This king Don Enrique the third was the son of the king Don Juan and the queen Doña Leonor, daughter of the king Don Pedro of Aragon, and descended from the noble and very ancient and illustrious succession of the Gothic kings and, namely, from the glorious and Catholic prince Recaredo, king of the Goths in Spain. And, according to what appears in the histories of Castile, the blood of the kings of Castile and their succession from one king to another has continued to this day, which is more than eight hundred years, without there being in it the alternation of any other lineage or succession, which, I believe, can be found in few lines of Christian kings which have lasted so long. . . .

And this king Don Enrique began to reign at little more than eleven years of age and he ruled sixteen, thus he lived more than twenty-seven years.)

Guaman Poma begins his biography of the Inca Manco Capac in a similar manner: in lieu of documenting his lineage, which Guaman Poma claims was infamous, he offers a statement about the duration of the Inca dynasty, which is reminiscent of the type of summary assessment given by Pérez de Guzmán:

Desde el primer Ynga Manco Capac Ynga que rreynó ciento sesenta años con el comienso y con el postrer Topa Cuci Gualpa Uascar Ynga lexítimo y de su ermano uastardo Atagualpa Ynga y desde que comensó a rreynar los dichos Yngas y acabar su rreyno, como se acabó y consumió su rreyno, los dichos lexítimos de derecho que rreynaron mil y quinientos y quinze años de señorear en la tierra estos dichos Yngas y rreys. ([1615] 1980:87)

(From the first Inca Manco Capac Inca, who reigned 160 years at the beginning, and at the end, Tupa Cuci Hualpa Huascar Inca, the legitimate, and his bastard brother Atahualpa Inca, and since the said Incas began to reign and their reign ended, how their kingdom was finished and extinguished, the said legitimate rulers by right, who reigned 1,515 years of ruling in the land, these aforementioned Incas and kings.)

The Spanish biographer continues with a description of King Enrique's physique and personal temperament, telling how he was of medium height and a good disposition, fair-skinned and blonde. However, illness during adolescence changed the prince's character. He spent most of his time alone and he was more inclined to incontinence than seriousness or prudence ([1450] 1924:12–13). Although Guaman Poma does not present this type of detailed information about Manco Capac, he follows the biographical model in the case of the other eleven Incas. Their appearances are described at length and, in a few notable cases, temperament is coordinated with physique.[5]

Returning to Pérez de Guzmán, we continue with his description of the reign of Enrique III:

El auia grande voluntad de hordenar su fazienda e creçer sus rentas e tener el reyno en justicia; . . . Ouo este rey algunos buenos e notables religiosos e perlados e dotores, con quien se apartaua a ver sus fechos e con cuyo conseio hordenaua sus rentas e justiçias. . . . E ansi, con tales maneras, tenia su fazienda bien hordenada e el reyno paçifico e sosegado. (Ibid.:14)

(He had a great desire to order his estates and increase his revenues and maintain the kingdom in justice; . . . This king had some good and eminent religious and prelates and doctors, whom he took aside to examine his actions and with whose advice he ordered his revenues and courts. . . . And thus, by such means, he maintained his estates well ordered and the kingdom calm and peaceful.)

The rule of Manco Capac is also described:

Y este Ynga ydeficó Curicancha, templo del sol. Comensó a adorar el sol y luna y dixo que era su padre. Y tenía suxeto todo el Cuzco cin lo de fuera. Y no tubo guerra ni batalla, cino ganó con engaño y encantamiento, ydúlatras. Con suertes del demonio comensó a *mochar* [adorar] *uacas*, ydúlos. ([1615] 1980:87)

(And this Inca built Coricancha, the temple of the sun. He began to adore the sun and moon and said that the sun was his father. And he had subjected all of Cuzco but nothing beyond it. And he had neither war nor battle; instead he won people over with deceits and enchantment, idolatries. With tricks of the devil, he began to adore idols.)

Guaman Poma also gives an account of each Inca's marriage. About Manco Capac, he says, "Y se casó, dando dote al sol y a la luna con su muger que era su madre, la señora Mama Uaco, Coya, por mandado de los *uacas* y demonios" ("And, giving a dowry to the sun and moon, he married his wife, who was his mother, the lady Mama Huaco, queen, at the command of the idols and demons") (ibid.).

Pérez de Guzmán concludes his portrait of Enrique III with an account of his death and a record of his children:

E vino a Toledo e alli mando juntar todas sus gentes e fizo cortes para auer dineros e hordenar los fechos de la guerra. Estando en Toledo, aquexolo mucha la dolençia, e murio dia de nauidad, año de mil e cuatroçientos e siete años. E dejo fijos a don Iohan, que despues del reino, e a la infanta doña María, que es reyna de Aragon, e la infanta doña Catalina, nasçida de pocos dias e caso con el infante don Enrique. ([1450] 1924:18)

(And he came to Toledo and there he demanded that all his peoples gather, and he set up court to gather money and order the affairs of war. Being in Toledo, this affliction bothered him greatly, and he died on Christmas day in the year 1407. And he left children, Don Juan, who reigned after him, and the princess Doña María, who is queen of Aragon, and the princess Doña Catalina, born only a few days [before her father's death] and married to the prince Don Enrique.)

Similarly, Guaman Poma describes Manco Capac's death and descendants:

Y murió de edad de ciento y sesenta años en el Cuzco. . . . Y tenía ynfantes, hijos lexítimos Cinche Roca Ynga, Chinbo Urma, *coya*, Ynga Yupanqui, Pachacuti Ynga. Y tubo uastardos y uastardas, *auquiconas* [príncipes] y *ñustaconas* [princesas]. ([1615] 1980:87)

(And he died at the age of one hundred and sixty years in Cuzco. . . . And he had legitimate children, princes and princesses, Sinche Roca Inca, Chimpu Urma, queen, Inca Yupanqui, Pachacuti Inca. And he had bastard children, princes and princesses.)

What is most striking about Guaman Poma's text is that it combines the Castilian formula of biography with elements of the autochthonous historiographic tradition. Guaman Poma exploits at least two types of indigenous source: the oral traditions recalled by himself and his informants, perhaps with the aid of *khipus* ("los *quipos* y memorias y rrelaciones de los yndios antigos de muy biejos y biejas sabios testigos de uista" [p. 8; see also El Inca Garcilaso (1609) 1963, Primera Parte, Libro Sexto, chap. 9: v. 2:204)]; and the pictorial tradition of native historiography (see Mendizábal Losack 1961:228–330; López-Baralt 1980:120–135). The prospect of such sources is suggested not so much by Guaman Poma's creation of visual portraits of the Incas as by his verbal description of them.

Each figure is described as though Guaman Poma were recalling a picture he had seen:

Mango Capac, Ynga, el primer padre de los dichos Yngas, tenía su *llauto* [cíngulo] uerde y su pluma de quitasol y su orexa de oro fino, *masca paycha* [borla real], *uayoc tica* [flor ornamental] y en la mano derecha su *conga cuchona* [hacha] y en la ysquierda un quitasol y su manta de encarnado y su camegeta arriua colorado y en medio tres betas de *tocapo* [paño de labor tejido] y lo de auajo azul claro y dos ataderos en los pies. ([1615] 1980:87)

(Manco Capac Inca, the first father of the said Incas, had his green headdress, and his feathers in the form of a parasol and his ear spools of fine gold, the royal fringe, and ornamental flower, and in his right hand his battle-ax and in the left, a parasol, and his flesh-colored mantle and his tunic, red on top, with three pieces of wovenwork cloth in the middle, and the lower part light blue, with two cords tied around his legs.)

He gives no clue about the sources of this visual information or whether he is referring to pictorial representation or symbolic values (see López-Baralt 1980:132). Yet from the perspective of the production of the text, the series of Inca biographies offers the best example of Guaman Poma's synthesis of the materials of both cultures.

From the viewpoint of the European reader, the biographies present the domestication of the exotic Incas. Whereas Pérez de Guzmán writes about the court of a king whose reign had ended some forty years prior to his writing, Guaman Poma brings the legendary deeds and lore of distant times into sharp focus. He adds prosaic detail to figures of mythic proportions and provides a kind of gossipy information that was typical of the biographical genre. At the same time, he destigmatizes (apparently fantastic) information that would shock a Western reader, passing off in a matter-of-fact manner the news that Manco Capac said that the sun was his father, that he married his mother at the command of idols and demons, that he died at the age of one hundred and sixty years. The accounts of Incas who lived for two hundred years ([1615] 1980:111), and *coyas* who made stones speak, communicated with demons, and ate their own children (ibid.:121, 129), are all couched in the benign and familiar formulas of the narrative biography. Guaman Poma tricks the reader, presenting these larger-than-life, godlike (or monstrous) figures as though they were ordinary kings and queens. Bringing them down to size, making them human, he lays the groundwork for his moralizing commentary.

The Prologue Always Comes Last

It is in the context of the concluding prologue that Guaman Poma's biographical subjects take on their full significance, not as unique historical personages, but as moral, human types worthy of emulation or condemnation. The prologue is one of the literary conventions that Guaman Poma seems to have misunderstood. Although he begins his book with a general "prologue to the Christian reader" (ibid.:11), he uses the formula for individual chapters as well as the book as a whole and he places these prologues at the end of the chapters they accompany. It is possible that the location of the prologue where an epilogue should be is a mechanical exigency. At the end of each chapter in the original manuscript, Guaman Poma set aside a final page or portion thereof on which to write a prefatorial message. Inasmuch as the prologue is in general an a posteriori phenomenon, written after a work is finished in order to justify, explain, or synthesize the important points of the text it prefaces, Guaman Poma's placement may simply reflect the original lineal order of his composition. But this version of the work is by all indications a final copy, according to Guaman Poma's own testimony (ibid.:918, 1084); therefore, his peculiar arrangement is more likely to be intentional.

Oddly enough, there are precedents in Guaman Poma's own time for making the prologue a concluding text rather than an introduction (Porqueras Mayo 1957:130). An item requested for the Lima book trade in 1583, Bartolomé de Albornoz's *Arte de los contractos* (1573) (Leonard 1942:28) offers a rationale for putting the prologue at the end of the discourse it accompanies. Albornoz favors the placement of the prologue in the final position, where it would serve not as a (probably) misleading invitation to the reader, but rather as a vehicle by which the reader might judge the work. Thus, the reader can use it to determine whether the text delivers on all that this "prologue" promises.[6] Guaman Poma likewise makes the lessons to be learned from his chapters the explicit topic of his "prologues." In the chapters dedicated to ancient Andean society he points out the good examples that contemporary Andeans should follow; in the discussions of colonial society in the *Buen gobierno*, he warns the Spanish reader to avoid the cruel behavior and moral folly attributed to the colonists.

The text that actually serves as introduction to Guaman Poma's chapters is often called the *primer capítulo*. With this designation, he follows a common literary convention (see Porqueras Mayo 1957:131–132); that is, when a formal prologue was not used, the first lines of a work commonly fulfilled the introductory function. Often the title *primer capítulo* meant, in effect, "prologue" (ibid.:131).[7] Fray Antonio de la Calancha tells why, in his *Corónica moralizada del orden de San Agustín* (1639–53), the *primer capítulo* will be used to introduce his work. He will put his introductory remarks in the first chapter of his chronicle, with the presentation of his main topic, because, although many readers skip over the prologue of a book, most read the first chapter (cited in Porqueras Mayo 1957:131).

Guaman Poma uses the first lines or page of his chapters in just this manner.[8] However, in almost all cases, he uses a picture, not a written text, to introduce the chapter. In only a few cases does a prose statement accompany or substitute for that introductory phrase. Thus, he uses the prologue and first chapter conventionally; the *prólogo* in the manner of Albornoz to close the chapters, and the *primer capítulo*, in the manner of Calancha to open them.

The prologue plays a very special role in Guaman Poma's rhetorical system; it is the arrow that points from the book to the world, that relates the text to the reader. All nineteen of Guaman Poma's prologues are moralizing commentaries on the chapters that precede them, but the ones of particular interest are those that accompany the biographical narrations. Such prologues reveal the moralistic orientation of the verbal portraits. Although the formal properties of the biographies follow the Castilian model to a great degree, they do not share—from the point of view of the text's production—the utilitarian conception of Pérez de Guzmán and Pulgar. Here we approach a fork in the road between historiography and moralistic literature, between works in the style of Pérez de Guzmán and Pulgar on the one hand, and Rodríguez de Almela on the other.

According to Pérez de Guzmán, history, in the form of biography, has as its aim the inspiration of virtuous men to perform noble deeds ([1450] 1924:7). "Las grandes hazañas," the historian promises, will be recognized and remembered. *La fama* appeals to the elite, rather than to the average citizen; the *Generaciones y semblanzas* are expected to inspire the leaders, the first among equals. Guaman Poma's biographies, in contrast, follow the orientation of Rodríguez de Almela and moralistic literature insofar as they attempt to move *every* person to action. This is true of the portrayals of the Incas and *coyas* as well as the viceroys.

Thanks to the prologues, the Incas and the *coyas* become examples less of heroic leadership than of moral and religious behavior to be either emulated or avoided. These examples are to appeal to Andean readers in their role as private citizens rather than as governing elites. The issue is personal conscience, not public duty, and it is defined in terms of Christianity versus paganism. Such is the message of Guaman Poma's concluding prologue, which frames the Inca biographies:

Letor de los Yngas: Aués de uer desde el comienso de Mango Capac Ynga hasta que se acabó el lexítimo Uascar Ynga. ¡O perdido Ynga!, así te quiero dezir porque desde que entrastes fuestes ydúlatra, enemigo de Dios porque no as seguido la ley antigua de conoser al señor y criador Dios, hazedor de los hombres y del mundo, que es lo que llamaron los yndios antigos Pacha Capac [creador del universo], dios Runa Rurac [hazedor del hombre]. Que así lo conocieron, que así lo decía los primeros Capac Apo Yngas antigos.

Así lo llamaron a Dios que es lo que entró en los corasones de bosotros. Y de buestra agüela Mama Uaco, Coya, Mango Capac Ynga entró los demonios, mala serpiente, y te a hecho maystro y herroniaco ydúlatra, *guaca mucha* [adorador]. Y te a puesto y enpremido la ley de ydúlatra y seremonias, aunque no la hizistes dexar los dies mandamientos y las buenas obras de misericordia. Así dexáredes de la ydúlatra y tomárades lo de Dios que fuera de bosotros, fuérades grandes santos del mundo. Y desde agora seruí a Dios y a la Uirgen María y a sus santos. ([1615] 1980: 119)

(Reader of this chapter on the Incas: You must consider, from the beginning with Manco Capac Inca, until the time the legitimate Huascar Inca was executed. ¡O lost Inca! Thus I call you, because since you appeared, you were an idolater, the enemy of God, because you have not followed the ancient law of knowing the Lord God and Creator, maker of men and the world, which is what the ancient Indians called the lord Pacha Camac [creator of the universe], Runa Rurac [maker of man]. Thus they knew Him, thus the first, ancient Capac Apo Incas [Incas, powerful Lords] told it.

Thus they called Him who entered your hearts God. And the devils, evil serpent, entered the heart of your grandmother, Mama Huaco, queen, and Manco Capac Inca, and have made of you accomplished and misguided idolaters, idol-worshippers. And he has placed and impressed on you the law of idolatry and false ceremonies, although that did not force you to abandon the Ten Commandments and good works of mercy. Thus, if you were to abandon idolatry and rely on that godliness that is within you, you would be great saints in the world. So, from now on, serve God and the Virgin Mary and their saints.)

Identical in tone, the prologue to the "letores mugeres" in the chapter on the *coyas* harangues idolaters: "Y así el primer ydúlatra comensastes, muger, y ciruistes a los demonios" ("And thus the first idolatry was begun by you, woman, and you served the devil") (ibid.:144). Such admonitions have a polemical as well as a moralizing purpose, for they defend the Incaic standard of justice and charity at the same time as they seek to challenge traditional Andean belief. Mostly, however, the moralizing thrust prevails.

The viceregal biographies (ibid.:438–475), too, are designed not to honor the elite and to inspire future leaders, but simply to condemn the base motives of the average individual. In spite of some laudatory remarks about certain viceroys, Guaman Poma does not emphasize their noble actions. Even in these descriptions of exemplary persons, he does not make heroism a category of Spanish behavior. Although he praises Antonio de Mendoza, for example, as "muy cristianícimo, amigo de los pobres y seruidor de Dios y de su Magestad" ("very, very Christian, a friend of the poor and servant of God and his Majesty"), he ends the discussion with this warning to the Spanish readers:

Ues aquí, tontos y encapases y pucilánimos pobres de los españoles, soberbiosos como Lusefer. De Luysber se hizo Lusefer, el gran diablo. Así soys bosotros, que me espanto que queráys ahorcaros y quitaros bos propio buestra cauesa y quartesaros y ahorcaros como Judás y echaros al ynfierno. (Ibid.:439)

(See here, foolish and incapable and faint-hearted, wretched Spaniards, proud as Lucifer. From being the bearer of light, Lucifer became the great devil. You are the same; I am astonished when I see that you want to hang each other and, yourselves, cut off your own heads and quarter yourselves and hang yourselves like Judas, and deliver yourselves to hell.)

He interjects a similar admonition into his laudatory biography of Luis de Velasco (ibid.:471), and he condemns Toledo for his execution of the Inca prince Tupac Amaru (ibid.:452).

Such instances typify the interpenetration of narrational levels, that of the events depicted and that of the language act that reports them (see chapter 1, pp. 32–35). In all the biographies, the author attempts to provoke the immediate introspection of the reader and to inspire a personal commitment to undertake moral reform; here the moralistic program of the *Nueva corónica y buen gobierno* comes fully into view. Working in tandem with the prologues, the biographical accounts become exempla to teach the reader how to do and be good.[9] Consistent with the goals of moralistic literature, which sought to convey good habits through that most widely used means, the exemplum (Hafter 1966:9–10), Guaman Poma rejects the historiographic goal of inspiring contemplation or promoting learning for its own sake. Instead, he attempts to persuade the reader to take action against a world filled with vice and corruption.[10]

The *Nueva Corónica* as Epic Story

Converting the historical anecdote into a moral example, Guaman Poma becomes the champion of the exemplum.[11] When the value of teaching a moral lesson prevails, historical facts themselves cede their privileged status to those attributes that can best persuade, and those might well be invented. As Guaman Poma's historical subject matter is taken over as an object of moral contemplation ([1615] 1980:369)—"Lo malo apartaldo para que sean castigos y con lo bueno se cirua a Dios y a su Magestad" ["Put the bad to one side so that the evil might be punished, and, with the good, serve God and his Majesty"]—the historical personage is re-created somewhere in the space that exists between history and precept, between the novelistic episode and the maxims that assimilate the biography to the didactic system (see Cros 1971:81).

In the *Nueva corónica y buen gobierno* there are two such cases that stand out: the account, repeated on various occasions, of the life of Guaman Malqui, Guaman Poma's father; and the story of the author's own life. These narrations, blending elements of fact and fancy, history and myth, are fictions founded on historical truths. According to sixteenth-century definitions, they are narrations in the epic mode.

The concept of the epic provisionally provides a productive approach to the problem of the *Nueva corónica*'s literary genre, and a closer consideration of that generic definition is merited. According to López Pinciano in his *Philosophía antigua poética* [1596], the epic is that "imitación de historia" ([1596] 1953:v.3:250) whose moral purpose requires that the events on which it is based be worthy of admiration[12] and its plot, or *fábula*, verisimilar (ibid.:178, 250). As the imitation of the thing rather than the thing itself ("ha de ser, digo, imitación de obra y no ha de ser la obra misma"), the *fábula* as the very substance of poetry ("la materia del ánima poética") can be of three types (ibid.: v. 1:10; v. 2:39). One is pure fiction, completely the work of the imagination, like the novels of chivalry. The second is of the type that we call the fable; like the apologues of Aesop, these consist of the elaboration of a truth on the basis of fiction ("sobre una mentira y ficion fundan vna verdad") and offer moral advice in the guise of a little tale (ibid.: v. 2:12). The third type of *fábula* is founded on history and gives rise to the epic and the tragedy: "There are others that, on the basis of a single truth, fabricate a thousand fictions, such as tragedies and epics, which always, or almost always, have their origin in some historical event, but in such a way that the amount of historical content is minimal in comparison to the fanciful. And thus the work takes the name of the genre of which it is mostly constituted. Fadrique added: "Because of that, Lucan is numbered among the historians; although his work contains fictional narrations, these are few in relation to the historical ones" (ibid.:12–13).[13]

The subject of the epic should be some worthy secular prince—virtuous, pious, and brave, not superhuman—whose history was neither so old as to be forgotten nor so modern as to be readily disputed ("ni tan antigua que

esté olvidada, ni tan moderna que pueda dezir nadie, 'esso no passó ansí' ")
(ibid.: v. 3:169, 178). Besides its heroic conception, viewed on the level of
either the individual or the collectivity, the epic offers latitude with regard
to what López Pinciano calls "truths" and "fictions," the mixture of factual information and invention. To make a point about the integrity of
such productions, he metaphorically describes poems based on history as
the making of cloth: the woof of this new fabric is history, and the warp
threads are poetic invention (ibid.: v. 2:98). The implication is that, woven
together, these generically different strands produce an unbroken and
sturdy fabric.[14] After debating the merits of the epic founded on truth and
that based on fiction, El Pinciano concludes, following Tasso, that the one
founded on history is superior.[15]

To the members of López Pinciano's generation, any long, fictional
narration in prose belonged to the epic genre. El Pinciano himself repeatedly extolls the *Historia etiópica* of Heliodorus, considering it in the same
category as the *Odyssey* and the *Aeneid* (ibid.: v. 3:165). Like Cervantes, he
proposes the application of epic theory to prose fiction (Shepard 1962:
214). Whether or not it is grounded on historical events, the epic is expected to teach the reader. El Pinciano states this explicitly, thus expressing an attitude that conforms to the general justification of all forms of art
in the period.[16]

My interest in applying the period definition of the epic to the specific
case of Guaman Poma is based on the observation that he founds his imitation of the action (*fábula*) in the *Nueva corónica* on history and weaves
into it a poetic imitation of events. On the basis of a single truth—that
Tawantinsuyu was conquered by foreign invaders—Guaman Poma elaborates a "thousand fictions." These include, of course, the fictional
welcome for the invading Spaniards and immediate acceptance of their rule
at Tumbes, the lack of native resistance to the conquest, and the successful
conclusion of the civil wars among the Spaniards, thanks only to the Andean *caciques*. These narrated events constitute the beginning, middle,
and end points of the poetic imitation. On this foundation, the author
reaches a "true" conclusion: the destruction of the Inca empire was carried out without any legal or moral justification. The model could be ex-
panded to comprehend the entire *Nueva corónica* narration and "Conquista." Again, on the foundation of a single truth—the rise and fall of
the Andean empire—a thousand fictions are concocted: one of the sons or
grandsons of Noah arrives in the Indies to found the Andean race; centuries later, a Spanish explorer stumbles inland and tells the Inca that he
and his horses eat nothing but gold; and on and on. This is not the short
fable, the story that dramatizes a moral lesson; it is, rather, the epic story

of Andean civilization, whose last phase is the tragedy of the Spanish conquest and colonization.

The second characteristic of the epic, that the work be the story of some worthy secular prince, is also present. Considering either the "Conquista" narration, or the *Nueva corónica* plus "Conquista," we find that Guaman Poma creates heroes from the fabric of his own family and his ancestral lineage. The conversion of the historically prominent figure into the exemplary hero heralded the birth of the epic poem out of the historical annal. Guaman Poma makes the same gesture in portraying his own forefathers as the heroes of ancient and contemporary Peruvian history. The first lords of this ancient dynasty brought civilization to its fullest flower in pre-Incaic times, according to Guaman Poma ([1615] 1980:65–75). Once conquered by the expansionist Incas, the Yarovilcas became the Incas' viceroys ("segundas personas") for all of Tawantinsuyu. Subsequently, Guaman Poma tells us that his own father, Guaman Malqui, likewise served as the Inca's chief minister; as we have seen, he is also credited with peacefully accepting the Spaniards' authority at Tumbes.

The heroic figure of Guaman Malqui is larger than life, for it transcends both the imperial Andean and the colonial Spanish spheres. Survivor of the conquest who had served in the palace of the Inca, Guaman Malqui later proved himself in battle loyal to the Spanish king by saving the life of a Spanish captain and subsequently helping to defeat the forces of the rebel conquistador Hernández Girón (see chapter 1, pp. 13–20). Guaman Poma's story of his ethnic lineage, from the dawn of Andean civilization until twenty years after the conquest, is summarized and exemplified by the heroic figure of Guaman Malqui. Pulling together the information that Guaman Poma relates about his father, the elements of a story—a narration with beginning, transitional, and terminating motifs (White 1973b:5)—appear. This is so either from the perspective of the biographical portrait of his father alone, or from that of the story that begins with the civilizing forefathers and ends with the loyalty to the Spanish king of the most recent of their descendants.

Guaman Poma thus attempts to draw to a stabilizing conclusion the tale that he tells of the genesis and flourishing of Andean civilization and its upheaval by foreign invasion. The life of Guaman Malqui serves as the narrative thread that shows that the first part of the work, the *Nueva corónica*, partakes of a poetic teleology, of that "internal purposiveness which justifies the way everything functions within that feigned reality" (Krieger 1974:59). Guaman Poma offers an epic story whose motific encoding can be identified either with the entire story of Andean civilization from the Yarovilcas through the Incas, or with that of one man, Guaman Malqui.

At this point, it will be helpful to consider Hayden White's distinction between the related formulas of chronicle and story: when the elements in the historical field are arranged such that events to be dealt with are organized into the temporal order of their occurrence, the result is a chronicle; the chronicle is organized into a story when the events are encoded into a motific pattern. In principle, the chronicle is open-ended, without inaugurations, culminations, or resolutions. The story, in contrast, has a discernible form, having transformed the diachronic, open-ended process into a completed process about which one can ask questions as if dealing with a synchronic structure of relationships (White 1973b:5-6).

Guaman Poma's *Nueva corónica* narration is actually a story that has the telic character of a poetic sequence, and teleology is what poetic form boasts as its essential characteristic. Murray Krieger points out that "it is just the poet's freedom to put teleology where his object of imitation had none that distinguishes him from even the most arrogant historian who would fashion the past in the shapes of his private fancy" (1974:56). Guaman Poma, too, creates a teleology where his object of imitation had none; he creates a vision of a moral world whose genesis and apocalypse consist in the appearance of the first Andeans and the death of the last Inca. An alternate reading stretches the span of this story from the era of the Vari Vira Cocha Runa to the conclusion of the conquistadores' civil wars. Within this design, "Conquista" would be another story, an allegory of Spanish greed and Andean good faith. "Conquista" is precisely the encounter of the principle of the Andeans' good faith with that of Spanish *codicia*.[17] Unburdened by the historian's accountability to "the facts," which imposes a referentiality on his or her work and inhibits the purity of the formal models (ibid.:53), Guaman Poma, as a poet, ignores the consideration of accountability. His story partakes of that internal purposiveness that comes wrapped in its own materiality (ibid.:59).

On the basis of such teleological principles, Guaman Poma's own critical commentary about other chronicle writers is revealing. He criticizes both Luis Jerónimo de Oré—whose work, as we have seen, he admires to the point of plagiarism—and his archenemy, Martín de Murúa—whom he detests as a horsethief and wife stealer—for not having told the whole story of the Incas: "Comensó a escriuir y no acabó para mejor dezir ni comensó ni acabó" ("He [they] began to write and did not finish; more properly speaking, he [they] neither began nor ended") ([1615] 1980: 1090). Guaman Poma's criticism is both substantive and formal; to impose a form on events is to impose meaning, or, rather, to impose form on the narration of events is to release a teleology contained in them. Thus,

Guaman Poma re-creates Andean history as though it possessed such completeness and closure. For the seventeenth-century interpreters of Aristotle, form was seen as the imposition of a latent if unrealized teleology in nature (Krieger 1974:60). For Guaman Poma, the real burden of history was to make sense of events, to give them a moral meaning. Thus, the story that he created portrays not a political or historical process, but serves as the basis for a moral meditation. The result is a kind of mimesis or historical fiction—an epic as "imitación de historia"—that exists somewhere between the historical example and the moral precept.

Although the contours of the epic conception are visible in Guaman Poma's work, the question remains as to the degree that he subscribes to their principles. To continue this assessment and to explore fully the problem of generic identification in the *Nueva corónica y buen gobierno*, we turn to Guaman Poma's favorite authors and preceptists, the writers of religious literature, notably *sermonarios* (collections of sermons) and catechisms. His goal, to create an epic replete with heroic figures and the expression of collective pride and faith in the ethnic group, must be reconciled with the discursive formation known as "the literature of good living" ("la literatura de bien vivir"); for if it can be inferred that Guaman Poma attempts to create order and meaning out of the events with which he deals by employing the techniques of storytelling, his engagement with ecclesiastical rhetoric must be considered for its implications as well.

3. From Story to Sermon

Both the theory and practice of ecclesiastical rhetoric in Guaman Poma's time offer much insight into his work, from its general conception to its specific rhetorical tactics. In the *Nueva corónica y buen gobierno* there are at least six quotations from Fray Luis de Granada's *Memorial de la vida cristiana*, though all but one lack citation of their source.[1] Fray Luis's writings are present throughout Guaman Poma's book. Obviously, he considered the Dominican writer to be an appropriate literary and intellectual model. Even more important, however, is the relationship of his text to what I consider to be its closest models, the collections of sermons that were published in Peru for the conversion of the native population. In my opinion, these doctrinal texts are more directly responsible for triggering his angry polemical reaction than are the chronicles written about the Spanish conquest of Peru.

The new, bilingual catechisms and *sermonarios* produced in Peru after the meetings of the Third Church Council in Lima (1583) are important to Guaman Poma in another way: they address the specific problems of cross-cultural communication. Written to solve the problems of the Spanish priests communicating with the Andean natives, these texts provide Guaman Poma with a theory and practice of communication that serve his needs in crossing the same cultural barrier, but from the opposite direction. The understanding of his rhetorical strategy depends on the examination of these works and Guaman Poma's pose as a preacher.

Ultimately, the discussion of the sermon—specifically the question of *inventio*—illuminates the history/fiction problem in Guaman Poma's rewriting of Andean history. Here the relationship of the sermon to the story emerges as the principal issue. In continuing the previous chapter's discussion about the *Nueva corónica y buen gobierno*'s implicit teleology, I shall examine the stories-within-sermons (the exempla) and consider the sermon's intrusion into the narration of the larger-frame story. By assessing the respective roles assigned to story and sermon, one discovers how the teleological design constructed in the *Nueva corónica* breaks down in the *Buen gobierno*.

Granadine Strategies

One of the most important religious writers of Counter-Reformation Spain, Fray Luis de Granada was also one of the most popular authors on the Peruvian book trade (Leonard 1940, 1941, 1942). He is the only author whom Guaman Poma cites as the source of any of his statements; the text happens to be a biblical anecdote about idolatry ([1615] 1980:367). Fray Luis is also the first of three writers whom Guaman Poma mentions as "los sabios que conponen los libros y lo escriuen para el seruicio de Dios" ("the wise men who compose books and write them for the service of God"); the other two are Domingo de Santo Tomás and Luis Jerónimo de Oré (ibid.:926).

Ironically, the works of Fray Luis de Granada and the catechisms written for Andean conversion provide antithetical models by which to interpret Andean experience. Where Fray Luis is magnanimous in his general, theoretical assessment of pre-Christian and pagan cultures, the New World literature of conversion is unforgiving in its treatment of pagan practices. Guaman Poma exploits both, relying on the Granadine outlook and using it to defend Andean society against the pragmatically oriented, pointed attacks in the works produced by the Third Church Council.

To understand Guaman Poma's appreciation of Fray Luis's works, we turn to the biblical anecdote for which Guaman Poma cites Fray Luis as his source. Concluding the first part of his work, that is, the *Nueva corónica*, Guaman Poma remarks,

Nos espantéys, cristiano letor, de que la ydúlatra y herronía antigua lo herraron como xentiles yndios antigos herraron el camino uerdadero, como los españoles[2] tubieron ýdolos, como escriuió el rrebrendo padre fray Luys de Granada: Que un español gentil tenía su ýdolo de plata que él lo abía labrado con sus manos y otro español lo abía hurtado. De ello fue llorando a buscar su ýdolo; más lloraua del ýdolo que de la plata.

Ací los yndios como bárbaros y gentiles lloraua de sus ýdolos quando se los quebraron en tienpo de la conquista. Y bosotros tenéys ýdolos en buestra hazienda y plata en todo el mundo. (Ibid.:369)

(Do not wonder, Christian reader, at the idolatry and ancient error the ancient Indians committed, they erred like Gentiles, they took the wrong road, in the same way that the "Spanish" had idols, as the Reverend Fray Luis de Granada has written: That a Gentile "Spaniard" had his idol of silver, which he made with his hands, and another "Spaniard" had robbed him of it. Because of that, he went weeping to look for his idol; he was more saddened by the loss of his god than because of the silver.

Thus the Indians, as pagans and Gentiles, wept for their gods when they were destroyed at the time of the conquest. But it is you, Spaniards, who have made idols of the wealth and riches that you have gained in the world.)

In the *Memorial*, Fray Luis had recalled this story about the tribe of Dan under the title, "De lo que se pierde por el pecado" ("Of that which is lost because of sin") ([1566] 1945, tratado 2, chap. 3: v. 2:219). His commentary on the story from the eighteenth chapter of the Book of Judges reveals a sympathetic attitude that Guaman Poma surely found heartening. In his own account, Fray Luis underscores the legitimacy of the pagan's sorrow:

Pues si este malaventurado lloraba tanto por haberle quitado un dios de metal que él mismo se había fabricado (teniendo por tan justas y debidas las lágrimas de esta pérdida), ¿qué será razón que sienta un cristiano, pues sabe cierto que todas cuantas veces pecó, perdió no al falso dios que él mismo hizo, sino al verdadero Dios que hizo todas las cosas? (Ibid., chap. 3: v. 2:219)

(Thus if this luckless one wept so much because of being deprived of a god of metal which he himself had fabricated [considering as just and proper the tears caused by this loss], with what right does a Christian grieve, since he knows with certainty that all the times he sinned he lost not the false god that he himself had made, but rather the true God who made all things?)

In the comparison, Fray Luis assigns greater blame to the Christian who willfully rejects God than to the pagan who lost his gods through no fault of his own, that is, as a result of destruction caused by others. Guaman Poma does not miss the opportunity, taken on the authority of Fray Luis, to point out that the Spaniards are more worthy of blame than either the ancient Andeans ("yndios antigos") or those who were the victims of the Spanish "en tienpo de la conquista."

Guaman Poma's admiration for Fray Luis can thus be attributed to the latter's tolerant sympathy for the humanity of the pre-Christian era and for those pagans who had never heard nor rejected the gospel.[3] Fray Luis's evocation of an ancient past that included the prefiguration of the Christian era, his reliance on the faculty of natural reason ("la luz natural") to show how the ancients came to know God,[4] and his presentation of Hebrew

kings and prophets as models of spirituality and good conduct, all give
Guaman Poma the authority to portray the first Andeans in the same
mode.

In this generous spirit, Guaman Poma likens the search of the ancient
Pacarimoc Runa, that is, literally "those of the dawn" ([1615] 1980: v. 3:
1098) to the quest of the prophet Habakkuk: "Señor, ¿hasta cuándo
clamaré y no me oyrás y daré bozes y no me rresponderás?" ("Lord, until
when will I implore and you will not hear me, and I will cry out and you
will not respond?") (ibid.:50). Guaman Poma copies the prayer from the
Memorial[5] ("¿Hasta cuándo señor, clamaré y no me oirás?" [Granada
(1566) 1945: tratado 5, chap. 2: v. 2:301]), and he uses it to describe the
spiritual yearnings of the first Andeans as analogous to those of their biblical predecessors. This prayer is similar to one in the Quechua tradition,
especially with regard to the motif "óyeme y respóndeme."[6] Guaman Poma
finds in this instance a comforting affinity between Old Testament culture
and his own. He repeatedly points out the similarity of the Quechua prayer
to that of the Old Testament prophet ("deziendo como los profetas") to
promote his thesis that biblical and ancient Andean spiritual traditions
shared the worship of the true God ([1615] 1980:78).

On the matter of the religious experience of the pre-Christian era,
Guaman Poma again takes his cue from Fray Luis. He proposes this dar-
ing thesis about indigenous civilization in counterpoint to both the cate-
chismal works written by the Peruvian missionaries and the Spanish
chronicles of Peru. Where both groups had identified modern and ancient
Andean society with paganism and barbarity, the breadth and tolerance of
Fray Luis's theological anthropology permit Guaman Poma to re-create
Andeans as God-fearing folk from time immemorial. The notion of harmony between ancient pagan and modern Christian experience, a constant
theme in Guaman Poma, was, in fact, the central idea of Fray Luis's
theology. The author of the *Memorial* faithfully followed the example of
the church fathers, trying always to find a supernatural, Christian meaning in the truths of nature and the thought of the ancients. His central
ideal was harmony: a real, physical harmony between the natural and
supernatural worlds, and a historical and providential harmony between
pagan antiquity and Christianity (Laín Entralgo 1946:227).

Besides the expansiveness of Fray Luis's outlook, there are two immediate and pragmatic reasons for Guaman Poma's election of ecclesiastical
rhetoric as the language of his exposition. One is that the rhetorical strategy of threat provides him with the perfect vehicle for arguing his
position.[7] The other is that the Lascasian model of argumentation for colonial reform is based on a principle of Christian doctrine. The personal,

religious obligation of restitution "de hacienda, de fama, de honra," that is, of an individual's goods or good name, whether tarnished by true or false accusations of wrongdoing (see Fray Luis [1566] 1945, tratado 2, chap. 1: v. 2:216), is the justification for Las Casas's political demands for the return of Peruvian lands to their owners.[8]

From the writings of Fray Luis de Granada, Las Casas, and possibly those of the archbishop of Lima, Jerónimo de Loaysa, Guaman Poma takes the principle of Christian restitution as the expressive vehicle by which he demands justice of the colonists:

Es muy justo que se buelba y rrestituya las dichas tierras y corrales y pastos que se bendieran en nombre de su Magestad porque, *debajo de consencia*, no se le puede quitársela a los naturales, lexítimos propetarios de las dichas tierras. ([1615] 1980:540, emphasis mine; see also pp. 477, 532, 573, 1086, 1087)

(It is proper that they reverse themselves and give back the said fields and yards and pasturelands sold in the name of his Majesty because, *according to* [Christian] *conscience*, they cannot take them away from the natives, the legitimate proprietors of the aforementioned lands.)

When he says that the Spaniards will go to hell if they fail to make restitution to the Andeans, he is short-circuiting the theological reasoning of Fray Luis de Granada: restitution is an act of penitence and contrition; the failure to make restitution, signifying the absence of penitence, would be cause for eternal perdition (see the *Memorial de la vida cristiana* [1566] 1945, tratado 2, chap. 1: v. 2:215–217). Guaman Poma turns this argument full force against the colonists and threatens the divine punishment forewarned by Fray Luis and Las Casas:

Disís que aués de rrestituyr; no ueo que lo rrestituýs en uida ni en muerte. Paréseme a mí, cristiano, todos bosotros os condenáys al ynfierno. . . . Aunque os metáys en el decierto y rreligión, ci no rrestituýs y pagáys lo que deuéys, serés condenados al ynfierno. ([1615] 1980:369, 1087)

(You say that you have to make restitution; I don't see that you give anything back either in life, or at the time of death. It seems to me, Christian, that all of you are condemning yourselves to hell. . . . Even though you were to abandon yourselves in the desert and become religious hermits, as long as you do not make restitution and pay what you owe, you will be condemned to the inferno.)

In this frame of reference, the political gesture becomes a personal one, reduced or elevated to the level of moral conscience; it is the preacher, not the historian or the storyteller, who focuses such intense attention on the designated reader.

For Guaman Poma, the historian, the teller of epic tales, and the preacher each provide features that hold respective values in his own discursive system. If at one extreme the lessons of history need to be taught, at the other, the preacher's strategy must convert those events into topics for religious and moral reflection and remedial action. Thus, Guaman Poma weds the moral function of history as *magister vitae*, and the structure of a poetic imitation, to the language of overt persuasion. From among the goals and strategies of history, epic, and ecclesiastical rhetoric, Guaman Poma leans ultimately in the direction of the last. He turns to the rhetorician and the preacher to fulfill his literary needs because his objectives are based first and last on extraliterary considerations.

In calling the system to which Guaman Poma appeals rhetorical instead of historiographic or poetic, I am following Bernard Weinberg's definition of a rhetorical system as "one in which a specific effect of persuasion is produced upon a specified audience by using the character of the audience, the character of the speaker, and the arguments of the speech as the means to persuasion" (1952:343). Guaman Poma argues for the rights of his people by dramatizing, not merely stating, his hypothesis. He avails himself of a fiction disguised as a historical narration as a kind of proof or demonstration of the claims of Peruvians to sovereignty in their own land. The special teleology that he imposes on the events of history reveals that he used the poetic *fábula* as well as historical data. Nevertheless, he adds to these the task of the orator, with whom the most direct form of the art of persuasion remained. To be victorious in his cause, he must move the affections of his readers. Only rhetoric, directing a specific message to a specific audience, explicitly serves this overarching purpose.

On Moving the Reader's Affections

Those aspects of rhetoric that are pertinent to Guaman Poma's literary enterprise are discussed in Fray Luis de Granada's *Los seis libros de la retórica eclesiástica, o de la manera de predicar*.[9] The relationship of the preacher to the orator was an intimate one, and Fray Luis, like many others, bases his theory of ecclesiastical rhetoric on that developed to deal with legal causes ([1576] 1945: v. 3:491). Unlike the dialectician who disputed with the learned in the schools, the preacher, dealing with the general populace, depended on examples and lively interpretations—not philosophical arguments—to win over his audience (ibid., book 2, chap. 2: v. 3:507).

One of the features that differentiates the sermon from oratory in general is what Fray Luis calls "accommodation or descent to particular matters"; this concept offers an important insight into the organization of Guaman Poma's work. Whereas the orator must evoke a single desired response in all listeners, the preacher must administer to the particular needs of each and every listener, different as these may be. He must "terrify some, inspire or console others, and apply to each the medicines most beneficial to personal health" (ibid., chap. 12: v. 3:524). According to Fray Luis, the preacher is to direct the sermon to the various estates, informing each as to its moral duty, in the manner that St. Paul was accustomed to doing at the end of his letters, and as John the Baptist also did: "Lo que también practicó San Juan Bautista, cuando a todos los que acudían a él, daba, según el estado de cada persona, varios preceptos de vivir" (ibid.:525).

When Guaman Poma names all the various groups to whom his own book is directed, he likens his project, too, to that of John the Baptist: "Como el precursor San Juan Bautista traxo los amenazos, azotes y castigos de Dios para que fuésemos enfrenados" ("Like the precursor St. John the Baptist [who] brought the threats, the calamities, and the punishments of God in order that humanity be restrained") ([1615] 1980:1). Paraphrasing Fray Luis's references to Jeremiah and John the Baptist from the first page of the *Memorial*, Guaman Poma tells how they warned their followers of the doom that would befall them if they did not reform their ways. His references to these prophets implicitly carry the same warnings to his own readers, and he fashions himself as the prophet of Andean doom. Envisioning the preservation of his book in the "archive of heaven, and that of the world" ("Lo tendrá en el archibo del mundo como del cielo") (ibid.:751), Guaman Poma evokes the Book of Judgment in which the lives of all humanity are to be written. Thus, he frames his work as an eternal account book.

Eternal accounts, according to Guaman Poma, have to be settled now; on the basis of his accounting, he expects to inspire the reader to take remedial action. In this regard, his strategies echo the practices prescribed by Fray Luis. On the question of moving the affections of the reader, the Granadine preacher suggests that the effect depends on two things: the greatness of the matter under consideration, and the ability to put it before the eyes of the listener ("mostremos ser en su género de grandísima importancia, y . . . propongámosle como patente a sus ojos") ([1576] 1945, book 3, chap. 10: v. 3:547). With regard to the question of making ideas "visible," Fray Luis gives the example of Jeremiah, who, in the *Lamentations*, not only describes but exaggerates the calamity he recounts (ibid.:547).

Another way of putting the matter before the reader's eyes is to focus on the character of the preacher himself. St. Paul commonly proposed himself as an exemplar for the imitation of the faithful, according to Fray Luis. He concludes that St. Paul put examples before the people's ears with his preaching and before their eyes with his person; at the same time as the listeners were struck with wonder, they were inspired to imitation (ibid., book 1, chap. 6: v. 3:501).

Fray Luis goes on to add that the real secret to moving others is to be moved oneself (ibid., book 3, chap. 10: v. 3:548). Yet how, he asks, can we move ourselves, since such effects are not in our power? By what the Greeks called "*phantasias*," which Fray Luis calls "visions": "Por las cuales de tal suerte se representan en el ánimo las imágenes de las cosas ausentes, que parece que las miramos con los ojos, y que realmente las tenemos presentes" ("Through which the images of absent things are represented in the soul in such a manner that it seems that we gaze upon them with our eyes, and that we actually have them present") (ibid.). According to Fray Luis, the need to envision scenes, useful to the orator, who ordinarily attempts to move his hearers either to commiseration or indignation, is of critical importance to the preacher, for the effects that he seeks to achieve are many and varied (ibid.).

To make these things "visible" to the parishioner, graphic devices were thus often used.[10] Sermons were often accompanied by hieroglyphs or paintings to be deciphered ("jeroglíficos impresos o estampados," or "pinturas a descifrar") (Maravall 1975:498). In Guaman Poma's desire to make things visible, he follows the same strategies, exaggerating (if only by focusing exclusively on) those criminal vices that he wishes to see corrected, presenting the character of the narrator as an exemplary figure, and animating the whole discourse with graphic representations. (I shall examine this last feature in the next chapter.)

With regard to the greatness of the matters to be treated in the sermon, Fray Luis quotes directly and extensively from the fourth book of Augustine's *Of Christian Doctrine*. Explaining how Cicero prescribed low, medium, and high styles of oratory for teaching, pleasing, and moving, respectively, the affections of the listeners, he adds that, although such styles are appropriate to judicial matters, they cannot be applied to ecclesiastical oratory because, here, every matter preached about is great ([1576] 1945, book 5, chap. 18: v. 3:603). It was Augustine's conviction that everything humanity encountered was to be interpreted with reference to its function in the larger design of God's providential dispensation. Living in such terms was a "continual exercise in translation, a seeing through the literal contexts of things (objects, events, persons) to the significance they acquire in the light of a larger perspective" (Fish 1972:25).

With a similar outlook, Guaman Poma makes every matter important by referring it to humanity's eternal destiny and the avoidance of eternal punishment. For him, there is no hierarchy of greater to lesser offenses; the outrages committed against the lowliest tribute-paying Andean ("*indio tributario*") are as serious as those committed against the ethnic lords. He translates all human experience—pre-Columbian as well as Spanish colonial—into the antagonistic forces of vice and virtue at the level of the individual, and each individual must fight that battle in his or her own life. As a member of a race whose historical progress foreign conquest and colonization has truncated, Guaman Poma rejects the conceptual matrix of European historiography that projected humanity's progress toward an ultimate goal and assumed the superiority of white, European peoples over other cultures in achieving it. Instead, he elects the theological conception that places humanity's great (and only) drama in the arena of individual salvation or perdition.

Thus, in Guaman Poma's work, that which happens in the world of human affairs raises to a higher power the factor of the story of "what happened." Although his exposition never leaves the spectacle of colonial Peru and Peruvians, Guaman Poma attempts to make sense of its specificity and to dignify it by placing that experience in a theological, not historiographic, purview. The specific events of history are devoured by the contemplation of the events that typify human nature. Hence the language of Christian morality, of vice and virtue, dominates. Guaman Poma abandons the project of telling what happened in Peru up through the time of the Spanish conquest in order to tell what generally happens in Peru in the day-to-day life of the colonized Andeans. His conceptual foundation of moral distinctions makes the happenings of contemporary Peru an example of the irony of the whole human condition. For its constant reiteration of certain types of actions (such as priests' and *corregidores'* abuses of the natives), the *Nueva corónica y buen gobierno* ultimately offers little insight into the chronological development of public events and illustrates and emphasizes instead the universal forms of human action.

The Literature of Conversion

Although possessing affinities for ecclesiastical rhetoric in general, the *Nueva corónica y buen gobierno* is in direct dialogue with the *catecismos* and *sermonarios* produced in Lima for the native Andean population. Only in this context do Guaman Poma's descriptions of his literary goals make sense. He declares that his book is to be a confessional guide for the Andeans:

La dicha corónica es muy útil y prouechoso y es bueno para emienda de uida para los cristianos y enfieles y para confesarse los dichos yndios y emienda de sus uidas y herronía, ydúlatras y para sauer confesarlos a los dichos yndios los dichos saserdotes. ([1615] 1980:1)

(The said chronicle is of great use and value and it is useful for the moral reform of Christians and infidels alike, for the said Indians so that they might make their confessions and mend their lives and correct their errors and idolatries and so that the said priests might know how to confess the aforementioned Indians.)

He repeats this statement about his purpose in the general prologue to the reader (ibid.:11).

Such claims come straight from the religious literature destined for the American natives. In the *Symbolo catholico indiano*, Pedro de Oré declares that the efforts of his brother, Luis Jerónimo, will be beneficial to the priests ministering to Indians as well as to the Indian themselves: "Las tengo por obras grandemente vtiles y prouechosas, assi para los curas de Indios como para los mismos Indios." The *Arte y vocabulario de la lengua general del Perú llamada quichua* also describes its purpose in the same manner:

El qual será muy util para todo género de gentes, así curas de Yndios, como otras personas eclesiásticas y seglares que ueuieren de tratar con los Yndios en poblado y yendo de camino. . . . Será también de mucho prouecho [para] el que comiença en la lengua Yndica para los que oyen confesiones. (1614: f 4 r)

([This book] will be very useful for all manners of people, for pastors of Indians as well as for other religious and lay persons having to deal with Indians in settlements or on the road. . . . It will also be of much use to those who are beginning in the Indian language, for those who hear confessions.)[11]

There are two points of contact between the Peruvian's chronicle and the Third Council's books of religious instruction. The first consists of the polemical arguments made about traditional Andean society and the spiritual potential of the Andeans; the second is the theory of communication put to practice within those didactic texts. In these works beats the pulse of the polemic to which Guaman Poma responds; these were the documents that circulated freely among the *indios ladinos* of Peru and the Spaniards, mostly ecclesiastics, who dealt directly with them (see Acosta 1982). Guaman Poma's defense of his race is a direct reaction to the biases expressed in these doctrinal texts. He mentions one or another of these works in his review of the "crónicas pazadas" ([1615] 1980:1089), and the *Tercero catecismo y exposición de la doctrina por sermones* can serve as an example of the missionary attitude expressed in such books.

The most damning charges made against the Andeans were the ringing condemnations of idolatry, drunkenness, sexual crimes, and promiscuity. Sermon XVIII of the *Tercero catecismo* is directed against the worship of the Andean *waqas*. As if final proof that they are false gods, the preacher asks,

¿Por ventura las *guacas* defendieron a vuestros antepasados de los *viracochas*?[12] Dadme acá la *guaca,* yo le pisaré delante de vosotros y la haré pólvora. . . . Todo es engaño y mentira. ([1585] 1773:243)

(Did, by any chance, the *waqas* defend your forefathers from the "Spaniards"? Give me the idol; I will step on it before your very eyes and smash it to bits. . . . All is deceit and lies.)

Those who continue to worship the *waqas* and obey the *hechiceros* will not learn the law of God, but rather remain as uncivilized as beasts of the fields:

El indio que no aprende la Ley de Dios es como bestia que no quiere mas de comer, y beber, no tiene otro gusto, sino en pacer yerua. ¡Hombre! tu no eres carnero, ni caballo. La lengua que tienes no es solo para comer, como el caballo, y el carnero, sino también para hablar como hombre. (Ibid.:288)

(The Indian who does not learn the Law of God is like a beast who neither knows nor wants anything but to eat and to drink; he has no other gratification but to graze on grass. Look, man! You are not a sheep or a horse. The tongue that you possess is not only for use in eating, like the horse or the sheep, but also for talking like a man.)

Like idolatry, the crime of ritual drunkenness is also attacked for its effect on human reason: drunkenness deprives man of "the best that God gave him, namely human reason and judgment," and reduces him to the level of a dog: "Lo mejor que Dios os dio que es el juicio y la razón de hombre, y de hombre os volvéis caballo y aun Perro" (ibid.:315, 316).

Fornication, adultery, and sodomy are also condemned in the strongest terms in the sermons. God's punishment for these sins is the ruin of the Andean nation:

Sepa que la causa porque Dios ha permitido que los Indios seáis tan afligidos, y acosados de otras naciones, es por ese vicio [la sodomía] que vuestros pasados tuvieron, y muchos de vosotros todavía tenéis. Y sabed que os digo de parte de Dios que si no os enmendáis, que toda vuestra nación perecerá y os acabará Dios y os raerá de la tierra. (Ibid.:347–348; see also pp. 304, 333).

(Know that the cause of God's permitting the Indians to be so afflicted and pursued by other nations is that vice [sodomy], in which your forefathers engaged and many of you still practice today. And understand what I tell you, by God's command, that if you do not mend your ways, your entire nation shall perish and God shall exterminate you and wipe you from the face of the earth.)

The claim that the subjugation of Peru is a divine punishment, and that the destruction of the Peruvian nation is the ultimate form of that punishment, is a spiritual explanation for secular affairs that Guaman Poma takes up in turn. He denies the sins of the fathers as well as those of the sons, and he turns the wrath of this divine punishment against the Spaniards themselves. His effort is made easier because he puts into practice the principles of cross-cultural communication as outlined in the "Proemio" to the *Tercero catecismo*.

A Theory of Cross-Cultural Communication

Entitled "Del modo que se ha de tener en enseñar y predicar a los Indios" ("How to go about teaching and preaching to the Indians"), the preface to the *Tercero catecismo* provides a wealth of advice on how to communicate with the aborigines. The first rule of rhetoric that the evangelizing priest is to follow—echoing Fray Luis—is to tailor the message to the listener: "Hase pues de acomodar en todo a la capacidad de los oyentes el que quisiere hacer fruto con sus sermones o razonamientos" (ibid.:vii). Second, the principal points to be taught should be repeated with such frequency that they are retained in the listener's memory (ibid.: viii). Next, the style should be simple, clear, brief; the language should be that of "conversation among companions, not theatrical declamation" (ibid.:ix–x). Fourth, and most important, the preacher must persuade his listeners to follow his advice as well as to make it understood: "El quarto aviso, y el más importante, es, que de tal manera se proponga la doctrina christiana, que no solo se perciba, sino que también se persuada" (ibid.:x). Thus, the preferred vehicle for communicating with a relatively sophisticated indigenous audience is not the dialogue of questions and answers (which format the first catechisms had followed) but rather the sermon:

Asi tambien es menester que esta misma Doctrina se les propusiese a los Indios en tal modo, que no solo la percibiesen, y formasen concepto de estas verdades christianas; pero también se persuadiesen a creerlas, y obrarlas como se requiere para ser salvos: y para esto es necesario diferente estilo, y ha de ser como Sermon, y

Plática del Predicador, y tal que enseñe, y agrade, y mueva a los oyentes, para que así reciban la Doctrina de Dios, y la guarden. (Ibid.:xiv)

(Thus, it is also necessary that this same doctrine be propounded to the Indians in such a way that, not only will they understand and form concepts of these Christian truths, but they will also be persuaded to believe them and put them into practice as is required for salvation: and for this a different style is necessary, and it is to be like a sermon and speech of the preacher, such that it teaches and pleases and moves the hearers, so that they receive the Doctrine of God, and keep it.)

Again, like Fray Luis, the missionary preceptist suggests that the Andean public, like any group listening to a sermon, can be moved best through the employment of lively interpretations, rather than reasoned arguments: "Estos Indios, como los demás hombres, mas se persuaden y muevan por afectos que por razones." Thus, exclamations, apostrophes, and other figures of the oratorical art are highly recommended to move the reader, and similes and examples figure prominently among them to make the unfamiliar intelligible (ibid.:xi–xii).

On all these counts, Guaman Poma follows the catechism's precepts. He adheres to the rule of accommodation by addressing all colonial groups separately; he repeats his contentions endlessly. He makes countless exhortative speeches, and his attempt to persuade his audience is patently obvious. On adapting the message to its receiver, Guaman Poma chooses the form of the sermon ("la Plática del Predicador"). Each of his nineteen prologues is, in effect, a sermon, and the chapters themselves conform to that format. To understand how the chapter narrations follow the rules of composition of the sermon, I turn again to Fray Luis's treatise on preaching (see also Adorno 1979a).

Fray Luis explains that the sermon, like any oration, consists of three parts: the exposition, the argumentation, and the amplification. The exposition is conceived as a narration—possibly but not necessarily historical—consisting of that which has happened, or *could* happen: "Exponemos pues con estilo sencillo, o con narración histórica, con la cual declaramos nuestro intento, o lo que ha sucedido o *puede suceder*" (emphasis mine). The argument serves as proof, with which the preacher attempts to make believable that which is doubtful: "Probamos con argumentos y razones, con las cuales intentamos hacer creíble lo dudoso." Amplification is understood to be that discourse designed to move the listener's affections:

Amplificamos cuando con una oración extendida, . . . concitamos el ánimo del oyente a ira, compasión, tristeza, odio, amor, esperanza, miedo, admiración o a cualquiera otro afecto. (Granada [1576] 1945, book 2, chap. 3: v. 3:508)

(We amplify when, with an extended speech, . . . we incite the spirit of the hearer to ire, compassion, sorrow, hatred, love, hope, fear, wonder, or other passions.)

Argumentation is directed to the *entendimiento* or understanding, which is, in Scholastic anthropology, the intellectual faculty of the soul. Amplification is directed to the faculty of the *voluntad* (the will) in order to mobilize the capacity to take action:

Pues por este medio abrimos camino para mover las pasiones, persuadir, disuadir, alabar o vituperar; porque para estas tres cosas principalmente conduce la razón de amplificar. (Ibid., book 3, chap. 1: v. 3:530)

(By this means, we open the path to move the passions, persuade, dissuade, praise, or vituperate; because the mode of amplification leads to these three things.)

Guaman Poma's narrative chapters fit the formula of the *exposición* with elements of *argumentación* interspersed. The chapter devoted to the Purun Runa, the third pre-Incaic Andean epoch in Guaman Poma's scheme, serves as an example of his procedure. He narrates the experience of an industrious and God-fearing people in the manner of the exposition. He moves into argumentation when he attempts to prove that these infidels were not Moors or Turks or Jews, but rather "españoles," that is, pertaining to the biblical cultural tradition to which the Christians lay claim. The prologue, which concludes the chapter, serves as an amplification insofar as it attempts to move the reader to action:

Mira, cristiano letor, aprended desta gente bárbara que aquella sonbra de conoser al Criador no fue poco. Y ací procura de mesclar con la ley de Dios para su santo seruicio. ([1615] 1980:62)

(Look, Christian reader, and learn from this barbaric people that that shadow of the knowledge of the Creator was not a small thing. And, thus, try to adhere to the law of God for the sake of His holy service.)

At this point, the sermon itself dissolves as it signals that which it hopes to achieve beyond its own confines. In most of the chapters, interpolated commentaries, directed from speaker to reader, break into the narration. Thus, the exposition, argumentation, and amplification are not kept completely discrete, but rather overlap as they would in any sermon. Only the prologues are consistently the center of amplification, as they seek to move the reader to action in the world of lived experience.

The Privileged Role of Invention

But how does the idea of the story, that is, the presence of a teleology, which I discussed in the previous chapter, fit into a frame that also embraces the sermon? If poetry proceeds by mimesis and rhetoric, by statement and proof (Howell 1975:93), how do the two coexist in the *Nueva corónica y buen gobierno*? I have claimed that the *Nueva corónica* of Andean experience is a story that begins with the creation of Adam and the generation of the Vari Vira Cocha Runa and ends with the recording of the death of the last Inca. Yet, within it, the sermon appears in the form of the prologues. These sermons have a corrosive effect, breaking the pace and pattern of the story and the esthetic distance between narrator and reader. Through the intrusion of the author's direct address to the reader, the characters in the story are matched up with the readers outside it. Thanks to the continual switching from one narrational level to another, the units of the story become examples in the sermon's context, even as they retain their identity as episodes in the story of Andean civilization.

The struggle that seemed to ensue between the impulses of history and mythic or epic fiction in the *Nueva corónica* give way completely in the *Buen gobierno* to a tension between poetics and rhetoric, with the latter definitively dominating. The triumph of rhetoric in the *Buen gobierno* settles the unresolved issue in the history/fiction discussion, which began this study. That problem concerns the status of truth versus that of verisimilitude and the relative role of invention. The *inventio* is as much a constituent of the sermon as of the story, and Fray Luis defines it as "el acto con que el entendimiento busca y halla cosas verdaderas o verosímiles, aptas a persuadir lo que se intenta" ("the process by which the faculty of the understanding seeks and finds things true or verisimilar, which are appropriate for persuading, as one endeavors") ([1576] 1945, book 2, chap. 1: v. 3:506). As Fray Luis indicated in describing the sermon's exposition, the writer may use that which has occurred or could happen, in other words, that which is true or that which is verisimilar. For rhetoric in general, verisimilitude occupies a privileged position. It is true that, in forensic oratory, the description of circumstances had to be the result of rigorous inquiry into the facts; but in demonstrative or deliberative rhetoric, the topics of didactic literature could be served by a wide range of means, so long as they fell within the bounds of verisimilitude (Cros 1971:85–86). Matters of description, for example, need not subscribe exclusively either to concrete reality or to the ideal projection (ibid.:88). When employed to praise or vituperate, rhetoric need not be objective (ibid.:83).

In matters of invention in ecclesiastical rhetoric, Fray Luis favors the *conformación* or *razonamiento fingido*, which he defines most generally as the invented speech. He attributes the practice not only to the classical orators, but also to Holy Scripture, and even—significantly—to the prophets. According to Fray Luis, the writer, like Jeremiah, is justified in presenting not merely what people generally say, but what they should say, or should have said. Through *conformación*, speeches and events that never actually occurred and people who never actually existed could be added (invented) for the sake of amplification and the arousal of commiseration ([1576] 1945, book 3, chap. 9: v. 3:545). For Fray Luis, the *razonamiento fingido* is the stock-in-trade of the preacher: "No sé yo si hay cosa que mas pertenezca al oficio del predicador" ("I don't know of any other thing that pertains more to the vocation of the preacher") (ibid., chap. 8: v. 3:544).

As the *inventio* takes into account not only the truthful but also the verisimilar, another possible justification emerges—under the rubric of rhetoric—for the fictitious episodes in Guaman Poma's history of the Spanish conquest of Peru. Events may be portrayed not as they were, but as they could have been: "lo que ha sucedido o puede suceder." Whether they actually happened is immaterial to the framing of the central proposition, to the presentation of the arguments. Whereas the historian would consider such episodes preposterous and without justification whatsoever, they are perfectly legitimate from the vantage point of the orator or the preacher—or of whoever would adopt the style of the "Sermón, Plática del Predicador." Thus, as Guaman Poma abandons rigorously historical fact, his *razonamiento fingido* is doubly justified—first, as he tells his epic tale, and second, as he uses the art of rhetoric to persuade the reader of the dignity and glory of Andean civilization.

The Simile of Lucifer

To frame his political arguments, Guaman Poma assimilates the oral style and figures of ecclesiastical speech, exploiting the simile to great advantage. His common term of comparison for the Spaniards is the pride of Lucifer: "Como el gran angel tan hermoso, Luysber, se hizo Lucefer, perdió el cielo por su soberbia" ("Like the great and so beautiful angel, the bearer of light, Lucifer, lost heaven because of his sinful pride") ([1615] 1980:560). He applies this simile to the colonists several times (see ibid.:439, 494, 551, 598, 813, 950, 961, 969, 1178), and his accusations against them for the sin of *soberbia* are legion.[13] He commonly associates acts of political treason with the sin of excessive pride, even as the *Tercero catecismo* describes the crime of Lucifer by comparing it to an act of treason ("Los condenó como a traidores a pena eterna") ("He condemned them like traitors to eternal punishment") ([1585] 1773:68). These fallen angels are no longer on God's side: "Y tienen su corazón lleno de rabia y de envidia contra Dios y contra los que son del vando de Dios" ("And their hearts are full of fury and envy against God and against those who are on God's side") (ibid.: 69).

From his Andean perspective, Guaman Poma begins by accusing the colonists of treason and translates the language of political crimes in the Christian rhetoric of sin. Thus he condemns Francisco de Toledo's execution of the Inca prince Tupac Amaru as an action by which the viceroy usurped the prerogatives of his own king. As a commoner, Toledo had no authority to kill the Inca sovereign; Guaman Poma calls it an act of sheer *soberbia*:

De los males que abía hecho en este rreyno, ací al Ynga como a los prencipales yndios y a los conquistadores deste rreyno, ues aquí, caualleros, la soberuia que tiene un mandado pobre. Se quiso alsarse como se alsó y mató a un rrey y señor deste rreyno. No pudiendo conoser la causa, cino el mismo rrey y señor a de sentenciar y firmar pa[ra] la sentencia y muerte de otro señor y rrey. Y ací la soberuia le mató a don Francisco de Toledo. ([1615] 1980:461)

(Concerning the evil things that he had done in this kingdom, against the Inca as well as against the illustrious lords and against the conquerors of this kingdom: see here, gentlemen, the enormous pride that a wretched envoy had. He tried to rise up in revolt, as he rose up against and killed a king and lord of this kingdom, not being able and lacking authority to judge the cause. But rather, the king and lord himself must judge and take responsibility for the sentencing and execution of another lord and king. And thus *soberbia* killed Don Francisco de Toledo.)

He accuses Toledo of *soberbia* for this deed (ibid.:452, 461, 948, 950, 951) and describes Francisco Pizarro's execution of Atahualpa Inca in the same terms, that is, as an act of political treason whose consequence will be eternal doom (ibid.:393).

So Guaman Poma gives the historical events of the conquest an interpretation that is simultaneously political and theological. Consistent with this conception, he explains modern Andean history as the consequence of the heavenly fall, in the midst of a harangue against the corruption of church inspectors and the suffering of the Andean laborers in the mines:

Y ací castigó a aquel Luysber, tan gran angel y tan hermoso, con sus seguaces. Y cayeron los ángeles malos del cielo como arena de la mar y mucho más, conforme la culpa como lo merecieron. Los primeros entraron al ynfierno con su Príncipe de las Tinieblas para rrecibir mayor castigo. Y otros quedaron en el mundo entre los hombres a estoruarnos la yda del cielo y engañarnos al pecado. (Ibid.:969)

(And thus he punished that Lucifer, so great and such a beautiful angel, with his followers. And the bad angels fell from heaven like sea sand and much worse, according to their guilt, as they deserved. The first entered the inferno with their Prince of Darkness in order to receive the greatest punishment. And others remained in the world among men and women to obstruct us on our journey to heaven and to lead us by deception into sin.)

At the same time as he brings the fallen angels into the world to explain the colonialist subversion of Andean souls, he threatens them with their earthly punishment: "A de sauer que ay un solo Dios y rrey y su justicia. Y los soberbiosos como Luzeber serán castigados en este mundo, ya que no en el otro mundo, con el castigo de Dios" ("One must realize that there is one God and king and his justice. And the prideful like Lucifer will be punished in this world, not in the next, with God's punishment") (ibid.: 1178). Unlike the *Nueva corónica*, which he concluded by threatening the Spaniards with eternal condemnation (ibid.:369), Guaman Poma brings the *Buen gobierno* to a close, promising punishment in this world.

The Voice and Character of the Preacher

As the sermon assumes a Christian audience at one end of the communication, it creates a voice of moral and spiritual authority—in the person of the preacher—at the other. Just as in the religious tracts and sermons written for the Andeans, the voice of any sermonizer positions itself in a status superior to that of the reader, be that reader king or *cacique* or commoner. The sermon exalts the superiority of the preacher, and so Guaman Poma takes advantage of it throughout his work.[14] It is in the context of the personal qualities outlined for the preacher that Guaman Poma's self-portrait is most meaningful. He must portray himself as a just, charitable, pious Christian; like St. Paul, he must be his own best example. Many of his autobiographical references emphasize his piety and Christian devotion to his fellows. His narration of his Christian service ends only with the story of his final trip to Lima, comforting his people en route and distributing *estampas*, prints or engravings depicting saints and other religious figures. It is nevertheless Guaman Poma's sermonizing, rather than his self-serving self-portraits, that creates the voice and character of the narrator as pious Christian.

An excellent example of his manipulation of the sermon style is found in the prologue addressed to his female readers with which he concludes his chapter of the biographies of the *coyas* (ibid.:144).[15] Here, rhetorical theory and semiotics together offer insights into the creation of the literary persona. Considering a single aspect of narrational viewpoint now, I shall explore it more fully in chapter 5. In both instances, I follow Uspensky's definition of narrational viewpoint as the position the describing subject establishes vis-à-vis the characters and events he or she portrays ([1970] 1973:1). In the prologue in question, Guaman Poma presents the narrator's viewpoint in such a way as to place the narrator in a position superior to that of his named addressees, the female Andean audience. He fashions this prologue out of the rhetoric of the haranguing sermon, and its message is to urge the female Andean readers to remember the sins of Eve and Mama Uaco, the wife (and mother) of Manco Capac Inca, who brought idolatry to the Andes (ibid.:144). The juxtaposition of the biblical and the Andean figures elevates the first *coya* to the ranks of humanity's greatest sinners and imports the alien, Christian concept of Original Sin into the ancient Andean world. The narrator's subsequent admonition that his compatriots should turn away from the failings of their biblical and native progenitors and look toward the Christian God for salvation represents the framing of a message whose literary mode is not that of the *cacique* but of the preacher. What is of interest here is to see exactly how Guaman Poma bends that alien voice and its texture to serve his own, very different, purposes (see Vološinov [1930] 1978:163).

The first feature of the salutation that strikes the reader is the use of the Quechua language to name and address all ranks of high and low Andean women to whom the prologue is directed: "A los letores mugeres, *Coya, Capac Uarmi, Curaca Uarmi, Allicac Uarmi, Uaccha Uarmi*" ("To the women readers: consorts of the Inca, consorts of the powerful lords, women of the *kurakas*, women of the lords promoted by the Inca, women poor and lowly") ([1615] 1980:144). The interjection of one natural language into a text written in another—here, the Quechua into the Spanish—constitutes what could be considered a position external to the narration at the level of phraseology. Normally, the writer's introduction of foreign or irregular speech represents the narrator's emphasis on his separateness from that speech act, for he assumes a deliberately external point of view with respect to the character described (Uspensky [1970] 1973:52). In the *Nueva corónica*, however, the device has the opposite effect, for the foreign phrase denotes Guaman Poma's internal position with respect to the world he represents; the Quechua invocation is native both to the narrator and to the character named. The phrase "A los letores mugeres, . . .

Uaccha Uarmi" is an emblem of the closeness, in fact, of the integration of the speaker and the depicted world, not an index of the distance between them.

This use of Quechua forges a link of authorial identification with the Andean audience as it weakens the connection between the speaker and the king to whom he directs his entire communication. As the use of Quechua emphasizes the distance between the Spanish king and the Andean realm of representation, the Quechua invocation establishes a hierarchical relationship within that represented Andean realm. At first glance, it might seem that the king has been replaced by a new receptor, Guaman Poma's female compatriots. I think, however, that this text should be viewed as a dramatization in which the narrator and his represented world act out a show of Christian piety for the benefit of the royal reader. The moralizing tone the Quechua-speaking voice assumes, as well as his verbal posturing with respect to his fellow Andeans, convert this monologue into a dialogue performed for the edification of the reader, a dialogue in which the narrator engages a group of silent interlocutors, in this case, the Andean women.

After addressing his Andean audience in his native tongue, the narrator's voice suddenly takes on the qualities of someone who is alien to them. His becomes the voice of the *Tercero catecismo*, threatening the native Andeans with doom and enjoining them to take up the paths of Christian faith and virtue. Thus Guaman Poma distances himself from the image of barbarity that he decries at the same time as he establishes his superiority over the Andean world he depicts. Through his harangue, which accuses the Andean women of the sins of Eve and idolatry, the speaker elevates himself above his fictional listeners, with whose world he had previously identified. Ethnic leader and *cacique* there, he becomes the spokesman of spiritual and moral authority here. Building levels of authority over his female compatriots, he is the preacher and counselor, they, the obedient flock. The injunction in Quechua, coupled with the sermon, allow the speaker to stand taller than his fellows while still remaining enclosed within their represented sphere.

The distance between the narrator and the noblewomen he addresses is smaller than the enormous gulf that separates him from the model of the sermon that he imitates. Properly speaking, Guaman Poma does not imitate but rather stylizes the sermon (Bakhtin [1929] 1978:181). According to Bakhtin, stylization occurs when typical features of a particular person, or of a particular social status, or of a particular literary manner are appropriated by another speaker. Stylization is separated from imitation by the fact that in stylization the author utilizes "the speech act of another in pursuit of his own aims and in such a way as to impose a new intention on the utterance" (ibid.:178–180). Guaman Poma's aim is to impose a hierarchical authority over the fictional "audience" that he addresses and to elevate his own stature in the potential view of his designated reader. Also, by recasting the discursive sermon style to suit his own purposes, the narrator domesticates and defuses its external voice of threat. By exhorting his people to undertake a collective effort at redemption and by speaking as someone from within the group appealing to his own, he nullifies the alien, paternal force of the words he employs. Thus Guaman Poma takes up arms against the threatening, racist language of the literature of conversion. More than merely distancing himself from that outsider's voice, he defeats it by turning it into an autochthonous call for internal reform.

The exhortation that closes the prologue is a case in point. This conventional ritual utterance is the ultimate consolidation of the preacher's and the *cacique*'s voices; that voice simultaneously identifies itself with the Andean audience: "Armémonos con la señal de la sancta crus de nuestros enemigos; líbranos, Señor, de todo mal del mundo, de la carne y del demonio" ("Let us arm ourselves with the sign of the Holy Cross against our enemies; liberate us, Lord, from all the evil of the world, of the flesh, of the devil") ([1615] 1980:144). With this exhortation, Guaman Poma definitively transforms a message of warning from without into an expression of solidarity from within. With these words, the narrator/preacher/ *cacique* concludes his exchange with his flock and drops the curtain on the drama enacted for the edification of the Spanish king. What Guaman Poma has done, in effect, is to convey the impression of his own leadership status as a *cacique* by assuming the voice of the preacher. His profound effort at cross-cultural communication is revealed in this translation of the concept of autochthonous spokesman and leader into terms that the foreigner can understand.

The Sermon Overtakes the Story

I return for the last time to the problem with which I concluded the last chapter, namely, the status of the *Nueva corónica* as a poetic imitation, as a story of Andean civilization from the dawn of time through the Spanish invasion and the destruction of Inca hegemony in the Andes. I would argue that in the *Buen gobierno* ecclesiastical rhetoric overtakes and supplants Guaman Poma's storytelling impulse. The internal purposiveness in the *Nueva corónica* is withdrawn in the *Buen gobierno*, in which the depiction of the status quo has no inaugurations, no culminations, and certainly no resolutions. The story of Andean civilization dissolves into a series of vignettes portraying the colonial oppressors and their corrupt exploitation of the Andean populace. The chapters of the *Buen gobierno* are not the episodes in a larger story, but simply a string of examples that make up the body of the sermon; they serve to illustrate the need for the recommendations for reform that become the chief points in Guaman Poma's political and social program. Exposition, argumentation, and amplification intermingle and multiply. The dozens and dozens of examples are never converted into a story; the contents of the *Buen gobierno* are too vast, and too diffuse, to be so confined. In the *Buen gobierno*, the sermon engulfs the fragments that might have constituted the story and becomes, ultimately, the favored mode of discourse.

Yet the compelling issue is not how Guaman Poma uses ecclesiastical rhetoric, but rather why he employs it. Although his book is, from cover to cover, a rhetorical enterprise devoted to persuading the Spanish king to institute radical colonial reforms, this charge apparently overwhelms the author as he goes about the task of describing colonial affairs. His desire to persuade his reader of the veracity of his version of Andean history was handled by letting the story tell itself, by creating the illusion of the narratorless narration. But his passion and the stakes are too high when he discusses the present. His need to persuade becomes acute and thus the story gives way to the sermon.

There are several possible implications of this shift from narration to oratory. The first is that the swelling of the sermon in the *Buen gobierno* constitutes Guaman Poma's recognition of his failure to make sense of Andean experience, given what has happened since the Spaniards' arrival. He simply cannot contain catastrophic and unheard-of events in an orderly pattern that can give place and meaning to all that has happened in the Andes. In its own right, the sermon is fragmentary; it is incomplete because its resolution or terminating motif—the reform of behavior, salvation, or whatever—lies beyond its reach. It is a discourse that can be completed only outside itself, and thus its pattern reflects the author's own, incomplete discourse, his own truncated search for the meaning of history.

In addition, the use of specifically ecclesiastical rhetoric among the rhetorical arts of persuasion is significant for two reasons. The first is that, according to the prevailing Augustinian theory of rhetoric, an external agent (the Holy Spirit), not religious oratory itself, was responsible for the preacher's achievement of his goals. Analogously, Guaman Poma's demands for colonial reform depend on external agents insofar as such reforms are to be achieved by Christian acts of restitution on the part of king and commoner alike. The author's pessimism about the achievement of this goal is explicit, because he considers the responsible agents—the

parish priests and landholding colonists—to be the Andeans' worst enemies. Clearly, he looks on his own discourse with little faith that it can
achieve its desired ends.

At the same time, by using religious language to assert his own claims
and those of his people, Guaman Poma moves the political problem and its
solution into the spiritual arena. As a consequence, the rewards or punishments for the colonists' compliance or failure to do their duty are also
moved to the realm of the transcendental. Such rhetoric, however powerful and persuasive it might have been from the lips and pens of Dominican
bishops and archbishops, becomes a pathetic instrument in the book of the
disenfranchised Andean petitioner. As valiant as his efforts were, Guaman
Poma's reliance on religious rhetoric reveals the lack of any real legal or
political threat on his part; it constitutes an admission of the lack of effective means with which he can defend his people.

Thus, Guaman Poma's attempt to write a story is fraught with ambivalence and inconsistency. As a result, that which would have a conclusion is open-ended, that which would produce unity results in fragmentation, that which would move toward identification leads to negation. This
is the overt message at one level of the text ("y no ay rremedio en este
mundo"), and it reflects the attitude responsible for the entire construction of the text at another. Because Guaman Poma expresses no hope of
achieving the colonial reforms he proposes, he builds, and accordingly
undermines, his own literary procedures. He sets up history, that is, a historical narration, only in order to deny its meaning. His reliance on language stands in front of his failure to believe in its power to communicate;
his use of the language of persuasion stands sentinel over his lack of belief
in its power. Whereas Guaman Poma seems to employ language naïvely as
though it could grasp the nature of things in figurative terms, he in fact
questions the very effort to capture adequately the truth of things in language (see White 1973b:36–37).

In this context, the disintegration of the story and the emergence of the
sermon in ever-clearer relief are mutually reinforcing effects of the attitude of negation that comes to characterize Guaman Poma's work. Denying that reality can be represented by a teleology, he abandons definitively the notion of the story. Before examining the final consequences of
this shift in authorial attitude, I shall turn to the pictorial text for evidence
of corroboration. How this rhetoric of denial is spelled out in the visual
narration is the subject of the next chapter.

4. Icons in Space: The Silent Orator

As Guaman Poma's favored genres of artistic signification, the chastising sermon and the narrative picture come together on the common ground of didacticism. Like the sermon, visual art in the sixteenth and seventeenth centuries was devoted to instruction and persuasion. Spanish culture on both sides of the Atlantic was concerned with the power of the visual image to educate and persuade. Pictures were much-used tools of Christian instruction, and Guaman Poma makes frequent references to "ymágenes,"[1] probably prints or engravings depicting saints and other religious figures, as necessary adjuncts to the Andeans' Christianization. Indeed, he claims that he himself often distributed such objects to his people ([1615] 1980:1122). So saying, he acknowledges his familiarity with Counter-Reformational instructional initiatives (see López-Baralt 1979a). The impact of Western, specifically Counter-Reformational, art is patent in his work, and, in his own view, his drawings are the feature of his book most likely to appeal to the visually oriented taste of his princely European reader ([1615] 1980:10).[2]

At the same time, the creation of visual representations is for Guaman Poma a natural extension of his own cultural tradition (see Mendizábal Losack 1961; López-Baralt 1980:120–135). He speaks of the importance of the vocation of the *qillqakamayuq*, or keeper of graphic information, in the Inca's administration, and he points out that these secretaries to the Inca and his royal council were nobles of his own Yarovilca dynastic lineage ([1615] 1980:193, 361). As noted in chapter 2, his acquaintance with the Incaic pictographic tradition is suggested by his prose descriptions of the twelve Incas, in which he sets forth details of their dress and appearance as if describing visual portraits of them that he personally had seen. From the viewpoint of either the autochthonous or the foreign culture, the visual medium offers Guaman Poma a trustworthy vehicle of communication. On examining his artistic practice, it will become apparent that he considers the picture a means of communication more powerful than written language.[3]

Baroque Sensibilities

As Mediterranean Latin culture crossed the Atlantic in the sixteenth and seventeenth centuries, completing its sphere of influence by "embracing Hispano-Portuguese America, the most brilliant America of the time" (Braudel [1949] 1976: v. 2:826), it brought with it the baroque art of the Counter-Reformation. It was in the nature of this art to be propagandistic, for it was preoccupied with convincing the public of the truth of certain contested notions:

Baroque art, then, often smacks of propaganda. In some respects, it was an art done to order, . . . Art was a powerful means of combat and instruction; a means of stating, through the power of the image, the Immaculate Holiness of the Mother of God, the efficacious intervention of the saints, the reality and power of the Eucharistic sacrifice, the eminence of St. Peter, a means of arguing from the visions and ecstasies of the saints. (Ibid.:832)

The notion of an art conceived not only to teach and entertain but also to move the spirits of the people was typically baroque. As a theoretician, López Pinciano (1596) spoke of this objective, and authors such as Suárez de Figueroa (1617) materialized it in works devoted to the reform of behavior and customs. The preoccupation for influencing the public was frequently expressed in theoretical treatises on painting in the period, such as Francisco Pacheco's *Arte de la pintura* ([1638] 1956).[4] The primacy of sight in the hierarchy of the senses was an idea that began with the baroque (Barthes [1971] 1976:65).[5] Maravall sums up the sentiment of the period toward art as a technique of persuasion; he describes the great cause of the baroque as the stirring of the passions ("la eficacia en afectar, esto es, en despertar y mover los afectos, es la gran razón del Barroco" (1975:168).

In the literary arts, poets lauded and seemed to envy the power of the visual image. In *Los cigarrales de Toledo* (1621), Tirso de Molina speaks of the license of the paintbrush:

En el breve espacio de vara y media de lienço, pinta lexos y distancias que persuaden a la vista a lo que significan, y no es justo que se niegue la licencia que conceden al pincel a la pluma. ([1621] 1913:126)

(In the brief space of about a yard and a half of canvas, one paints faraway views and distances that persuade the faculty of sight of what they signify, and it is not fair that this license granted to the paintbrush be denied to the pen.)

In his increasingly cited protocol (1677) on behalf of the painters of Madrid, Calderón speaks of the same potential of the visual gesture:

Pues sabiendo que es un manchado lino de minerales, y licores, hace creer (o quando no lo crean que lo duden) que se vé presente lo historiado, y real lo fabuloso. (Curtius 1936:92)

(In spite of knowing that a painting is merely a strip of linen, stained with minerals and liquids, it makes one believe [or if not believe, then at least raise the possibility] that one is seeing the historical made present and made real that which is feigned.)

For Calderón, there is no question that the faculty of sight has the advantage over that of hearing (ibid.: 93). Aside from pointing out that the visual image can materialize events that happened long ago (or that never happened at all), these laudatory evaluations celebrate the awesome dignity and creative power of the visual. Painting is related to the supernatural, according to Calderón, for painting is an activity that emulates divine creation, since God, in effect an artist, portrayed Himself in His greatest works: "Buelve á acabar donde empezó, ratificándose en ser la Pintura remedo de las obras de Dios, pues Dios, en cierto modo Pintor, se retrató en sus mayores obras" (ibid.: 97).

Similar sentiments had been expressed earlier, when a *Memorial* (Bib. Nac. Madrid. MS 2350, ff 272–281) was sent to Guaman Poma's own King Philip III from the painters of Madrid, requesting the foundation of an academy of painting (Volk 1977: 393–397). The court painters remind the king that the Holy Spirit compensates for human limitations through this miraculous medium, because it makes clear in an instant that which many books and much time would be required to tell (ibid.: 393). They summarize their argument about how painting can serve the urgent need for religious decoration of an instructive character, especially for those who cannot read. With regard to the effect of the visual image on the viewer, they recall the anecdote about St. Gregory: he fell to weeping on seeing a certain thing represented pictorially, even though he had read about it many times without being so moved (ibid.: 394).

The prestige of visual art and its association with religious instruction make its extension to secular purposes quite logical. The flourishing of illustrated literature in the seventeenth century was such that it is difficult for us to imagine the extent of its influence on the arts and on life in general (Gállego 1972:87); it was capable of enthusing an entire society (ibid.: 88). The literature of good government—dedicated to the education of princes and offering political advice to the king's ministers—constituted a great part of the literature of emblems or *empresas*. *Arbitristas*, be they gentlemen or friars, did not just send the king memoranda; they dedicated entire books to him. And, to etch their advice in the monarch's memory, the shrewdest of these authors used engravings to delight while instructing, and thus lighten the solemnity of their lessons (ibid.: 92–93).

Guaman Poma's work might be viewed in the broad context of this tradition.[6] In any event, his pictures communicate a bald, straightforward meaning unlike the esoteric constructions of the literature of *empresas*; his interest in the didactic value of the picture is much more akin to the attitudes expressed by the court painters and their defenders, who were concerned with the public utility of the visual image as "silent orator and living text" (see chap. 3, note 10, and Volk 1977: 393–394):

The sight of images moves to compunction those who look at them, and to the ignorant and coarse, they give a living story of Jesus Christ, our well-being. And thus it is, because who with greater vivacity and passion impresses in our hearts the sweet gravity, the divine beauty and marvelous aspect and celestial authority, perfect purity and divinity of the Most Holy Virgin, than this mute orator and living text?

The picture, as silent orator, plays a decidedly rhetorical role. As an integral part of his own "sermon," Guaman Poma uses the drawings to please, to teach, and, most important, to persuade. His subtle manipulation of the visual image—exploiting it on some occasions, failing to materialize it on others, and elsewhere using it to soften the blow of his virulent prose—indicates that he was in tune with the sensibilities of his period and that he, too, became a propagandist in the use of art.

Visual Representation and Suppression

The picture takes the polemical argument out of the realm of the assertive and gives it the gloss of fact; it removes the element of strangeness or incredulity from unheard-of or miraculous events, and conveys a system of values as though it were a system of facts (Barthes [1957] 1972:123–131). The power of the visual image resides in the fact that it signifies not by argument but by imperative; it appears at the same time generalized, neutral, and innocent (ibid.:125). The difference in Guaman Poma's visual and verbal treatments of a single event indicates that he is sensitive to this fact; I believe that it explains his heavy reliance on pictorial narration. A telling example appears in his account of the Hernández Girón rebellion.

In a picture of Hernández Girón's troops battling against the king's forces, a soldier firing a harquebus appears in the foreground (plate 5). A tiny caption over the barrel of the gun reads: "Este mato cien hombres" ([1615] 1980:432). In the prose narration on the accompanying page, however, Guaman Poma validates the report only as hearsay: "Dizen que un solo arcabusero mató cien hombres" ("They say that one infantryman alone killed a hundred men") (ibid.:433).[7] Here the narrator makes it clear that his account is secondhand and that he takes no personal responsibility for its authenticity. Yet in the picture the written statement lacks the qualifier "They say." Within the pictorial frame, language floats free from the constraints placed on it in verbal narration. Indeed, it would be absurd to materialize an event in pictorial form, then add a qualifier that would place its occurrence in doubt. For Guaman Poma, the picture does not abide by the rules that govern written language. The Hernández Girón example shows how the pictures impose themselves on the reader without linguistic constraints or reference to the potential verification of assertions. Altogether, the drawings allow the author to impose on the reader his views about Andean civilization as a harmonious social order and the contemporary colony as a "world upside-down."

The thesis that Guaman Poma views pictures as more powerful than writing is best corroborated by examining his restraint in picturing certain kinds of events. Although expressing the hope that the variety of his drawings will amuse his royal reader, he deliberately limits the range of subjects that he depicts visually. Certain themes are conspicuously absent from Guaman Poma's pictorial text, suggesting that what he does *not* communicate in the pictorial mode is revealing. In other cases, the presence of a picture neutralizes or domesticates the stridence of his attendant verbal assertion, creating an ironic distance between picture and prose as they send conflicting messages.

There are several instances in which a picture tames or destigmatizes the narration that follows it. Typically, these are pictures of the social types or categories that make up Guaman Poma's representation of colonial society. In the *Buen gobierno*, he devotes entire chapters to certain groups, whom he characterizes almost exclusively for their abuses of the Andean population. Nevertheless, the pictures that serve as "primer capítulo," or introduction, to these chapters are all dignified portraits of such

Plate 5. "This soldier killed a hundred men"
    ([1615] 1980:432)

individuals. The priest (ibid.:575), the *corregidor* (ibid.:493), the *encomendero* (ibid.:563), and the church inspector (ibid.:689, 692, 695, 698) are all visually portrayed as distinguished personages, although the accompanying narrations are stinging attacks against them.

Guaman Poma exercises restraint in representing these local colonial authorities, as, for example, when he pictures a worthy priest at the opening of the chapter called "Los padres de las dotrinas" and flanks him with Saints Peter and Paul (ibid.:575). Yet the opening lines of the accompanying text tell how the priests are typically given over to greed for riches and sins of the flesh:

Los dichos saserdotes y padres y curas questá en lugar de Dios y de sus sanctos . . . no hazen lo que estas bienauenturados hizieron. Antes se uan a la cudicia de la plata y rropa y cosas del mundo y pecados de la carne y de apetitos y daños que no se escriue, que el buen lector luego los sabrá para buen castigo, exemplo. (Ibid.: 576)

(The said priests and fathers and ministers who represent God and his saints . . . do not do what these blessed ones did. Rather, they give themselves over to the greed of silver and clothes and things of this world and sins of the flesh and of desires and abuses about which I do not write; the good reader will presently understand them for their value as punishment and example.)

The "primeros capítulos" of the chapters on the church inspectors, the *corregidores*, and the *encomenderos* similarly preface virulent verbal criticism of these officers with portraits that seem to contradict his words.[8] Here he seems to follow the esthetic doctrine of imitation by visually portraying the colonial officials most directly responsible for the Andeans' welfare, not as he claims they *were*, but as they *should* have been. He indulges his anger when depicting the other groups who make up colonial Andean society: the "lieutenants, judges, and clerks," the miners, majordomos, and *corregidores* of mines, the "prideful Creoles and half-castes and mulattoes" are consistently shown exploiting the native Andeans.

In this respect, Guaman Poma never forgets who his first reader is, and the restraint he exercises seems to subscribe to a premodern respect for authority characteristic of the absolutist order of the seventeenth century "in which the traditional structure of society and especially kingship, were seen as part of a divinely established hierarchy and in which politics, morality, and religious belief were taken as inseparable" (Hodgart 1969: 56; see also Maravall 1975:48, 351). Such a perspective criticizes society but never attacks its foundations, and Guaman Poma follows the rule, whether exercising a European-style respect for monarchy or adhering to an Andean belief in the cosmological character of political leadership (see Ossio 1976–77). Denying the rights of all colonists with regard to the Andeans, but accepting the authority of the king himself, Guaman Poma attacks only the king's officials. In this effort, Guaman Poma's combinations of idealizing pictures and accusatory prose allow him to criticize without offending, to protest without showing disrespect for the king, and to persuade his princely reader with an indignation that does not threaten. By the same token, he employs a similar softening technique in portraying his own race. While severely criticizing in writing the conduct of native Andeans under the colonial regime, he visually guides the reader away from his own passionate judgments or, at least, tempers them with the illusion of the Andeans' Christian obedience and well-being.[9]

The type of visual decorum that Guaman Poma maintains can be appreciated best by examining the presumably historical events that are narrated in the prose text but are never represented graphically. At various points in his book, Guaman Poma claims that his father, Guaman Malqui, saved the life of the Spanish conquistador Luis de Avalos de Ayala during the conquest of Peru. He dramatizes the point by inventing a speech for Avalos de Ayala in which the Spanish captain praises the author's father:

¡O señor deste rreyno, don Martín de Ayala, seruidor de Dios de nuestro muy alto enperador don Carlos de la gloriosa memoria! ¡Aunque a yndio, tendrá cuydado de dalle su encomienda su Magestad! ([1615] 1980:16; see also pp. 750, 917)

(O lord of this kingdom, Don Martin de Ayala, servant of God, of our most exalted emperor Don Carlos of glorious remembrance! Although it be for an Indian, his Majesty, with great solicitude, will give you his grant and estate.)

Whether the *cacique* actually saved the conquistador's life is not known. It seems, though, that Guaman Poma would have pictorially commemorated the event, as he illustrated his claims that Guaman Malqui had met with Pizarro at Tumbes to turn over the keys to the Andean kingdom in 1532 and that his father had aided in the defeat of Hernández Girón several years afterward (see plates 1 and 4). Yet Guaman Poma does not portray the event, even though he narrates his father's heroic deed with considerable verve.

I believe that this can be explained by the fact that the political and military superiority of the Andean over the Spaniard is, for Guaman Poma, a taboo subject, because such depictions could potentially offend the king.[10] Otherwise, Spaniard and Andean normally meet as equals (see plate 4). Guaman Malqui's act of bravery and mercy toward the Spanish captain Avalos de Ayala would necessarily upset the pictorial equilibrium that Guaman Poma carefully establishes.[11] His desire to express his ethnic and racial pride is mitigated by his need to cultivate, not alienate, his Spanish reader. The conspicuous absence of Guaman Malqui's heroic deed is testimony to Guaman Poma's attempt to manipulate his reader's reactions.

At the same time that he is careful not to show Andean might as more powerful than that of the Spaniards, he creates and maintains the visual dignity of the Andean lords, including the Incas. In spite of his accusations about the suspicious background and devilish ways of Mama Huaco and her son/husband Manco Capac Inca, Guaman Poma portrays them both in poses of great dignity. Although he narrates the civil war between the Inca princes Huascar and Atahualpa at the time of the Spanish conquest (ibid.:380), he never draws any picture of combat in that conflict. While describing Atahualpa's confrontation with the Spaniards at Cajamarca, he explains how the horses frightened the Inca prince, causing him to be thrown from his royal litter to the ground (ibid.:385). In pictures, however, he does not illustrate the incident or the confusion that resulted from it. Instead, he draws the preceding moment, when the Spanish horsemen approach the still enthroned Atahualpa (ibid.:384). From first to last, Guaman Poma portrays the Incas with dignity, even commemorating the end of their line with a picture of Don Melchor Carlos Inca in European costume (ibid.:753).

Guaman Poma's distinguished portraits of all Andean lords, including the Incas, toward whom he was ambivalent, can be explained by his understanding that the forces in opposition in his world were no longer Inca/non-Inca, but rather Andean/European. According to Saavedra Fajardo, the art of "good government" required that all good leaders be remembered with edifying, exemplary portraits in order to stimulate the noble performance of their successors (Maravall 1960:218). In accordance with such conventions, Guaman Poma begins his own *Good Government* with the exemplary portraits of the first ten viceroys and offers occasional representations of the Roman Catholic popes in his papal history in the *Nueva corónica*. Missing are commemorative portraits of the Spanish monarchs. Although Philip III appears as interlocutor in the dialogue "Pregunta Su Magestad" ([1615] 1980:975), he occupies only a secondary position in the title page drawing. Where we might expect to see portraits of Philip II, or Charles V as emperor at the time of the New World's discovery, we find none. The minimal visual role of the Spanish monarchs seems odd in light of the king's role as addressee. Such absences tell us that

Guaman Poma's book is not as conventionalized as it seems. For their manipulation of visual codes of representation, Guaman Poma's pictures conceal more than they reveal. Still to be discovered are the complexities of his pictorial articulation.

The Symbolic Values of Pictorial Space[12]

In the semiotic analysis of art, the interest of the objects represented lies not only in their mimetic value as copies of objects in the real world, but also in the symbolic value of the place that they occupy on the pictorial field and the relationships that they may have to the objects surrounding them. In the present case, a specifically Andean pattern of spatial signification is pertinent. I propose reading the pictorial text by superimposing on it a grid of Andean spatial symbolism; I would argue that the arrangement of icons in space allows for an additional visual interpretation and is responsible for an additional level of pictorial meaning. Thus, although pictorially expressing himself in ways that are comprehensible to the European reader, Guaman Poma employs and remains true to his own autochthonous values of symbolic representation.

My point of departure for this examination is Guaman Poma's *mapamundi*, in which he transforms the conventionalized model of symbolic European geography into a quadripartite image of the Andean universe (plate 6). The center of this particular *orbis terrarum* is occupied not by Rome or Jerusalem, as was customary, but by Cuzco. What makes this representation uniquely Andean are the two diagonal divisions of space. The first division separates upper and lower fields (with the upper position carrying the preferred value); the second diagonal, an intersection of the first, simultaneously fixes the center of the design (the fifth sector) as well as the positions to right and left. The system of oppositions thus created can be translated into the following hierarchy of preferences. The center is the position of preferred value. Among the four quadrants, however, the scale of values can be read first from left to right (from our vantage point) and then from top to bottom; the first position (to the left of center from our viewpoint) is occupied by Chinchaysuyu; the second (to the right of center), by Collasuyu; the third position (above center) by Antisuyu, and the fourth (below center) by Cuntisuyu (see Wachtel 1973:180–181). Because of the reversal of the visual field, which gives the same effect as a mirror image, the conceptual right will always be found on the pictorial left from our viewpoint as external observers. It should be emphasized that the superiority/inferiority dichotomy does not signify absolute values, but rather articulates a system of oppositions and a hierarchy of

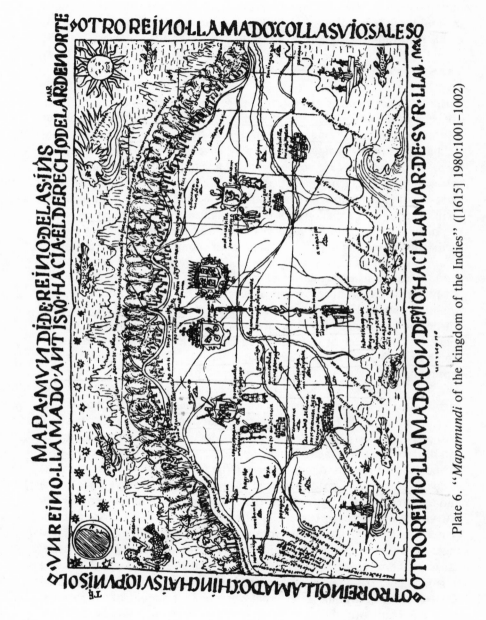

Plate 6. "*Mapamundi* of the kingdom of the Indies" ([1615] 1980:1001–1002)

preferences. The systematic, complementary quality of terms in opposition is central to this consideration, and the concept of opposition is substantive because it is structural.

Complementing Guaman Poma's model of the Andean universe is Juan de Santacruz Pachacuti Yamqui Salcamayhua's drawing of a design found on the wall of the Temple of the Sun, Coricancha, in Cuzco ([1613] 1879: 256). This cosmological scheme consists of a masculine/feminine duality mediated by a center (Isbell 1976:38–40). The relational structure of the Coricancha drawing is such that the male elements are represented on the conceptual right (pictorial left) and the female elements on the left (pictorial right). Isbell has analyzed this model not as a paradigm of superiority/inferiority but as a concept of necessary complementarity (ibid.:38, 55; see López-Baralt 1979c).

Both the Coricancha drawing and Guaman Poma's diagram of the model of the empire can be resolved into a single symbolic model: the opposition upper/lower (*hanan/hurin* in Andean terms), which R. Tom Zuidema has called the basic structure of Andean culture (cited in López-Baralt 1979c:84). El Inca Garcilaso's verbal description of the imperial city of Cuzco resolves the Coricancha model and Guaman Poma's *mapamundi* into one fundamental opposition:

Thus our imperial city began to be settled: it was divided into two halves called Hanan Cuzco, which as you know, means upper Cuzco, and Hurin Cuzco, or lower Cuzco. . . . The distinction did not imply that the inhabitants of one half should excel those of the other in privileges and exemptions. All were equal like brothers, the children of one father and one mother. . . . And he [the Inca] ordered that there should be only one difference and acknowledgment of superiority among them, that those of upper Cuzco be considered and respected as first-born and elder brothers, and those of lower Cuzco be as younger children. In short they were to be as the right side and the left in any question of precedence of place and office, since those of the upper town had been gathered by the men and those of the lower by the women. (Garcilaso [1609] 1966: v. 1:44–45)

Recent investigators (Wachtel 1973:177; Ossio 1973:179) have identified the position to the right of center with *hanan* (upper), the left of center with the notion of *hurin* (lower). Thus, the Andean concept of *hanan* unites the positions of upper and right with the qualities of maleness or superiority (depending on whether the relationship is one of complementarity or domination); *hurin*, then, unites the positions of lower and left, representing the qualities of femaleness or inferiority, that is, the concepts of complementarity or subordination, respectively (López-Baralt 1979c:88).

The complete design of Guaman Poma's *mapamundi*, consisting of four sectors arranged around a center, can be found in only a few drawings in the book. By that, I mean that the icons, whatever their content and connotations, are arranged into a composition that repeats the arrangement of the original *mapamundi* design. Thus, for example, the kingdoms of Castile and Peru, and the Christian concept of the city of Heaven, are represented in drawings whose icons are arranged in a pattern that consists of four domains organized around a center sector ([1615] 1980:42, 952). As these non-Andean entities and concepts are formally materialized according to the Andean pattern of spatial signification (Wachtel 1973:209–212), the whole corpus of Guaman Poma's drawings might well be scrutinized for evidence of the same articulation. Thus, an initial interpretation of events depicted in his drawings, based on the denotative and connotative values of the icons themselves, can be reinforced (or altered) by taking into consideration the values of the positions that the icons occupy on the pictorial field. Of the 399 drawings in the work, approximately two thirds of them (about 265) can be analyzed for spatial contrasts and directional orientation.[13] If Guaman Poma organizes all the phenomena of real and hypothetical, historical, fictional, and mythical experience according to that grid, then the scale of values inherent in it should serve as a powerful tool for interpreting the scenes and events visually recorded.

Using pictorial signification, Guaman Poma diagrams the historical defeat of his people by the Spaniards. If there is truly a historical reflection in the *Nueva corónica*, it resides in the way the author conceptualizes events pictorially; in picture after picture, he dismantles the chief symbol of the Andean political paradigm. In effect, he creates the fundamental and perfect model of the Andean universe in his symbolic map of the world and he charts his pictures of pre-Columbian times according to the map's positional values. In his portrayals of colonial times, however, he often contradicts those same values. Thus, through the fragmentation and subversion of the original design, he shows how colonization turned autochthonous cultural and social order into chaos and ruin.

Perhaps the most fascinating question about Guaman Poma's pictures is whether he consciously composed them in light of these Andean values. Since it is impossible to answer this question with certainty, we can at least frame a different but equally pertinent one: Are the patterns repetitious enough to be significant and consistent enough to be meaningful? Although the inevitable repetition of certain types of pictorial composition may run counter to the idea of variety that Guaman Poma hoped his pictures would achieve, the principle of repetition and structural consistency that it implies makes possible the analysis of the drawing's spatial composition. By determining the positional value of clusters of visual elements, categorized by pictorial theme, the reader can appreciate how the substitution of one group by another traces the process of paradigmatic transformation itself and reveals how the perfect *mapamundi* model is disarticulated.

One can see, for example, how the spatial slot of priority, the center, is consistently occupied by the Inca in depictions of Inca times, but also how, in the colonial era, this slot is emptied of figures of Andean leadership. Instead, it is filled either by impersonal symbols of the Spanish monarchy, or by human figures representing not the Inca as lord but the Andean as helpless victim. In other words, the blocking of the five positions on the Andean spatial grid is like the syntactical arrangement of the elements in a grammatical sentence: the members of various paradigms or sets of icons are placed in the various positions; that is, to borrow terms from the linguistic analysis of poetry, the principle of equivalence is projected from the axis of selection to that of combination (Jakobson 1960:358). Entities become equivalent in value or meaning because of the equivalent positions they occupy on the syntagmatic plane (see Levin 1962:30–41).[14] That which we "read" in order to understand pictorial meaning is the syntax or arrangement of the composition.

The idea of a secret or at least implicit interpretation is found in two pictures that narrate the Spanish takeover of Andean society. One of these pictures records a historical event: the fateful encounter between Atahualpa Inca and Francisco Pizarro at Cajamarca. By disordering the signs of Andean spatial representation, Guaman Poma symbolizes the threat to Andean political order occasioned by this event. The other picture is the author's imaginative title-page drawing, in which the Roman Catholic pope and the Spanish king are shown in their respective relationships to the Andean world. In both pictures, the superimposition of the Andean grid on the pictorial field makes possible an interpretation that lends special meaning to particular icons.

Guaman Poma's frequent verbal complaint that the Spanish conquest turned the Peruvian world upside-down is rendered graphically by the reversal of the positions of the signs identifying the four subdivisions of the empire. Apart from the *mapamundi* itself, Guaman Poma presents a model of the arrangement in his collective portrait of the "Gran Consejo del Inca," in which the four lords of the subdivisions of the empire occupy their rightful ceremonial positions (plate 7). From left to right they are the lords of Chinchaysuyo, Antisuyu, Cuntisuyu, and Collasuyu ([1615] 1980:366). They are accompanied by the counselors of Hanan Cuzco and Hurin Cuzco, to the right of Chinchaysuyu, and to the left of Collasuyu,

Plate 7. "The Royal Council of these realms"
([1615] 1980:366)

respectively (Wachtel 1973:178). The Atahualpa-at-Cajamarca tableau represents the unwanted permutation of this order, for the positions of the lords are reversed and confused (ibid.:386; plate 8). The lord of Chinchaysuyu is now to the left, rather than to the right, of the Inca; the lord of Antisuyu is nowhere visible. The other identifiable figure in this drawing, the lord of Collasuyu, normally on the Inca's left, is now at his right. Representing the incarnate center of the universe, the Inca is the traditional guarantor of harmony (Wachtel [1971] 1977:30). Here, he still occupies that privileged central position, but the disorder around him forewarns that he is about to be toppled.

A second *hanan/hurin* (upper/lower) hierarchical distinction pertains to the band of Spaniards in the foreground of this drawing. These Spanish intruders are in the inferior position, as they encroach for the first time on Andean space. Placed below the Andean lords, these four figures on the horizontal axis are themselves ranked on a scale of descending value, from Almagro to Pizarro to Fray Vicente de Valverde to Felipillo the interpreter. On this left-right axis, Almagro occupies the position of greatest positive value; Felipillo, the most negative. This arrangement is not accidental, for the prose text corroborates it.[15] According to the spatial signs, the position of the priest makes him a more negative figure than the soldier-conquerors, but the Indian liaison is by far the most despicable. Thanks to this spatial configuration, "Atahualpa Inca in the City of Cajamarca" is the essential statement about a paradigm of order about to be overturned. The center will be emptied, and alien elements (the conquistadores, their rivals, the clergy, and the co-opted Andeans) will replace the traditional heads of Tawantinsuyu.

The title-page drawing is a colonial transformation of the original paradigm (plate 9). No Inca appears, and all the indigenous elements have been substituted by European symbols and figures. All the vanished lords are replaced by a single sign of indigenous authority: the image of an Andean prince, dressed as a Spanish courtier. The author identifies this figure as himself; his clan names, Guaman (falcon) and Poma (lion) ("águila y león rreal, Guaman Poma," ibid.:1037) are depicted in the heraldic bearings on the shield adjacent to him. Since the Andean figure is adorned and identified by European symbols (see also ibid.:167), the whole composition suggests acquiescence and assimilation to foreign ways. However, a reading of the picture according to the Andean design tells a different story.

When the Andean grid is superimposed on this drawing, the importance of the vertical line of crests, representing the Roman Catholic papacy, the Spanish monarchy, and Guaman Poma's (invented) coat of arms, is

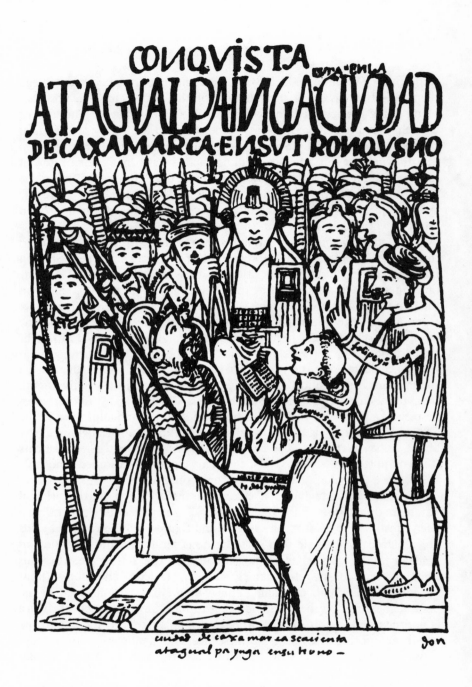

Plate 8. "Atahualpa Inca in the City of Cajamarca"
([1615] 1980:386)

Plate 9. "The First New Chronicle and Good Government by Don Felipe
Guaman Poma de Ayala, Lord and Prince" (title page)

diminished. In the *mapamundi* model, the vertically arranged sectors represent not first and second but rather third and fourth positions. Hierarchical Andean authority is symbolized not by the vertical arrangement but rather by the diagonal line that divides upper and lower fields. In this drawing, that line connects the Catholic pope and the Andean prince. A sort of mediation between the two is effected by the institutional sign of the kingdoms of Castile and Leon, which occupies the place reserved for Cuzco, or for the personal figure of the Inca in the traditional pattern (see plates 6 and 7). In this drawing, the center is a position imperfectly filled; the lack of any personalized sign of authority is a departure from the original model, which suggests that this center of authority is a weakened version of the traditional one.

Although the personal signs of the pope and the Andean prince enter into a hierarchical relationship, the figure of the king is pushed off to the side. He is not merely removed from the expected central position, where he would ideally be placed, but he occupies the position of Collasuyo, the second subdivision of the empire. Because he might have been placed in the privileged but empty slot of Chinchaysuyu, sector I on the grid, his placement on the field in this secondary position can be read as a sign of pejorative value. In Guaman Poma's description of the Collas, he commonly characterizes this regional group as physically degenerate and ruthlessly greedy for the riches of the Potosí mines found in their territory (ibid.:77–78, 180, 338): "Y to[dos] de la casta son gordícimos y floxas, encapases, pucilánimos, pero rrica gente llámase *Colla capac* [un poderoso Colla] rrica de plata de Potocí y de oro de Carauaya, el más fino oro de todo el rreyno" ("And all of that caste are very fat and lazy, good-for-nothing, faint-hearted, but rich people called *Colla capac* [powerful Colla], rich in the silver of Potosí and the gold of Carabaya, the finest gold in all the kingdom") (ibid.:180). The theme of *cudicia* is used to describe the Collas on another occasion: Guaman Poma tells how their earthly greed prevents their true conversion to the Christian faith ("Pero con engaño se puede hazerse cristiano. No se puede con la cudicia de la plata como aquí; es echarse a perder y murir una ues") (ibid.:77). Reading Guaman Poma's text, Wachtel suggests that the Chinchaysuyu-Antisuyu versus Collasuyu-Cuntisuyu division of the Andean grid connotes the terms of a double opposition: order or culture versus barbarity or nature, and prosperity as opposed to poverty (1973:180).

At the same time, Guaman Poma accuses the Spanish colonizers of uncontrollable greed. The Collas' exploitation of the riches of Potosí is, in fact, superseded by that of the Spanish. The author reminds the reader that the king of Spain would be nothing without the wealth of Potosí:

"Por la dicha mina [Castilla] es Castilla, Roma es Roma, el papa es papa y el rrey es monarca del mundo" ("Because of the said mines, Castile is Castile, Rome is Rome, the pope is pope, and the [Spanish] king is monarch of the world") ([1615] 1980:1065). Like Guaman Poma's verbal interpretation, his manipulation of the spatial positions places the Spanish monarch where the Collas belong. The king of Spain has replaced the greedy, exploitative, and hypocritical Collas on the new map of the Indies of Peru.

In this new symbolic map, Guaman Poma summarizes his dreams about the ideal relationship of Europe to Peru by placing the Roman Catholic pope and the Andean prince in the priority relationship. Guaman Poma foresees an autonomously ruled Christian Andean state. Thus, the pope represents spiritual authority, not political domination. But between the original model of Tawantinsuyu and this idealized map of the future lies Guaman Poma's interpretation of Andean history. I am increasingly convinced that his assessment is to be found in the pictures themselves, and that his viewpoint undermines and denies the ideal relationship that he proposes in his title-page fantasy.

To examine Guaman Poma's visual interpretation of Andean history, I turn to the major compositional patterns of his drawings, as these are articulated along the primary diagonal axis and its mirror-image reversal and the horizontal left-right opposition. The succession of uses to which the central position is put serves as a final comment on Guaman Poma's views about the historical destiny of the Andean peoples.

Lines of Authority and Hierarchy

Guaman Poma uses the oppositions gods/humanity, male/female, master/servant, and good/evil both to show how certain European institutions reflect the values of Andean culture and how, in other spheres of experience, the Spanish invasion and conquest have perverted and destroyed those cherished values (see Adorno 1981a).

In all the compositions arranged along the primary diagonal, a figure at the upper right-hand portion of the field (the viewer's upper left) is balanced by a figure at lower left (our lower right). The diagonal line thus created signifies a pattern of hierarchy. Of the 265 pictures that can be studied for positional relations, approximately 20 percent follow this pattern. The drawings that depict humanity's relationship to its gods, religious and moral hierarchies, and social relationships based on patriarchy and gender, are charted along this diagonal axis in such a way as to suggest that Guaman Poma is interpreting Incaic and colonial phenomena according to the Andean paradigm. So, for example, the patriarchal order suggested in the drawings of the first Andean man and woman, the Vari Vira Cocha Runa, is reiterated in the drawing of Adam and Eve (ibid.:22, 48; plates 10 and 11). Because of the chronological ordering set up in the text, Adam and Eve seem to prefigure the first natives of the New World. Such a visual interpretation would have been the effect that Guaman Poma desired, for he continually emphasizes that the first inhabitants of the Andes descended directly from Adam: "Vari Vira Cocha Runa, primer generación de yndios del multiplico de los dichos españoles que trajo Dios a este rreyno de las Yndias, los que salieron de la arca de Noé, deluuio" ("Vari Vira Cocha Runa, the first issue of the multiplication of the said 'Spaniards' that God brought to this kingdom of the Indies, those who came forth from the ark of Noah, Flood") (ibid.: 49). Nevertheless, it is Adam and Eve who are conceived in imitation of the Andean prototypes. The setting of the Andean sierra and Adam's employment of the *taki chaclla*, the Andean digging stick, make the Vari Vira Cocha Runa the effective models for their biblical predecessors. Thus, the use of Andean values to depict the foreign culture reaffirms those values.

In the drawings that illustrate humanity's relationship to its gods, the deity is always placed in the upper right-hand position, and the human figures worship below, at the lower left (upper left and lower right, respectively, from our viewpoint). The *hanan* (upper right)/*hurin* (lower left) relationship prevails throughout the representation of biblical, Incaic, and modern Andean, Christian spiritual orders; thus, the Andean principle is clearly the graphic symbol by which Guaman Poma articulates his views of ancient and modern persons as religious beings. We find, in succession, the Old Testament patriarchs (Noah, Abraham, and David) kneeling in supplication before the image of the venerable, bearded old man who conventionally represents the Judeo-Christian god (ibid.:24, 26, 28). Subsequently, the Inca and his court kneel in worship of the *waqas* located high atop rocky peaks (plate 12; ibid.:268, 270, 272, 274), and the modern Andeans devoutly worship at the feet of the images of the crucified Christ and one of the titles of the Virgin Mary, Santa María de la Peña de Francia[16] (plate 13; ibid.:835, 837, 847, 933). This is a hierarchy never substantially altered; the pictures seem to say that, in Andean experience, the Christian Messiah comes to replace the old gods of the Incas peacefully.

The category of human relationships defined by a religious or moral authority is depicted in the same manner; that is, the *waqa*/Inca opposition is replaced by that of the priest/parishioner. In these tableaux, a priest or other officer of the church is pictured with the humble friar, nun, or

Plate 10. "The first world: Adam and Eve"
([1615] 1980:22)

Plate 11. "The first generation of Indians: Vari Vira Cocha Runa"
([1615] 1980:48)

Plate 12. "Idols of the Incas: Inti, Huana Cauri, Tambo Toco"
  ([1615] 1980:266)

Plate 13. "Good conduct and Christianity: the confraternity of twenty-four" ([1615] 1980:933)

Andean parishioner for whom he is the spiritual superior. Consistent with the relationship of the Roman pope to the Andean prince, set up on the title page, spiritual authority over the indigenous population in colonial times is always portrayed as European. In other words, the terms of opposition are identified along ethnic as well as religious lines. Even though Guaman Poma is vehemently anticlerical, he acknowledges the priest/ parishioner hierarchy by arranging its forms along the Andean primary diagonal axis. This preferred descending line defines the position and counterposition of hierarchy and permanence (ibid.:476, 478, 482, 486, 641, 643, 645, 647, 649).

Patriarchal relationships are similarly executed; the right/left axis for sex signs, which, we have seen (plates 10 and 11), is normally followed throughout Guaman Poma's drawings. This arrangement is one that explicitly follows a cardinal feature of the *mapamundi* and Coricancha models.

When political relationships are articulated along this preferred Andean diagonal, however, the depiction of colonial times brings an unhappy transformation of the original hierarchy. Here, the graphic design explicitly reiterates the point that the prose text argues. Institutional political domination is usually signified by the figure of authority or superiority in the upper right-hand section of the field, whereas the subjugated or the inferior group is located at the lower left. This arrangement prevails in the drawings of Andeans with other Andeans, as in the pictures of the Inca and his subjects: he is pictured above and to the right; they are below and to the left (ibid.:153, 161). Moving backwards in time, we discover that Guaman Poma portrays the ancient lords of his local region in a similar relationship vis-à-vis the warring, conquering Inca. There, the Andamarcas and Lucanas stand above and against the Inca foes, who will eventually defeat and absorb them into their growing empire (ibid.:157). Political relationships among Spaniards are similarly represented, as in the picture of the emperor Charles V with President Pedro de la Gasca, who is about to be sent to Peru, or the drawing that shows President de la Gasca interviewing the courier of the rebel Gonzalo Pizarro (ibid.:419, 428).[17] The consistency with which political relationships are thus represented suggests, once again, that this graphic pattern of Andean origin signifies the ideal order.

The problematical subject for this axis of hierarchy, however, is the integration of the Spaniard and the Andean into a single political order. Throughout the work, there are no pictures in which the Europeans appropriate centrality or hegemony in the area of political organization, in contrast to their acknowledged predominance in the ecclesiastical hierarchy.

When one looks for Andeans in the *hanan* position in the pictures representing colonial times, only the figures of the victim and the martyr appear. In one such drawing, Guaman Poma depicts an Andean man before a life-size cross, the sign of Christian martyrdom (plate 14). In the meantime, the priest below harasses him: "Con la dotrina se venga el padre porque se quejó y pidió justicia [el yndio]" (ibid.:605). In the other, a *cacique* hangs dead at the gallows, executed at the request of the *encomendero* and by order of the *corregidor* (ibid.:571; plate 15). The Andean portrayed as victim in *hanan* position cannot represent political authority, which the icon itself denies. On the contrary, the silenced Andean at *hanan* stands instead for a moral superiority over the evil men who victimize him. Guaman Poma's portrayal lends only dignity to an Andean whose power and authority have been destroyed. In both pictures, the Andean figure emulates, through suffering and the signs of cross and gallows, the symbol of supreme sacrifice.

Thus, Guaman Poma depicts the disappearance of native rule in the Andes; indigenous political authority has been definitively destroyed. The only indigenous presence is that of the panderer to the colonists' will (ibid.:900), or of the helpless victim (ibid.:571, 605). The spatial metaphor of identification, continuity and order from pre-Columbian to colonial times works in the categories of spiritual, patriarchical, and social-moral experience, but not in the political. Here, Guaman Poma's vision is ironic; the Andean figure placed at the preferred, *hanan*, position is victim, not lord. At the same time, the political prerogative is denied to the colonists; the *hanan* space rightly occupied by the Inca or other ethnic lords is left empty by their execution at the hands of the foreign invaders (ibid.:392, 453, 571). Such pictures constitute the visual rendering of Guaman Poma's thesis that the world is upside-down ("el mundo al rreués").[18]

Disorder on the Horizontal Axis

A second major compositional pattern, which repeats a portion of the *mapamundi* design, reiterates the Chinchaysuyu/Collasuyu opposition. In the Andean world, this conceptual right/left configuration has been associated with political domination and subordination (Isbell 1976:38–41). Guaman Poma employs it in his drawings, to describe concrete social and political situations; about 28 percent (75) of the 265 drawings are articulated in this pattern. In other words, if the diagonal composition gives us the theory of the system and its rules of combination in the spiritual, social, patriarchal, and moral hierarchies, the horizontally oriented compositions offer the actual articulation of those relationships; that is, the

Plate 14. "Recite the doctrine, Indian troublemaker! Tell it to me at once!
([1615] 1980:605)

Plate 15. "The *encomendero* has the *cacique* hanged; the *corregidor* orders it to please the *encomendero*" ([1615] 1980:571)

paradigmatic relationships of the system are unfurled on the diagonal axis while the syntagmatic aspects are played out on the horizontal axis. Here the relationship of humanity to its gods is not a topic for representation, and only two basic oppositions are depicted: male/female and good/evil, the latter of which turns out to be synonymous with the distinction Andean/non-Andean. In drawings where this positional order is disrupted, the spatial signifier corroborates the negative values that the pictorial objects themselves convey.

In the Coricancha and *mapamundi* models, the horizontal arrangement of sex signs is of fundamental importance. El Inca Garcilaso corroborates the placement of the male on the right, the female on the left. As we saw, he likens the relationship to that of older and younger children, and the idea of the complementariness of different parts (*hanan/hurin*) that make up the whole has been underscored in contemporary studies (ibid.:37–38). Guaman Poma follows this pattern when sex signs are involved, and, when the image-signs form an opposition Andean/non-Andean, the former normally occupies the position of privilege. Because this right/left opposition constitutes an unmistakably Andean ordering pattern, one can assume that Guaman Poma's use of it is never accidental. At the same time, I would argue that his violation of its order is also meaningful; the scenes thus depicted carry negative values.

Looking first at the drawings in which sex signs are present, one discovers that the reversal of the male (right)/female (left) order connotes disorder or misguidedness. This is the message, for example, in the picture of the ancient Andeans of pre-Incaic times who search for the true God. The Vari Runa man looks up and leftward (not rightward, as all other worshippers ancient and modern had been portrayed by Guaman Poma), and utters a prayer in Quechua, "Pachacamac, maypim canqui?" ("Creador del mundo, ¿dónde estás? / Creator of the world, where are you?"). As Guaman Poma claims that the previous generation had lost its full knowledge of God ("perdieron la fe y esperansa de Dios") while retaining the intuitive awareness of God by the light of their natural reason ("una sonbrilla de conocimiento del Criador") ([1615] 1980:50), so he pictorially indicates spiritual confusion by reversing the signs whose right/left orientation normally signifies order (ibid.:53). The reversal of the sex signs underscores the disorientation of the Vari Runa generation occasioned by their imperfect and intuitive spiritual quest (see chapter 2).

In like manner, crimes from Inca times, themselves indications of social disorder, are portrayed such that the reversal of sex signs emphasizes the negative values depicted. Thus, for example, adulterers are pictured as they are stoned to death (plate 16; ibid.:308), and a woman who poisons

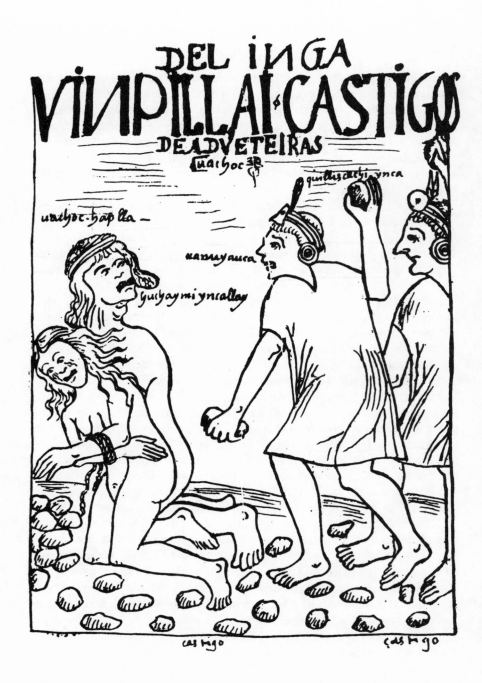

Plate 16. ''The Inca's punishment for adultery''
([1615] 1980:308)

people for a living ("*hanpiyoc collayoc runa uatoc*") is beaten to death by an Inca executioner (ibid.:312).

In colonial times, Guaman Poma complains, Andean women are coerced and corrupted by the Spaniards; these sexual abuses and offenses constitute for him the worst manifestation of social disorder. Only *mestizos* will be born; the Andean race will perish! Thus, he portrays Andean girls being delivered to *encomenderos* (ibid.:381, 565), and an Andean girl attempting to defend herself from a lascivious Spaniard (ibid.:882; plate 17), in pictures where the sex signs are reversed. In both of these cases from colonial times, the reversal of sex signs occurs only within the Andean ethnic group; that is, there is a male in the *hanan* position, but he is the Spaniard. In opposition to him, the Andean male and female occupy the *hurin* position to his left. However, within the Andean group, the female occupies the *hanan* position; the male, that of *hurin*.

The only gross, sexually explicit representation of Spanish/Andean sexual relations is found in a drawing that includes no Andean males, and the reversal of sex signs is complete and unmistakable. The drawing, called "El corregidor i padre, tiniente anda rrondando y mirando la güergüenza de las mugeres," shows a brazen Andean woman displaying her naked body before her visitors and exposing her genitalia (ibid.:507; plate 18). Her placement on the conceptual right, with the Spaniards at the left (our right), unequivocally defines the threat to Andean racial integrity and social order that her actions represent.

When European and Andean political adversaries, either real or potential, come together on the horizontal axis, the confrontation is usually stated such that the Andean is placed on the right, the non-Andean on the left. This arrangement is articulated in drawings that begin with the Spaniards' arrival and reception at Tumbes by the author's father (see plate 4), and continue through colonial scenes.

For the conquest era, there are very few pictures in which Inca lords meet peacefully with Spanish viceroys and captains (ibid.:442, 462), and these are idealized representations. In these rare pictures, Andean and non-Andean meet as equals, on the same plane, with neither exercising authority or force over the other. In most of the drawings, however, the placement of the Spaniard at the right signifies disorder and violence (ibid.:523, 810).

Thus, when Guaman Poma depicts the functioning of social and political relationships in colonial times, order breaks down and dissolves. The violation of the pictorial spatial code denies again and again the notion that justice and order could reign under the Spanish colonial regime. The symbolic placement of images on the horizontal axis reiterates the story of the destruction of Andean society.

Plate 17. "The Indian parents defend their daughter from the lascivious Spaniard" ([1615] 1980:882)

Plate 18. "The *corregidor*, the priest, and the lieutenant make their rounds"
([1615] 1980:507)

From these drawings, Guaman Poma's language of denial begins to emerge. Whereas the pictures articulated on the primary diagonal axis put new entities into old hierarchical molds, identifying European institutions with Andean cultural values, the spatial articulation on the horizontal axis contradicts the most fundamental (*hanan/hurin*) expression of order. The basic symbolic structure of the Andean world thus begins to disintegrate in the drawings, undermining and rendering futile all Guaman Poma's fervent calls for colonial reform.

Paradigms Lost: The Reversed Diagonal and the Empty Center

The pictorial language of negation can be further observed in a third compositional pattern. The subversion of the traditional hierarchies is the subject of this pattern, which is the mirror reversal of the primary diagonal design. Consisting of a diagonal directed from lower right to upper left (our lower left to upper right), this line traces the second division of space in the Andean model. Approximately 16 percent (forty-three) of the drawings that can be analyzed subscribe to this compositional pattern.

But the second division in the absence of the first is itself an aberration; accordingly, the majority of drawings organized along this axis can be described as contradictions of the structural hierarchy implicit in the drawings that are organized according to the primary diagonal. In this perversion or mirror image of the original order, the *hanan* position alternately places Satan, the forces of evil, and the colonial usurper at the upper left-hand (our right-hand) position. There are dozens of pictures in which this diagonal arrangement is found, and most of them are doubly expressive of the chaos of colonial life as described by Guaman Poma.

Condemning the Spaniards' presence and practices as thoroughly in drawings as in writing, Guaman Poma draws dozens of pictures that reiterate the reversed diagonal pattern. The majority of these drawings show murderers, corrupt *corregidores*, vagabond ruffians, and lascivious and wicked priests in the upper left-hand position (our upper right). In most cases, the figures are juxtaposed to their Andean victims, who occupy the position at the lower right (our lower left). A visual summary of the reversal of all the pertinent visual principles is found in the drawing called, "Cómo le maltratamiento de los corregidores y padres españoles deste rreyno a los yndios, yndias pobres" (ibid.:936; plate 19). The *hanan/hurin* arrangement of the pairs male/female and priest/parishioner have been reversed; the reversed primary diagonal is twice reiterated in the priest's club and the *corregidor*'s staff, and the Andean victim falling to the ground rehearses once more the colonial martyrdom of Atahualpa and

Plate 19. "How the *corregidores* and priests of this kingdom abuse the Indians" ([1615] 1980:936)

Tupac Amaru. Nearly all the organizational principles of the Andean paradigm have been violated in this picture, and Guaman Poma's *hanan/ hurin* articulation of Christian spiritual order has been subverted.

As the distortion and fragmentation of the original *mapamundi* model thus increase, one final factor must be considered: the position of the center. Very few drawings represent the original, perfect design, and although the primary diagonal establishes a certain hierarchy of values in some drawings, the prevalence of its mirror image in others contradicts it. On the horizontal plane, the *hanan/hurin* order is also often reversed. The position of the center itself is articulated on the horizontal or the diagonal axis in only a few cases. Where it appears, it mediates the terms of opposition.

Both in the *mapamundi* itself and in the "Gran Consejo" drawing (plate 7), the personal figure of the Inca occupies the center. In pictures of colonial times, the only symbols that replace that image are the coat of arms of Castile and the institutional emblem of the Catholic church. If we search for other icons that occupy the central position, we find very few. In the pictures composed along the primary diagonal, only Christian religious symbols are to be found. The historical Cross of Carabuco, which Guaman Poma attributes to St. Bartholomew's evangelizing visit to Peru in apostolic times ("San Bartolomé que ganó más primero y como dejó la santa cruz de Carabuco") (plate 20, p. 92; ibid.:45), is at the center of two diagonal compositions (ibid.:92, 653); tiny crucifixes, usually as part of rosaries, appear in others (ibid.:649, 835, 837, 847). Still others are centered by wall-size or life-size crucifixes (ibid.:633, 643, 687). In these pictures, as in the St. Bartholomew drawing in which the apostle speaks to a kneeling Andean, the chief emblem of Christianity serves as a symbolic mediator between European and Andean worlds (see Adorno 1981a).

Andean figures appear in horizontal compositions that have an articulated center. No longer the Andean-as-lord, as in Incaic times, this figure stands alone without the symbols of empire (that is, the four lords of the imperial subdivisions) around him. In this manner, Guaman Poma stands at the center of a drawing entitled "Pregunta el autor," in which he interviews his people (plate 21; ibid.:368). Here, the headdresses indicating traditional ethnic identification are obscured, in painfully ironic contrast to the orderly portrayal of the same in the "Gran Consejo" picture that immediately precedes it (plate 7). In another drawing, a *cacique*, again dressed in courtier's costume, writes down the grievances dictated to him by the Andeans who flank him to right and left (ibid.:784). Here, the humble garb of the petitioners suggests that, in this and the previous picture, the Andean-as-lord is now simply the Andean-as-adviser or petitioner.

Plate 20. "St. Bartholomew at the Holy Cross of Carabuco; the Indian was
baptized" ([1615] 1980:92)

Plate 21. "The author inquires of his people"
([1615] 1980:368)

Still other horizontal compositions are centered by Andean infants being baptized (ibid.:627, 852).

The last example of the Andean at center shows an *alcalde* being whipped by a black slave while the *corregidor* who demanded the beating looks on. The drawing is called "Corregidor afrenta al alcalde hordenario por dos guebos que no le da *mitayo*" (plate 22; ibid.:503). The scene is reminiscent of the paintings of the Flagellation of Christ because the victim is bound to a pillar, a common symbol of the Passion. Ironically, the exploited Andean is the ultimate link between the native and foreign worlds. As a Christian symbol, the pillar is exclusively an emblem of suffering and martyrdom; it does not share with the empty cross the promise of redemption. Yet even most of Guaman Poma's crosses leave an image of suffering uppermost in the viewer's mind, because, as instruments of torture and death, the nails are conspicuously present.

In the overall course of Guaman Poma's pictorial narration, the imperial Inca has been replaced by the humble petitioner and the brutalized victim with whom the Christian symbols of suffering are associated. In sum, the pictorial transformation represents a number of kaleidoscopic changes by which Cuzco and its Inca, originally at the center of the traditional order, are ultimately substituted by the figure of the anonymous Andean, degraded and abused, as well as by the emblems of foreign institutions. Standing empty, the center of the design lacks resonance.

In Guaman Poma's depictions of the colonial era, the original Andean model with its five sectors is never reproduced. That perfection exists only in the Andean past (the *mapamundi*) or in the other-worldly future (his representation of the Christian heaven, referred to earlier). The compositional patterns Guaman Poma uses in the *Buen gobierno* constitute only portions of the archetypal design; the great majority of drawings reproduce only broken bits of the prototypical scheme. So, his *Nueva corónica y buen gobierno* drawings tell a grim tale, as they exploit part but never the whole of the fundamental and perfect Andean design. By pictorial means, Guaman Poma reiterates the destruction of the Andean world as he graphically reenacts the dismantling of its chief symbol. Together with other patterns of visual and verbal signification, to be examined in chapter 5, these compositions lead the reader to the full revelation of Guaman Poma's despair.

Plate 22. "The *corregidor* punishes the magistrate for failing to collect a couple of eggs from an Indian laborer" ([1615] 1980:503)

5. Mediating among Many Worlds

The final destination of this excursion through the *Nueva corónica y buen gobierno* is the relationship of the narrator Guaman Poma to the percipients he names and the characters he creates. The role he assumes between the external world he addresses and the fictional world he presents is one of many mediations. He portrays his viewpoint as being internal to the moral world of the king but external to the corrupt sphere inhabited by colonial exploiters. Satire and allegory here serve as fictional forms of representation. With regard to the contemporary Andean audience, the narrator positions himself in an attitude of social and moral superiority (as *cacique* and Christian) and he likewise places himself both inside and outside the world of the ancient Andeans.[1]

Guaman Poma's representation of narrational viewpoint is multifaceted but consistent, and I turn to its consideration in the face of the author's contradiction of his own efforts on other fronts. What he says about the history of the Spanish conquest of Peru is at odds with what he really means (chapter 1). His attempt to create heroes and to integrate the many strands of Peruvian experience into a meaningful, cohesive whole (chapter 2) fails to result in an epic synthesis and produces instead an endless sermon (chapter 3). The silent orations of the pictures often say one thing and mean something more or something other (chapter 4). In all cases, the voice of the social reformer and orator overtakes those of the historian, the storyteller, and the *cacique*. Thus the issue of narrational voice surfaces as a central and final perspective from which to evaluate the Andean writer's efforts.

As noted earlier, narrational viewpoint consists of the position the describing subject establishes vis-à-vis the characters and events he or she sets forth (Uspensky [1970] 1973:1). In considering Guaman Poma's point of view as it pertains to his critique of colonial society, one must recall that he belonged to the premodern world, which normally questioned only the manipulation of power, not the structures that created it (Maravall 1975: 48, 351). Guaman Poma criticizes the local practices of the colonial institutions of church and state but he does not reject the theoretical principles of "good government" on which they are founded. His use of the literary topos of "el mundo al rreués" ("the world upside down") reveals his classical attitude: on more than a dozen occasions, he complains that the proper order of things is reversed (see chapter 4, note 18), but he never questions the idea and potential of order itself. In fact, all his recommendations for governmental reform reveal that he accepts the existing structures of power and authority. Accordingly, he argues that the Andeans are victimized and exploited as he paints a picture of how the Spanish colonists increase and prosper.

Guaman Poma sees the impossibility of the situation that he and his people face, yet he refuses to give up hope of the existence of a moral or rational universe, in spite of his doubts about ever coming to inhabit it personally. In spite of the incongruity between what he professes—the reform of the colonial order—and what he admits he believes—that reform in Peru is impossible ("Todo es acá mentira") [(1615) 1980:1114])—he must resolve two pressing rhetorical problems to address effectively his princely *destinataire*. The first is how to attack and condemn the colonists, who are the vassals and subjects of the Spanish king; the second is how to situate himself vis-à-vis the ancient Incas whom the king, as champion of Counter-Reformational and missionary efforts, would view as pagan idolaters.

Allegory, Satire, and the Sermon

In all of Guaman Poma's virulent denunciations of the Spanish colonialists, the issue at stake is how he expresses his anger and simultaneously controls it, how he varies the expression of his argument or message to make it forceful. Satire is one of the channels through which he gives vent to and contains his rage and modulates the monotone of his angry voice; its use probably comes directly out of his experience with ecclesiastical rhetoric. The association of satire with preaching goes back to the Hebrew prophets (Frye 1962:21), and since medieval times sermons had been typically full of exempla—either animal fables, folktales, or gross anecdotes—that were intended to catch the attention of the congregation (Hodgart 1969:170). No doubt many of the sermons that Guaman Poma listened to were embroidered with satirical portraits of the Indian neophytes. In any case, Guaman Poma's satire is born of passion, not detached cynicism; he is a satirist more by default than by choice of a literary avocation. Satire is for him the last resort of an impassioned preacher who must enrage the listener and move him or her to moral action without causing personal offense.

The typical problem of satirical technique is finding a way to criticize an object without antagonizing the reader (Feinberg 1967:86). For an attack on anything to be successful, speaker and audience must agree on the undesirability of the object of criticism. Yet in the *Nueva corónica y buen gobierno*, writer and designated reader—the Andean petitioner and the Spanish monarch—are located on opposite sides of the cultural boundary that separates them.   Guaman Poma solves this problem by moving beyond the personal level to the impersonal and by committing himself to a high moral standard (see Frye [1957] 1973:225). By identifying the reader with an attitude of moral superiority, the author invites, and probably assures, the reader's good will. The theory of satirical technique precludes the reader's identification with the characters depicted, and Guaman Poma makes it clear that the Spanish king to whom he writes and the Spanish colonists whom he describes belong to different moral categories within the European cultural sphere as he defines it.

The cardinal feature of Guaman Poma's fictional re-creation of the monarch is the king's devotion to the cause of justice for all. By creating the illusion of a community of morality with his designated reader, the narrator implicitly minimizes the differences between the ways of understanding the world that separate them. The use of the visual and verbal codes of Christian rhetoric, from iconography to allegory, serve as the strategic solution to the formal problem (see Adorno 1981a).

Many metaphors constitute an allegory, according to López Pinciano ([1596] 1953: v. 2:144), who points out that the most noteworthy practitioners of the art use it more to accuse than to defend.[2] Guaman Poma likewise creates clusters of visual and verbal metaphors as weapons of attack. With the prolonged doubling of meaning that allegory offers, Guaman Poma uses the technique ironically, creating a blame-through-praise celebration/attack on the Spanish voyages of discovery, giving them an allegorical interpretation that has the bitter humor of a political cartoon. On two occasions ([1615] 1980:46, 375), he draws a Spanish galleon on the high seas (plate 23). Aboard are figures whom he identifies as Columbus, Vasco Núñez de Balboa, and Juan Díaz de Solís, the explorer of the coasts of Yucatan and Brazil. Almagro and Pizarro, the conquerors of Peru, appear on the same deck (ibid.:46). In the second drawing of the same scene, an additional figure is present, the Spanish geographer and explorer Martín Fernández de Enciso (ibid.:375).

In the written narration that accompanies these drawings, Guaman Poma

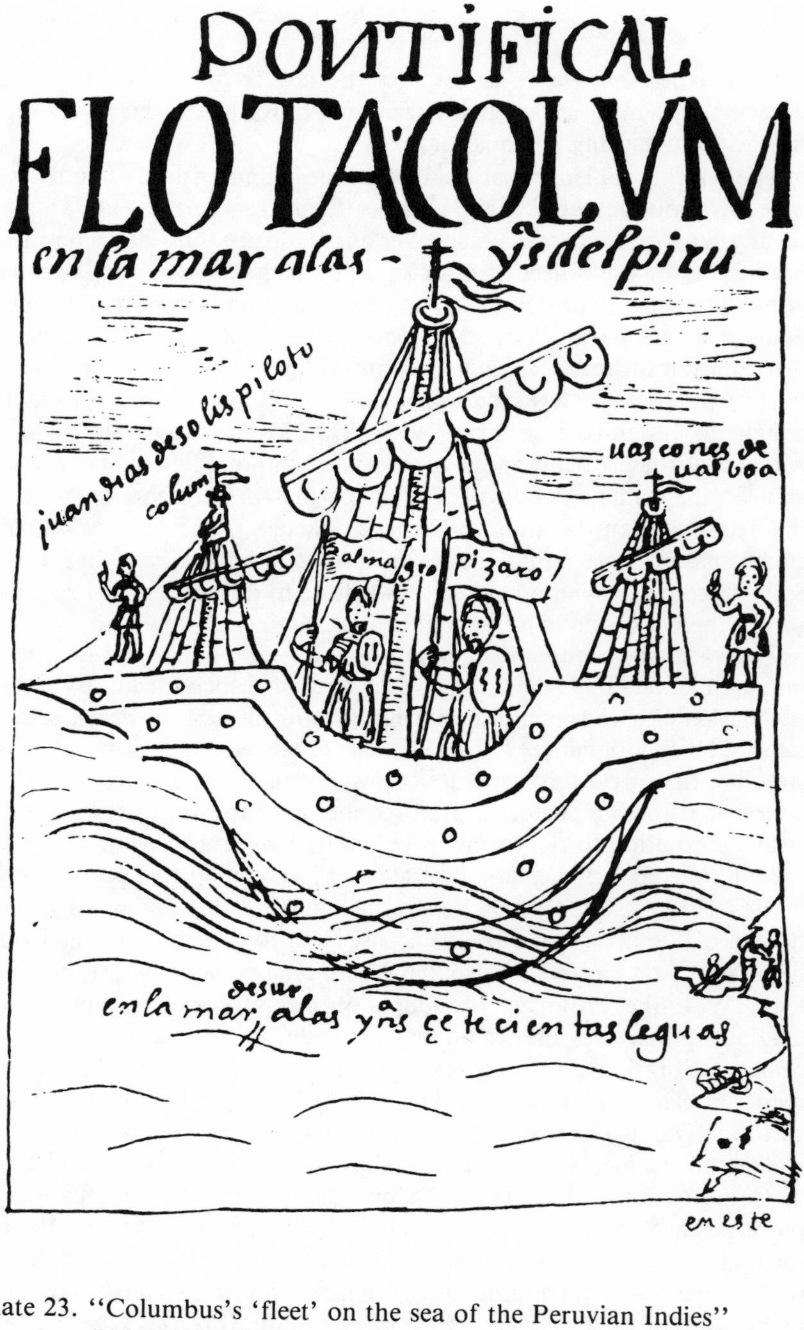

Plate 23. "Columbus's 'fleet' on the sea of the Peruvian Indies"
([1615] 1980:46)

offers a chronology of the events associated with these various historical figures, but makes simultaneous these various deeds in the drawings entitled "Flota Colúm" and "Enbarcáronse a las Yndias." Allegorically speaking, the drawings combined with the narration deal with a single phenomenon; that is, the various expeditions together compose the act by which Europe arrived definitively in the New World. The resulting picture is an encomium of the Spanish discoveries, made allegorical and ironical by the single visual summary of various voyages and by the verbal text. Describing the explorers and conquistadores, Guaman Poma tells that they had become deranged in their greed for gold:

Y no quicieron descansar ningún día en los puertos. Cada día no se hazía nada, cino todo era pensar en oro y plata y rriquiesas de las Yndias del Pirú. Estauan como un hombre desesperado, tonto, loco, perdidos el juycio con la codicia de oro y plata. A ueses no comía con el pensamiento de oro y plata. A ueses tenía gran fiesta, pareciendo que todo oro y plata tenía dentro de las manos. A cido como un gato casero quando tiene el rratón dentro de las uñas, entonces se huelga. . . . Así fue los primeros hombres; no temió la muerte con enterés de oro y plata. (Ibid.:376)

(And they did not want to rest a single day in port. Every day they did nothing but think about the gold and silver and riches of the Peruvian Indies. They were like desperate men, foolish, crazy, their judgment lost with the greed for gold and silver. Sometimes they didn't eat for thinking of gold and silver. Sometimes they had great celebrations, imagining that they had gold and silver in their hands. They were like the house cat, when it has the mouse in its claws, then it rejoices! . . . So were the first adventurers; they did not fear death because of their desire for gold and silver.)

So as not to overlook the historical consequences of this phenomenon, he adds, "Peor son los desta uida, los españoles corregidores, padres, comenderos. Con la codicia del oro y plata se uan al ynfierno" ("Even worse are those of this generation, the Spaniards, *corregidores*, priests, *encomenderos*. With the greed of gold and silver they are going to hell") (ibid.).

The visual allegory and verbal satire take on explicitly moral meanings; in fact, they can be seen as aspects of Guaman Poma's sermonizing. Devoted to teaching a lesson, these satirical pieces touch what López Pinciano considers the heart of allegory; leaving esthetic pleasure aside, allegory here concentrates only on teaching (López Pinciano [1596] 1953: v. 3:247). Although the narration may be nonsense as history, the allegory is vivid and useful as instruction. Using historical events as a point of departure to offer a moral lesson, Guaman Poma is squarely in the domain of the preacher. Likening the greed of the explorers to the glee of a house cat with a mouse in its clutches, Guaman Poma follows the rules for clear expression—using common similes and comparisons as prescribed in the *Tercero catecismo.*

His other extended visual and verbal allegory, exploiting a whole series of animal metaphors in the manner of the sermon,[3] continues the point made about greed. In the tradition of the medieval bestiary, Guaman Poma draws a picture that assigns animal identities to various groups of colonial functionaries (plate 24). With jaws open and tongues extended, the tiger is the vagabond Spaniard, often a soldier; the lion represents the *encomendero*; the "cierpe" is the *corregidor*; the fox, the parish priest; the cat, the clerk; and the *cacique principal*, a mouse ([1615] 1980:708). His metaphors reiterate the Plautine topos *homo homini lupus* (man against man is a beast [wolf]), an aphorism that gave expression to a common sentiment of the baroque period (Maravall 1975:326). The same verbal description is reiterated on other occasions ([1615] 1980:709, 832, 913–914). The bestiary motif or animal fable plays a role in the prologue-sermon that concludes the chapter entitled "justicia yndios." As moral allegory gives way to simple forms of satire in the sermon (Hodgart 1969: 170), so too Guaman Poma exploits metaphor to make satirical identifications. He tells the Spanish reader to love his neighbor and defend the Andeans, as poor sheep, from the ferocious animals that would devour them:

Cristianos letores: Y comunica en tu ánima y rrumia dentro de tu corasón y procura de ser cierbos de Jesucristo. Ama a buestros prógimos y defendelde a buestro basallo, los pobres obejas, para que no le coman los ferós animales, serpientes, ticres, leones, sorras, gatos y rratones, para que de ellos Dios te lo pague en el cielo. ([1615] 1980:832)

(Christian readers: Communicate with your soul and meditate in your heart and try to be servants of Jesus Christ. Love your neighbor and defend your vassals, the poor sheep, so that the ferocious animals—serpents, tigers, lions, foxes, cats and mice—do not devour them, so that God will reward you in heaven because of them.)

Thus satire strikes a moral chord of invective and denunciation. The central point of this fablizing is that humanity, seeing itself as different from the beasts, portrays its fellows in animal guise to make a point about human conduct. But Guaman Poma does not use animals as symbols of human types and vices, as is usually the case, to make moralizing palatable and to provide a detached reader with amusement (see Feinberg 1967: 52, 55). Guaman Poma's satire turns in a darker direction and corresponds

Plate 24. "Six devouring beasts feared by the poor Indians of Peru"
([1615] 1980:708)

to the "satirical device of reduction, of revealing the non-human drives behind human pretensions to grandeur" (Hodgart 1969:172). As the transformation of the primitive animal tale into moral satire usually results in a
satirical polemic in the form of a political or social protest (ibid.), so
Guaman Poma's satire is exclusively that of denunciation, removed as far
as possible from fantasy, the opposite pole of satire in Frye's scheme (see
Frye [1957] 1973:224–225).

This satire of invective is closely allied to preaching and is generally
based on an encyclopedic scheme of the seven deadly sins in which a sense
of nightmare and the demonic prevails in spite of any humor (ibid.:225).
Enfolded in his sermonizing, Guaman Poma's satire is devoid of laughter
and deprived of its regenerative ambivalence (see Bakhtin [1965] 1968:12,
21). Not merely defeated but deprived of dignity as well, the Andean,
whipped and naked, stands bound to a pillar of suffering in the center of a
universe where once the enthroned Inca held sway (cf. plates 7 and 22).

Guaman Poma's satire is that of the nightmare of social tyranny, in
which experience culminates in a vision of the source of evil in personal
forms (see Frye [1957] 1973:238–239). The personal forms of the sources
of evil reside in his satire of the colonists. Making them speak in their own
voices, he parodies the missionaries' Quechua sermons and creates satirical dialogues and monologues that dramatize the colonists' greed. In these
parodies and satirical sketches, as is common in these genres, the central
emphasis is on the attack of abuses, not the portrayal of characters or
situations that might be of interest for their own sake (see Booth 1974:137).

Most significant is Guaman Poma's parody of the sermon in Quechua.
The genre that provided the model for his discourse becomes, ironically,
the target of his greatest scorn. In an exaggerated imitation of sermon
style, he ridicules both the priests' stylistic mannerisms and their speech
patterns. He parodies the speech of his most hated enemies, the *padres de
doctrina*, so that the alien voices might condemn themselves. Most of the
sermons demonstrate what the author promises at the outset: "Mexcla el
sermón de su hazienda y rrescates y otras ocupaciones que ellos pretenden"
("They mix up the sermon with finances, barter, and other businesses in
which they deal") ([1615] 1980:624). Significantly, he does not translate
these Quechua discourses into Spanish for the benefit of his readers of
Spanish; at this level, his satire is clearly oriented to the Quechua speaker.
Urioste's translations of Guaman Poma (ibid.:625) reveal the covert irony
of these pieces:

El padre dijo: ¡Tejan! El padre dijo: ¡Acábenlo! Sepan que el padre es mejor que el
corregidor, mejor que el *kuraka*, mejor que el encomendero y que el mismo virrey.

Debes escuchar mis buenos mandatos que te dije que trabajaras, ¡porque te voy a azotar hasta las nalgas! Esto es lo que les ordeno hoy en el Evangelio. Este es el sermón. Se lo digo como representante de Dios. ¡Reciban esto en el corazón!

(The priest said, "Weave!" The priest said, "Finish it!" Understand that the priest is better than the *corregidor*, better than the ethnic lord, better than the *encomendero* and the viceroy himself. You should listen to my good commands because I'm going to whip your ass! This is what I ordain today in the gospel. This is the sermon. I tell it to you as a representative of God. Accept this in your hearts!)[4]

With these sermons, Guaman Poma renders as vicious and cruel the voices of the parish priests; he effectively takes the language of the gospel out of their mouths. As he makes religious rhetoric his own, he uses dramatizations to take it away from those to whom it is entrusted. Imitating the speech of the preacher, he empties the preacher's voice of religious content. In this way, Guaman Poma puts his criticisms of the colonists in their own mouths and those of their countrymen. It is significant that, throughout, the Andean is silent. Suffering, degraded, and dehumanized, the Andeans are portrayed without a voice, without hope.

These cruel Spanish voices form a chorus that becomes an essential part of Guaman Poma's anticolonialist attack; what makes them ironic is the meaning of immorality that the reader attaches to them. Alternating between his own speech and such parodies and impersonations, Guaman Poma succeeds in highlighting his central argument in ways that the use of a single technique could not. Yet his experimentation with a variety of literary genres may simply register his sense that any—or even all—formulas are inadequate to convey his interpretation of colonial reality. Hence, the feverish production of pictures and prose with its extensive repetitions and reiterations attempts to communicate a message that is larger than any single utterance or even the sum of them all.

Guaman Poma obsessively repeats his assertions that the Andeans, since time immemorial, have lived by the Ten Commandments and that the Spaniards, from Francisco de Toledo to the local parish priest, suffer from *soberbia*. Although he uses metaphorical identification of Andean and non-Andean phenomena, he is skeptical of its ability to explain things; as a rhetorical strategy, metaphor is insufficient to explain the orderly system of Andean society, or to elucidate fully the consequences of Spanish behavior in the Peruvian colony. Each reiteration betrays the emptiness the phrases represent and exposes their inadequacy to describe a view of reality that can never be submitted to formulas. Dwelling even more on the evils of colonialism than on its reform, Guaman Poma confesses the moral cynicism that he feels: "Acá se acauan los yndios y no ay rremedio en este mundo" ("Here the Indians are being exterminated, and there is no recourse in this world"). The victory of satire over every other literary form, most especially that of the satiric dialogue over the exemplary biography, moves our reading further in the direction of the ironic despair against which hope cannot compete.

Thus, on one hand, Guaman Poma desires to promote the restoration of order in society and he perceives that there exists a certain potential for doing so. On the other, his despair paints a terrifying picture of colonial experience that contradicts and overwhelms the reformer's zeal. At bottom, the issue is not merely sin and greed, or Christian morality and its absence, for these are rhetorical devices; the issue is the lack of fundamental understanding between the two cultures. Unlike the European chroniclers who could judge cultural similarities with a distant look or a squint of the eye, or the Scholastic thinker who posited likenesses at the philosophical or theological levels, Guaman Poma lived through the differences and experienced the lack of comprehension and understanding between vastly different cultures.

Yet where does the metaphorical strategy end and the ironical attitude begin? How can Guaman Poma make countless types of identification between the two cultures and, at the same time, deny that any such identification is possible? In my estimation, there is no such contradiction in the *Nueva corónica y buen gobierno*. I would argue that the metaphorical formulation is, for Guaman Poma, a pose, not a conviction. He elaborates a system of resemblances for the reader without believing in it himself. Behind the smiling face of naïveté lie the bitter fruits of the self-critical attitude. It is satire that serves as the bridge that links the metaphorical strategy with the ironic outlook.

Of *Caciques* and *Coyas*

A final inquiry concerning Guaman Poma's narrational viewpoint centers on his relationship to the long-gone Incas and the contemporary Andeans. We now move away from the focus on the speaker-percipient relationship that has oriented this study to consider, at last, the Andean world with which the speaker identifies. I have selected for the problem of his narrational viewpoint one Andean figure toward whom the narrator's attitude is ambivalent from the outset: Mama Huaco, *coya*, mother and wife of Manco Capac Inca. According to Guaman Poma, Mama Huaco is a sorceress of unknown origins and the author of the Inca dynasty, which replaced the original Incas and subjugated the ancient dynasty of Yarovilca

Allauca Huanoco, from which Guaman Poma claims descent and lordly status (see Adorno 1980, 1981b).

In considering his treatment of Mama Huaco, we discover that his depiction of Andean characters is more complex than his depiction of the Spaniards. Whereas the narrator simply criticizes or praises one colonist or another, he does not enter into a system of relationships with these characters; they stand outside the Andean cultural space that he has defined in his book. In creating Andean figures, however, the author presents a narrator who must enter into the hierarchy of relationships that he creates. As a result, these portrayals are more problematic in conception and richer in execution than those of the Spaniards. By probing the relationship of picture to prose in the *Nueva corónica y buen gobierno*, one discovers that the apparent distance between the speaker and the object of his description ironically masks their identification.[5]

Of particular relevance in the case of Guaman Poma's bifocal text is Boris Uspensky's development of a theory and terminology to describe the composition of verbal and visual artistic productions. Pertinent to the consideration of the visual text is the question of internal and external viewpoints and their relationship to linear and inverse perspective. To describe the texture of Guaman Poma's verbal discourse, I rely on the works of Bakhtin and Vološinov, on whose work Uspensky grounded his own system of analysis (Uspensky [1970] 1973:5–6). Examining the spatial and temporal positions assumed by the subject in both pictures and prose, I shall show how Guaman Poma articulates a point of view that is alternately internal and external to the sphere he describes.

Throughout the visual and verbal texts, Guaman Poma as narrator approaches the sphere of the European as though he were simultaneously alien and native to it. In order that his account be received with full confidence in its authenticity and veracity, the narrator must convey his message with the ring of credibility. Thus he insists on his status as a native Peruvian and an eyewitness to the events that he describes: "Y ancí lo e uisto a uista de ojos para el rremedio de los pobres y seruicio de Dios y de su Magestad. Como e uisto tantas cosas ques de espantar" ("And thus I have seen it with my own eyes, for the remedy of the poor and in service to God and his Majesty. It is frightening how much I have seen") ([1615] 1980:715; see also pp. 285, 893, 908). At the same time and to avoid alienating his courtly reader, the narrative persona plays down his role as an exotic informant who speaks in a foreign tongue. The essential drama that Guaman Poma faces is how to cast the narrator as the trustworthy confidant whose very authority derives from his condition of exotic strangeness. He resolves this contradiction through the syntactics of composition.

Guaman Poma's local ethnic patriotism allows him to express a degree of anti-Inca sentiment. Yet he treats the Incas with considerable subtlety, for he describes them in three ways: from his perspective as a descendant of the Yarovilca dynasty, he identifies them as usurpers; from his perspective as a Christian, he calls them idolaters; as a native informant of the potentially racist foreign king, he finds it advantageous to treat them as distinguished historical personages. Through the manipulation of certain compositional techniques, Guaman Poma creates the illusion of standing both inside and outside the historical realm that he portrays, as one position or the other variously suits his purpose. Thus he establishes the authority of his views for a remote historical period of which he has only secondhand knowledge.

Inside the *Coya*'s Chamber

The "First History of the Queens, *Coyas*" opens with the portrait of Mama Huaco, *coya* (plate 25; ([1615] 1980:120). She is shown seated in her palatial quarters while three female servants—two young women and a dwarf—attend her. Holding up a mirror that contains her own reflection, Mama Huaco engages in her toilette. Several features of this charming tableau suggest that an internal point of view, and possibly inverse perspective, are at work. Viewpoint is considered to be <u>internal</u> when the eye that observes and records a scene seems to be located within the represented sphere, and external when it seems to stand outside the area depicted (Uspensky [1970] 1973:2). Perspective in visual art is linear when the object portrayed is viewed from a single static vantage point and conveys the impression that the observation is made at a given moment and from a fixed position; perspective is inverse when a plurality of viewpoints is represented, because the artist's position is dynamic (Uspensky [1970] 1976: 221–228). In inverse perspective, the "formal fractures of every sort, the distortions of form in comparison with what we would see from a single point of view" stem from the desire to portray the object in the fullness of its existence (ibid.:228). Thus, the artist using inverse perspective views an object from several different angles and conveys the simultaneous impression of those many successive viewpoints.

In Mama Huaco's portrait, there are three features that suggest that the artist's viewpoint is internal to the scene. First, the carpet on which she is seated is tilted upward toward the viewer. This distortion suggests that the artist is representing the rug as though he were standing on it, and looking down at it. Only from such a position would the four corners that we can see be simultaneously visible. A second feature is the relative smallness of

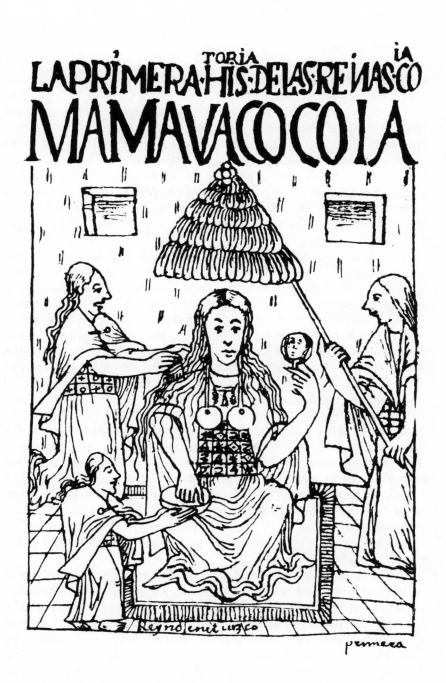

Plate 25. "Mama Huaco, *coya*, reigned in Cuzco"
([1615] 1980:120)

the dwarf in the foreground, compared to the larger size of the ladies-in-waiting in the background. If the dwarf were being pictured from our vantage point as external observers to the scene, her head would loom larger than those of her companions in the background. However, the diminutive size of the dwarf's head tells us that her figure is articulated by an artist who creates the illusion of being an observer internal to the scene. To that recording eye, the background figures would be closer, and therefore larger, than those in the pictorial foreground. This particular gradation in sizes is considered a typical feature of inverse perspective insofar as the latter presupposes, for the moment, an internal viewpoint (Uspensky [1970] 1973:135-136).

A third feature of the drawing makes impossible a single, fixed, internal viewpoint on the part of the artist, for the specific feature of mobility associated with inverse perspective comes into play. Mama Huaco holds up a mirror, and we see both her face and its reflected image in the glass. Even the vantage point of someone within the scene, if in a fixed position, does not make possible the view offered here; only a mobile viewpoint can realize this contiguous representation of successive visual impressions. The image of the face can be attributed to an external viewpoint, the image of the reflection, an internal one. Thus, we have the play between internal and external viewpoints, which is common to inverse perspective. The effect of this alternation is the illusion of the removal of the frame that separates the artistic production from the world outside it. The overall visual impression is that the recording eye is inside the room portrayed. This royal domestic tableau is represented, as it were, from within the boundaries of its own purview. Since this portrait presents a historical figure, the manipulation of spatial values carries with it an implicit temporal meaning. The artist creates the illusion of having achieved the impossible: he has taken an anachronistic position within an ancient historical portrait as though he were recording his impressions of it from within its own confines.

Although the visual representation of the first *coya* offers the illusion of an internal view of the vanished Inca world, it would seem that the verbal narration of the *coya*'s biography could only be told in a retrospective manner, with respect to which the narrator would necessarily assume an external viewpoint. The time of his reporting, after all, is not synchronous with that of the events he describes. Yet even in the historical narration, Guaman Poma contrives an internal viewpoint, which alternates with an external one. In the written text, our point of orientation is defined by the "temporal relations of the describing subject (the author) to the described event" (ibid.:57). In general terms, Uspensky regards the position of the narrator to be internal to the narration when his "present time" is the same as that of the character represented; external, when he views the deeds of those figures retrospectively (ibid.:67). These positions are typically alternated through the manipulation of the tense and aspect of the verb (ibid.:69). Such an alternation occurs in Guaman Poma's account of ancient history.

The Present in the Past

Mama Huaco's biography is narrated primarily in the imperfect and preterite tenses of the retrospective verb system in Spanish. Benveniste's distinction of the verbal systems of history and discourse illuminates the contrastive values of the imperfect and preterite tenses, and their respective relationship to internal and external viewpoint ([1966] 1971:205–215). (Although his analysis is undertaken for French, his conclusions are equally relevant for Spanish.) For Benveniste, the verbal system of discourse, as opposed to that of history, resides in the relationship of the first and second grammatical persons, thus assuming the presence of a speaker and a hearer and the intention of the former to influence the latter (ibid.:208–209). He defines the verbal system of history as the narration of past events, which are presented without any intervention of the speaker in the narration; such events are "characterized as past from the time they have been recorded and uttered in a historical temporal expression" (ibid.:206).

In Spanish the historical utterance is quintessentially captured in the preterite tense (Alarcos Llorach 1969:110–112; Bull 1960:17, 94–98). In Mama Huaco's biography, the preterite tense, that is, the historical verb system that attributes actions to a time period that precludes any personal intervention by the speaker, predominates. Utterances constituting final assessments of Mama Huaco's life are described in their perfective, usually terminative, aspects as points of time without duration (Bull 1960:17). Her physical appearance, time and place of death, and spiritual legacy are all treated from the perspective of overview and summation: "Fue muy hermosa . . . dejó la ley del demonio muy entablado a todos sus hijos. . . . Murió en el Cuzco de edad de duzientos años" ("She was very beautiful . . . she left the law of the devil very well established for all her children. . . . She died in Cuzco at the age of two hundred years") ([1615] 1980:121). In Uspensky's system, the use of the perfective aspect of the verb defines the retrospective position of the narrator: "Looking from the future time back into the characters' present," the narrator's point of view is external to the ongoing narration (Uspensky [1970] 1973:67).

In other parts of the biographical narration, however, temporal references connoting the narrator's internal position as based on the use of the imperfect aspect of the verb appear. Since the imperfect tense in Spanish describes the middle or durational aspect of an event viewed retrospectively, as a process as yet unconcluded (Alarcos Llorach 1969:111–112; Bull 1960:17), it conveys the idea of an utterance made in the present time concerning a retrospective temporal domain. Because the imperfect occupies an intermediate location that blurs the boundary between the historical and discursive verbal systems, Benveniste locates the imperfective aspect of the verb on both planes of utterance ([1966] 1971:209). According to Uspensky, the imperfective aspect of the verb conveys a sense of "present in the past." Like the present-tense form of the verb, the imperfect allows the narrator to "carry out his description from within the action—that is, synchronically, rather than retrospectively—and to place the reader in the very center of the scene he is describing" ([1970] 1973:74). This narrative tactic is found in the following excerpts from Mama Huaco's biography:

Según cuentan su uida y historia que hablaua con los demonios . . . hacía hablar a las piedras y peñas . . . dixo que era hija del sol y de la luna. . . . Tenía su bestido de rrosado . . . gouernaua más que su marido Mango Capac . . . hazía milagros de los demonios . . . hazía mucho bien a los pobres en la ciudad. ([1615] 1980:121)

(According to the way they tell her life story, she spoke with the demons . . . she made stones and boulders speak . . . she said she was the daughter of the sun and moon. . . . She had a rose-colored dress . . . she governed more than her husband Manco Capac . . . she performed diabolical miracles . . . she did much good for the poor of the city.)

Through the use of the imperfect tense, the speaker creates the illusion of bringing actions begun in past time into his own arena of intervention.

The notion of the "present in the past" can also be analyzed with regard to the preterite tense. In this light, Guaman Poma's statement that Mama Huaco "dixo que era hija del sol y de la luna" has a special meaning. An atemporal function of the simple past tense allows the verbs of inner action, such as thinking and even saying, to constitute "presentification." The preterite "dixo," representing an action articulated internally and perceived externally, indicates not temporality in this case, but rather a semantic meaning-content by which Mama Huaco decided to pose as, or believed that she was, the daughter of the sun and moon. This inner action, recorded in the form "she said," lends to all other narrated actions in her story a sense of "being there" that can be likened to the representation of the plastic arts (Hamburger 1973:98). The "presentification" of Mama

Huaco in the picture, which also creates "a static Here and Now" (ibid.: 98), corroborates this effect.

In using the imperfect, the narrator offers not final assessments, but rather a verbal moving picture of the individual practicing witchcraft and idolatry, dressing in a certain manner, and reigning forcefully but with compassion over the Inca's domain. The narrative voice creates the illusion of observing these actions in progress and of noting their repetition. Overall, the impression the narrator gives is that of an internal viewpoint, of materializing *in situ* the deeds of the historical personage as she moves with grandeur and superstition through the routine of her daily life. The alternation of preterite (external viewpoint) and imperfect (internal vantage point) tenses creates the illusion of the narrator's movement in and out of this historical scene at the level of the sentence. That is, he frequently recalls events that he orients to retrospective points in time and others that he does not so focus. Thus, the speaker organizes his account not as a sequence of events but in terms of a series of retrospective axes that allow him to choose which aspect—beginning, middle, or end—of the action to use in recalling the event (Bull 1960:100). Just as the spatial articulation of pictorial viewpoint has implications for temporal meaning, so the temporal manipulation of the verb carries spatial signification. The imperfect tense creates the illusion of the narrator's encroachment into the spatial domain of the ancient Incas, where he witnesses Mama Huaco's acts of charity and feats of sorcery.

Another syntactic construct that introduces the narrator into the represented realm is an element that probably derives from the author's native Quechua. This the use of the nonwitness validator, "dizen que" ("they say that"), which I have already described in another chapter (chapter 1, pp. 20–22). Here we find that the Quechua discourse-marker, superimposed on the narrator's Spanish prose, expresses at both the phraseological and spatial-temporal levels the narrator's identification with the represented Andean world. The type of utterance in question combines within the same sentence events that are viewed as past, historical, and external and those that are present-time, discursive, and internal from his point of view. Here, the internal position is marked by the use of the regular present tense (Uspensky [1970] 1973:71), as present and past tenses are brought together:

Dizen que fue gran hechizera. . . . Y dizen que [a] ella no le fue conocida su padre. . . . Para se casar, dizen que pedió a su padre al sol dote y le dio dote y se casaron madre y hijo. ([1615] 1980:121)

(They say that she was a great sorceress. . . . And they say that her father was not known to her. . . . To marry, they say she asked her father the sun for a dowry and he gave her a dowry and mother and son were married.)

Although Benveniste's history/discourse contrast corroborates Uspensky's analysis of cases like these, the major argument for internal viewpoint comes from the validation feature of Quechua discourse. "Dizen que" may be a translation of the nonwitness validator, the Quechua suffix -si, which signifies that the speaker cannot vouch for information as an eyewitness, but has acquired it through hearsay (see Urioste 1973:45, 49). Whether the origin of "dizen que" in this instance is Spanish or Quechua, the relevant point is that Guaman Poma makes it clear that he cannot personally verify certain of the legendary attributes of Mama Huaco. This device places the narrator beyond the confines of Mama Huaco's world and makes his point of view external with regard to her actions.

On the other hand, this alternation of grammatical tenses within a single sentence effects what Uspensky calls a "sudden change in point of view" ([1970] 1973:72). Whereas the narrative voice is external to both the character and events depicted by the historical tense in the subordinate clause, his temporal position is internal to the represented world at the level of the main clause ("they say that"). The reporter is privy to special information, which places him, as a result, inside the world he describes, at least at the level of his own base time in the discourse. "Dizen que" means "I have it on the authority of others that . . ." For Benveniste, this construction represents the interruption of historical narration by the intervention of discourse; the historian's commentary on the events reported, or his reproduction of someone else's words or account, requires the use of the discursive tense system ([1966] 1971:209). Thus, the phrase "they say that," like "according to how they tell her life and story" ("según cuentan su uida y historia"), places the narrator within reach of the native oral traditions. "Dizen que" and its analogues tell us that the accounts are taken on the authority of contemporary Andeans who are acquainted with the Inca past. Thus, the narrator places himself inside the Andean world, at a temporal remove from the events of the ancient past but nevertheless retaining a spatial position within the realm of Andean experience on which he relies for his report.

From the initial portrait to the final pronouncement, the spectacle of the coya's life unequivocally represents a view of that lost world from within. The biography and the pictorial tableau are both representations of the Andean world as dynamic and ongoing. The manipulation of space in the picture and verb tense in the narration endow the composition with a sense of dynamism and an image of potency for both ancient and contemporary Andean worlds. This illusion of "presentification," of the bringing-forth of the Andean world, is due to the mobility of the authorial viewpoint. At close temporal range, the narrator verbalizes Mama Huaco's actions as they were happening; at another moment, distantly removed in time, he renders her deeds in their perfected state, capturing them, as it were, in a still photograph. At other moments, he bends his ear close to contemporary oral accounts of the Andean elders, who recall reports of those bygone times. Each of these facets of the temporal complex suggests that the notion of inverse perspective proper, even more than the simple internal viewpoint, may be the most pertinent factor in describing Guaman Poma's construction of temporal relations. The same feature of inverse perspective characterizes the spatial relations in Mama Huaco's portrait. Her picture is not a simple, static rendering but a composite view of many successive visual impressions.

In addition to the portrait and biography, the evidence of this mobility unfolds even in the prologue (see chapter 3, pp. 74–77). Summoning the noble ladies by their titles in Quechua, Guaman Poma portrays himself as their equal, that is, as a *cacique* himself, until he moves head and shoulders above them in his stylized sermon. Then, in his final prayer, he creates an illusion of solidarity with them. He establishes his position as primarily internal to the world he depicts, lending himself authority vis-à-vis his princely *destinataire*, and, within that world, he creates himself as superior to its other inhabitants, thus granting himself a prestige greater than that of his characters.

The Author as Hero

Ultimately, the heroes and heroines that Guaman Poma creates in his book do not measure up to the stature and dignity with which the author endows the image of the narrator. Only he has a panheroic conception that can bridge the world of the ancient warrior and noble statesman (Guaman Chaua) and the Inca's viceroy and Spanish king's captain (Guaman Malqui). In his book, only Guaman Poma (Christian *cacique* and princely author) unites the heroism of the past with that of the present. His is a chivalric enterprise, righting wrongs and defending the defenseless. Hence, the relationships that the narrator establishes with both the royal reader and with the Andeans he addresses—fictional characters all—serve ultimately to enhance his own position even more than that of his historiographic and biographical subjects. Here, finally, the figure of Guaman Poma appears, for it is the author's creation of himself as narrator that offers the most complete information about him. From this discussion of viewpoint, the narrator Guaman Poma emerges not as informant, but as author(ity), not as the Spanish king's servant but as the Andean lord. Where he seems to present a picture of himself as the assimilated *indio ladino*, we find instead that he remains true to his own cultural heritage in an identification that is as intimate as it is consistent (see Adorno 1981a).

As for his hero's reward, it appears only in the writing of the book itself. The evidence that I have discovered regarding his literary production, especially his extensive textual emendations and the insertion of additional pages into the already-sewn quires, corroborates this view (see Adorno 1980). The repetitions and repetitiousness for which he is notorious seem to be an indication that to finish his book would be for him to admit defeat. Guaman Poma's ultimate irony is that he pours himself into the writing of a book that, he fears, cannot achieve the goals that he has set for it. To finish the book, to let it go, would be to subject it to a fate that he less welcomes than wishes to postpone.

Guaman Poma's Final Critique

Looking over the *Nueva corónica y buen gobierno* one last time, we can see how Guaman Poma sows the seeds of irony in his whole production. His employment of Andean spatial symbolism challenges the reader's assessment of his apparently assimilated artistic style; his metaphorical identifications, apparently innocent and well intended, possess a dark underside that overwhelms his interpretation of both the European and Andean sides of colonial experience. As a tool of irony, metaphor denies the illusion of unity and wholeness; it disguises differences but acknowledges that they cannot be ignored.

Guaman Poma's utopian proposal of making his son the prince of Peru in a universal kingdom where Philip III would be the "monarca del mundo" and his recommendation that a cardinalate of the Indies be established both seem to declare a faith in a political and religious structure that he doubts can fulfill its goals. He separates himself from his entire project when he declares that the world is upside-down: "Es señal que no ay Dios y no ay rrey. Está en Roma y Castilla. ("It is a sign that there is no God and no king. They are in Rome and in Castile") ([1615] 1980:1136). Calling himself a servant of "Cristóbal de la Cruz," his mission, he says, is to serve "los pobres de Jesucristo" (ibid.:1118). So he strips himself of his self-proclaimed identity as counselor to the king. These efforts, too, end up by denying what they had once affirmed. The lament with which he ends his meditations echoes an ancient refrain—the one that he had associated with Andean man's original search for God, and that, in fact, reiterates the traditional Quechua prayer theme. On raising his voice to ask, "¿Adónde estás, nuestro señor rrey Phelipe?" (p. 1122) ("Where are you, our lord king Philip?"), Guaman Poma identifies himself wholly with his own race and rejects the image of the colonial imperial counselor. As in the pictures, he completely isolates the Andean from the European cultural sphere (see Adorno 1981a).

In spite of his efforts to create unity and wholeness in his treatise on good government, Guaman Poma's project fails. At the formal level, the *Buen gobierno* is nothing but a series of starts and stops. It stands in sharp contrast to the *Nueva corónica*, where Guaman Poma had carefully woven the threads of biblical, papal, and Andean histories into a single fabric. The *Buen gobierno*, meanwhile, becomes tiresomely repetitious; it seems to move ahead but goes nowhere. It has no culminations, no resolutions, save the tale of the broken old man who takes his manuscript to Lima. "Camina el autor" is one small story whose effect is to stand in contrast to the formless or motifless corpus into which it is inserted. The disjointed and fitful prose of the *Buen gobierno* reflects Guaman Poma's frustrated attempts to control the reality he wishes to describe. About this part of his book we may say, just as he complained about Murúa's work, "ni comensó ni acabó" ("He neither began nor concluded"). This narration takes the form of a chronicle, not a story, and its very lack of motific encoding denies the attribution of positive value to the experience that it recounts; "todo es acá mentira."

Where Guaman Poma had set up a story to give past Andean experience meaning, he denies it in the case of the present. Although seeming to construct an illusion of unity, the *Buen gobierno* leaves us with only a collection of disparate pieces. Although giving himself over to language both written and pictorial, Guaman Poma questions its power to communicate, to change things. Constructing a model of morality for the present and the future, he doubts the prospects for its fulfillment. This is the tragic degree of irony through which life is seen as unrelieved bondage. Guaman Poma had his own way of putting it, and it is the epitaph of his ironic vision: "Y no ay rremedio en este mundo."

Reflecting not only the author's assessment of future prospects for Andean-Spanish relations, his picture/prose book signals another problem: the author's doubts about the possibility of communication across the cultural barrier. The existence of his book itself is a testimony to the importance that Guaman Poma attaches to the problem. The twin movements between, on one hand, the picture that idealizes and the prose that criticizes and, on the other, the picture that criticizes and the prose that condemns, belie a fundamental uncertainty about the prospect of cross-cultural communication. Guaman Poma is engaged not only in a search for solutions, but also in a search for the best ways to make them and himself understood. Far from being a kind of straightforward illustration of the verbal text, the pictures, as carriers of their own independent meaning, enter into different types of relationships with the written text, and all testify to a desperate attempt to bridge the communication gap. In this context I would express one final reflection that concerns the conflicting tensions and tendencies that attended the birth of narrative in Spanish America.

Guaman Poma's experience reveals that, although the seeds of narrative fiction were planted in a field that was presumably historiographic, the shoots of history, oratory, and fiction were not kept separate. Literary discourse was constructed, in short, out of the variety of models at hand. Guaman Poma was present at that historical moment that Octavio Paz has described as "the response of the real reality of Americans to the utopian reality of America" ([1961] 1966:13). The Americans countered the providentialist histories written by Europeans with their own brand of narrative. Due to their circumstances, these early Amerindian texts were filled with models of experience that seemed more mythical than real, with solutions that they knew were doomed, with contradictions that they could not resolve but only ratify. The interpenetration of the models of history, fiction, and rhetoric reflect the effort to work through antithetical concepts that represent contradictory realities. The limits of creative combination were imposed only by the imagination or despair.

And so, within such imaginative spheres, fiction could mask itself as history, and historiography could be exchanged for oratory. For Guaman Poma, the history that he would order and contain within the bounds of the story refused to be so confined. Reality itself overwhelmed any effort to make sense of things. Guaman Poma's chronicle of fragmented vignettes is an early example of the response of Andeans to the dream that was dreamed by others. His book came to life in a moment when the historical and the fictional were hopelessly bound, and yet each separately and both together were inadequate to render comprehensible the whole of experience.

The larger issue raised by Guaman Poma's enterprise is not whether he succeeds or fails in his own autodidactic literary apprenticeship. The greatest implications of his effort lie, I think, in the critique of European letters that he performs. In his dedicated and desperate attempt to understand and re-create the world of his experience, he struggles with the full range of means that the Europeans used to interpret and give expression to reality: the chronicles and *relaciones*, the juridical treatises, the polemical tracts, the catechisms and sermons, the heroic epic formulation, biography, allegory, and satire. Ironically, this work so long dismissed summarily in the manuals of literary history as crude and naïve possesses an extraordinary variety of discursive strategies.

By sampling the range of possibilities within European discourse, Guaman Poma reveals their respective inadequacies in reporting and interpreting native American experience both before and after the Spanish invasion and conquest of Tawantinsuyu. By rewriting Andean history to include the preconquest Christianization of the Andes by one of the apostles, he unmasks the pretentiousness of the European histories he had read. Even as he takes up and adheres to parts of the Scholastic philosophy of the just war, he challenges the purely theoretical juridical formulations about the rights of the conqueror. As he casts the mythical/historical Inca heroes and heroines in the mold of the exemplary biography, he usurps the mantle of Christian nobility and morality and uses its formulas to praise and condemn the "barbarian" ladies and lords. He reveals the racism of the proselytizing sermon by turning its cruel attacks on the colonists themselves. His most ringing and dramatic condemnation of the foreigners' discourse comes, however, in the satirical Quechua sermons in which he replaces the ministry of the gospel with expressions of criminal greed.

Yet it is not merely a sense of the foreigners' smugness and superiority that Guaman Poma rejects in responding to this discourse. It is, more profoundly, the European concepts of history, religion, and justice that he finds wanting. The histories that he knew were created to justify and celebrate colonial domination; religious tracts that simply augmented the extirpation of idolatrous campaigns aimed at controlling native society; the debate over the just war that took place well after the conquests, when the institutional machinery of colonization was already in place—Guaman Poma tested each of these means in succession and together to help make sense of the world around him. His failure to find in any an acceptable explanation of events, a possible resolution of the colonial situation, reflects the failure of European discourse itself to lay the foundations on which to build a just society in that brave, New World. Guaman Poma's book stands as a testimony of that real response of Americans to the utopian reality of America dreamed by others.

Notes

Introduction

1. I have examined elsewhere (1974b) the racial and critical biases to which the writings of the early Spanish colonial Amerindian authors have been subjected; such judgments were due in large part to the *mestizaje* or *indigenista* political interests of the critics or to their rigid application of the esthetic standards of the traditional literary canon.

2. "El colonialismo no sólo destruye a partir del momento en que se instala violentamente en territorios subyugados, sino que arrasa y rehace en beneficio de su propia empresa imperial, la historia previa de esos territorios. Los mecanismos de esa destrucción y re-escritura interesada son visibles, con una claridad que nunca deja de sorprender, en la literatura colonial hispanoamericana. Por ello, el proceso de descolonización implica siempre una contraofensiva en la que se rescatan no sólo territorios geográficos, sino mentales; no sólo espacio sino tiempo. Es decir: historia" (González Echevarría 1976:21).

3. For attempts to piece together Guaman Poma's biography from evidence internal and external to his own work, see Adorno (1979–80, 1980, 1981b), and Varallanos (1959, 1979).

4. All citations of the *Nueva corónica y buen gobierno* text are from the 1980 Murra-Adorno edition and are reproduced with the permission of the publisher. When citing Guaman Poma's own text, I have used his original page numbers as we corrected and reproduced them in the edition. When referring to the accompanying critical apparatus, I have used the volume and page numbers of the three-volume 1980 edition. Bracketed Spanish translations within Quechua quotations are by Jorge Urioste; English translations of Guaman Poma's original Spanish, and of all other texts in Spanish, are my own.

Due to the difficulties presented by Guaman Poma's Spanish, such as the lack of agreement in number between noun and verb phrases (see Urioste in Guaman Poma [1615] 1980: v.1:xxviii–xxxi), I have attempted to render his prose according to a criterion of intelligibility, for literal translation is often impossible. One of the particular features of his Spanish prose, which I have retained in English translation, is his use of the adjectival qualifier, "the said," or "the aforementioned." His use of the term in Spanish comes from the Quechua *ñisqa*, which is conventionally used in that language to refer to a noun phrase already mentioned in the discourse (ibid.: xxx). His exaggerated use of this feature in Spanish will remind the reader of the extent to which the author's native Quechua influenced his Spanish.

5. Among the few, named native Andeans of the period whose transcribed testimony or writings are known (Titu Cusi Yupanqui, Juan de Santacruz Pachacuti Yamqui Salcamayhua, El Inca Garcilaso de la Vega), Guaman Poma is unique in being the only one who presents an extensive, direct commentary on native Andean life in the Spanish viceroyalty. It seems that he took up his literary vocation after an apprenticeship of reading religious works, such as those of Fray Luis de Granada, which constituted the mainstay of Spanish Golden Age literary culture in the colonies. Guaman Poma claimed that it had been his half-brother, a *mestizo* priest whom he identified as "Padre Martín de Ayala," who originally taught him the skills of reading and writing (ibid.:15–16).

6. "In hidden polemic . . . the author's discourse brings a polemical attack to bear against another speech act, another assertion, on the same topic. Here one utterance focused on its referential object clashes with another utterance on the grounds of the referent itself. That other utterance is not reproduced; it is understood only in its import; but the whole structure of the author's speech would be completely different, if it were not for this reaction to another's unexpressed speech act" (Bakhtin [1929] 1978:187).

7. In his *Proemio* to the *Historia natural y moral de las Indias*, Acosta remarked, "Así que aunque el Mundo Nuevo ya no es nuevo sino viejo, según hay mucho dicho y escrito de él, todavía me parece que en alguna manera se podrá tener esta Historia por nueva, por ser juntamente historia y en parte filosofía y por ser no sólo de las obras de naturaleza sino también de las del libre albedrío, que son los hechos y costumbres de hombres" ([1590] 1962:13). That is, Acosta saw his history as "new" because it treated human affairs as well as natural phenomena and because it attempted to study causes (the work of the philosopher) as well as to narrate effects (the task of the historian). The latter was a distinction formulated by the Italian theorist of history Francisco Patrizi (see Mignolo 1982:86–87).

8. Guaman Poma outlined as separate but related issues the question of the existence of history and that of its being recorded. He affirmed the validity of a variety of historiographic sources, which included the *khipus*, the Andean system of knotted cords used for preserving information, and the recollections and oral accounts of Andean elders and eyewitnesses ("los *quipos* y memorias y relaciones de los yndios antigos de muy biejos y biejas sabios testigos de uista") ([1615] 1980:8).

9. The terms "history"/"historian" and "chronicle"/"chronicler" were used interchangeably during Guaman Poma's time (see Mignolo 1982:75–77, 82).

10. Since John Murra coined the term in his 1961 article in *Natural History*, it has been repeated by nearly everyone who has written on the *Nueva corónica*. As a *probanza de méritos*, Guaman Poma's appeal to the king stood out from the petitions typically written by conquistadores and other Europeans. He staked his claim

not on a series of previous personal (usually military) deeds of which the written account simply provided verification, but rather on those efforts and personal sacrifices whose very end was the writing of the book. El Inca Garcilaso and other indigenous and *mestizo* chroniclers did likewise.

11. Guaman Poma indicated that he was born after the fall of the Incas: "Porque yo no nací en tienpo de los Yngas para sauer todo que destas cordilleras lo supe y lo fue escriuiendo; adonde estube más tienpos fue aquí" ("Because I was not born in the time of the Incas to know everything about these cordilleras that I found out and went about writing; where I spent most of my time was here") ([1615] 1980:860). His linking of spatial and temporal categories reflects an Andean conception of the convergence of time and space; see Wachtel (1973) for an analysis of Guaman Poma's attempt to coordinate Andean and Western spatial-temporal systems.

1. Contradicting the Chronicles of Conquest

1. In his study, *El cronista indio Felipe Huamán Poma de Ayala*, Porras points out the factual errors in Guaman Poma's historical and geographical accounts. Repeating his assessments, historians of literature and other commentators have denigrated Guaman Poma's work.

2. This is the part of the work that has provided, and continues to offer, so much documentary information about Andean practices; since its publication in 1936, the *Nueva corónica* has been unrivaled as a source of information about Andean institutions (Murra 1970:6).

3. This passage reveals some of the native Andean observations made about the strangers from abroad:

Cómo tubo noticia Atagulpa Ynga y los señores prencipales y capitanes y los demás yndios de la uida de los españoles: Se espantaron de que los cristianos no dormiese. Es que decía por que uelauan y que comía plata y oro, ellos como sus caballos. Y que trayýa *ojotas* [sandalias] de plata, decía de los frenos y herraduras y de las armas de hierro y de bonetes colorados. Y que de día y de noche hablauan cada uno con sus papeles, *quilca* [representación gráfica]. Y que todos eran amortajados, toda la cara cubierta de lana, y que se le parecía sólo los ojos. Y en la cauesa trayýa unas ollitas colorado, *ari manca* [olla sin estrenar], y *suri uayta* [adorno de pluma de avestruz]. Y que trayýan las pixas colgadas atrás larguícimos, decían de las espadas, y que estauan bestidos todo de plata fina. Y que no tenía señor mayor, que todos parecían ermanos en el trage y hablar y conuersar, comer y bestir. Y una cara sólo le pareció que tenía, un señor mayor de una cara prieta y dientes y ojo blanco, que éste sólo hablaua mucho con todos. ([1615] 1980:383)

(How Atahualpa Inca and the illustrious lords and captains and the rest of the Indians learned about the life of the Spaniards: They were frightened by the thought that the Christians might not sleep. This was because they kept nightly watches. It was reported that they, as well as their horses, ate silver and gold. And that they wore sandals of silver; the same was said of their bridles and horseshoes and of their weapons of iron and their red headgear. And that night and day they talked with their papers. And that they were all shrouded like corpses, their entire faces covered with wool, and that only their eyes could be seen. And on their heads they wore colored pots and ornaments of ostrich plumes. And that they carried their penises, very long, hanging behind; this they said of the swords. And that they were dressed completely in fine silver. And that they did not have a greater lord, that all seemed to be brothers in their dress, in speaking and conversing, eating, and dressing. And it seemed that they had one single face. It seemed there was one greater man among them; with a dark face and white teeth and eyes, he talked a lot with everyone.)

For a similar account, also based on Andean oral traditions, see Titu Cusi Yupanqui ([1570] 1973:15).

4. Compare Guaman Poma ([1615] 1980:420–429) with Zárate ([1555] 1947, book 6, chap. 7; book 7, chap. 8:547–569).

Ramiro Condarco Morales (1967) was the first to observe the correspondence between the texts of Guaman Poma and Zárate; he also noted the similarity between the Peruvian writer's chapter on Inca law ("hordenansas") and Fray Martín de Murúa's discussion of the same topic in his *Historia del origen y genealogía real de los Reyes Incas del Perú* ([1590] 1946). In the first case, there is no doubt that Guaman Poma copied Zárate, and the examples are more prolific than Condarco Morales indicated. On the coincidence of Guaman Poma and Murúa, however, it is unclear who copied from whom. According to his own testimony, Guaman Poma considered Murúa his avowed enemy ([1615] 1980:920), a scoundrel (ibid.:521, 625, 661–663), and, at the same time, a learned man ("gran letrado") (ibid.:521).

5. See Guaman Poma ([1615] 1980::430–434), and Fernández ([1571] 1963, *Segunda parte*, book 2, chaps. 24–25 and 43–45; v. 164:327–333; v. 165:10–20).

6. Guaman Poma begins at Zárate's book 6, chap. 7, by paraphrasing Carlos V's letter to Gonzalo Pizarro; Guaman Poma's version of the document mirrors and abridges Zárate's text. Whereas Zárate's transcription of the letter recognizes the "loyalty" of Gonzalo and announces the appointment of de la Gasca as president of Peru, Guaman Poma makes the letter exclusively one of pardon for Pizarro. Only his last sentence alludes to de la Gasca, insofar as it expresses the emperor's demand that Gonzalo obey the newly appointed royal official (cf. Zárate [1555] 1947, book 6, chap. 7:547, and Guaman Poma [1615] 1980:420). Guaman Poma illustrates this event with a picture of Carlos V giving the letter for Gonzalo to President de la Gasca ([1615] 1980:419).

Guaman Poma also follows Zárate's text regarding Gonzalo's gathering of his forces while de la Gasca arrived at Trujillo and organized the royal army. Again, Guaman Poma visually illustrates the account taken from Zárate, depicting the reception for Captain Carvajal given by Gonzalo on the arrival of the former to Lima (ibid.:421) (cf. Zárate, book 6, chap. 10:553, and Guaman Poma ([1615] 1980:422).

Guaman Poma carefully follows Zárate's text in the account in which Gonzalo organizes his troops and names his officers (see Zárate, book 6, chap. 11:554; Guaman Poma [1615] 1980:422). Finally, as Gonzalo's officers prepare the ceremonial banners that will accompany them into battle, Guaman Poma again repeats the Zárate text (compare Zárate, book 6, chap. 11:554, and Guaman Poma [1615] 1980:422).

7. This textual comparison was previously noted by Condarco Morales (1967:307–308).

8. Compare Zárate, book 6, chap. 14, book 7, chaps. 6–8, with Guaman Poma ([1615] 1980:423–429).

9. Although the immediate context for this citation suggests that the reference might be to Gonzalo rather than de la Gasca, this particular account describes the president's gathering of his troops ("Yua haziendo más gente") while Gonzalo had returned to Cuzco ("Tornó al Cuzco con quatrocientos soldados") (Guaman Poma [1615] 1980:427; see Zárate [1555] 1947, book 7, chaps. 3, 4:565).

10. Zárate ([1555] 1947, book 7, chap. 4:566) offers a list of the royal army's officers, which Guaman Poma reproduces, adding to it the name of his father's benefactor ([1615] 1980:427). Although Zárate does not mention Captain Luis de Avalos de Ayala, he was apparently in Peru at the time of this encounter (Porras Barrenechea 1948:14).

11. "Dizen que" may be a Spanish linguistic means of disavowing the author's responsibility or authority for the remarks that follow it. However, it may also be a Spanish translation of the discourse or sentence marker in Quechua, the suffix -si, which signifies that the speaker has acquired the information through hearsay and cannot vouch for its certainty as an eyewitness (Urioste 1973:49). The hearsay or nonwitness validator and the witness validator are regular features of Quechua discourse (ibid.:45).

12. This particular title of the Virgin Mary, which has its origin near Salamanca, Spain (Chevalier 1944:531–532), is a Dominican devotion. Tirso de Molina's hagiographic *comedia*, entitled "La Peña de Francia" and published in the *Parte cuarta* (Madrid, 1635), tells the story of how the devotion originated during the reign of Don Juan II of Castile, when a French university student discovered the image of the Virgin hidden in the rocky crags of the Peña de Francia south of Salamanca. On disinterring the image, hidden since Rodrigo lost Spain to the Moors, the king of Castile pledged to build a shrine on the location; as the student, Simón Vela, lies dying, his mission of finding the image of the Blessed Virgin fulfilled, he summarizes the history of the Virgin of the Peña de Francia (Téllez [1635] 1970, Acto Tercero, vv. 1028–1039:174):

Rey Don Juan, sol de Castilla, esta Imagen soberana está aquí desde los tiempos que Rodrigo perdió a España; haz, pues, que aquí se fabrique una generosa casa, y que su gobierno tengan los Padres de la Orden sacra del grande español Domingo; porque ya el Cielo me llama para darme en dulce muerte hallazgos de tal ganancia.

(King Don Juan, sun of Castile, this sovereign image has been here since the time that Rodrigo lost Spain [to the Moors]. Order, then, that a noble home be built here and that the fathers of the holy order of the great Spaniard Domingo be responsible for its management; because now Heaven calls me to give me in sweet death the rewards of so great a discovery.)

Santa María de la Peña de Francia is Guaman Poma's favorite devotion; he frequently mentions her miracles, feast day, and his personal devotion to her ([1615] 1980:405, 654–655, 665, 922, 947, 1115, 1117). He draws her image on several occasions (ibid.:404, 653, 841, 933, 946), and attributes to her name a parish and settlement in Suntunto, Huamanga (ibid.:745, 833) as well as chapels in Chocllococha, Castrovirreina (ibid.:1110, 1119), and in the church of Santa Clara in Lima.

13. Although *encomienda* was officially abolished in 1542 (Ots Capdequí [1941] 1975:25–26), it continued to be an odious form of servitude for the ethnic Andean. Guaman Poma's frequent complaints against *encomienda* and his dedication of an entire chapter to the *encomendero* problem ([1615] 1980:561–574) attest to the turn-of-the-seventeenth-century existence of this colonial institution.

14. Compare Las Casas ([1560] 1958: v. 5:465–468) with Guaman Poma ([1615] 1980:510, 514, 563, 972).

15. Guaman Poma's silence with regard to Las Casas's name is not surprising, given the times. Luis López, a Jesuit brother of José de Acosta in Perú, was put under accusation of the Inquisition for holding opinions similar to those of Las Casas. This helps to explain why Acosta, although following Las Casas's doctrines in the *De procuranda indorum salute* ([1588] 1954), neither uses his name nor cites his books (Hanke [1959] 1975:90).

16. Las Casas refers to natural law in the same *Principio II* in these terms:

Tienen todas éstas [naciones] sus reinos, sus señoríos, sus reyes, sus jurisdicciones, altas y bajas, sus jueces y magistrados y sus territorios, dentro de los cuales usan legítimamente y pueden libremente usar de su potestad, y dentro dellos a ningún rey del mundo, sin quebrantar el Derecho natural, es lícito sin licencia de sus reyes o de sus repúblicas entrar, y menos usar ni ejercitar jurisdición ni potestad alguna. ([1564] 1958:489)

(All these nations have their kingdoms, their dominions, their kings, their jurisdictions high and low, their judges and magistrates and their territories, within which they use legitimately, and can use freely, their power, and within them, it is not lawful that any king in the world, without breaking natural law, should enter without the permission of their kings or their republics, and much less that they should use or exercise any authority or power whatsoever.)

17. Such accounts were not uncommon. For example, Juan de Santacruz Pachacuti Yamqui Salcamayhua ([1613] 1968:283–284) attributed the cross to the visit of St. Thomas: "Pues se llamó a ese barón *Tonapa viracochampacachan*, ¿pues no

será este hombre el glorioso apóstol Sancto Tomás?'' (''Since they called this gentleman *Tonapa viracochampacachan* can it not be that this man is the glorious apostle St. Thomas?''). Many other chroniclers also gave assurances that St. Thomas had visited the Indies in ancient times in order to preach against the diabolical religions of the indigenous peoples (Esteve Barba 1964:11).

18. Here, before the fact, Guaman Poma refers to his father by the Hispanic surname that he says was conferred on Guaman Malqui sometime later by the conquistador Luis de Avalos de Ayala.

19. Almost as a footnote, Guaman Poma continues:

Bastaua que sólo fuera el excelentícimo señor don Martín de Ayala a darse de pas y serbir a la corona rreal por todo el Pirú, pues que fue gran señor, *Capac Apo* [poderoso señor], segunda persona del Ynga y su bizorrey destos rreynos. ([1615] 1980:564)

(It would have been sufficient if only the illustrious lord Don Martín de Ayala had gone and offered himself in peace to serve the royal [Spanish] crown for all of Peru, for he was a great lord, a powerful lord, and second minister of the Inca, his viceroy in these realms.)

Thus he emphasizes the historical role that he insistently attributes to his father.

20. In his *Relectio de Indis*, Vitoria had declared invalid and illegitimate the claim to Spanish hegemony based on the aborigines' willing acceptance of Spanish rule. He argued that fear and ignorance, which should never intervene in the making of such choices, were precisely the prevailing factors in such situations. The natives would not have understood what they were doing, nor what the Spaniards were asking. Besides, those doing the asking bore arms as they surrounded the defenseless and timorous masses (''Además, esto lo piden gentes armadas que rodean a una turba inerme y medrosa'') ([1532] 1967:73). Vitoria argued that only by a complete familiarity with the Spanish administration could aboriginal peoples legitimately accept by their own free will the rule of foreigners (ibid.:94–95).

21. Guaman Poma is not the first ethnic Andean to make this claim; it was presented in the Spanish court in the 1560s by Felipe Huacra Paucar. Son of one of the lords of Jauja, Huacra Paucar went to Spain to plead his case personally. In his estimation, his own father should have been named the *encomendero*, if the establishment of the labor-controlling institution were inevitable (see Murra 1980; Espinosa Soriano 1971–72).

22. In his *Introducción del símbolo de la fe*, Fray Luis de Granada defines the light of reason and compares it with that of faith ([1582] 1944, Parte Tercera, Tratado Primero, chap. 1:400): Humanity can know its Maker by virtue of ordinary human reason; Christian faith, however, makes knowledge of this truth certain, firm, and infallible. The most felicitous circumstance is the combination of the two:

Pues cuando desta manera la lumbre de la razon se casa con la fe (que es cuando lo que la fe nos enseña, testifica tambien la razon) recibe el ánima con esto una grande alegría y consolacion, con la cual se confirma mucho mas en la fe; porque mas alumbran dos lumbres juntas, que sola una. (Ibid.)

(But when, in this way, the light of reason is joined with that of faith [which is when that which faith teaches us is also attested by reason], the soul receives a great joy and consolation, with which one is much more confirmed in the faith; because two lights illuminate more together, than one alone.)

23. In this case, Guaman Poma has taken advantage of Andean religious categories to suggest—even if only implicitly—the analogy of Andean and Christian understandings about deity. He describes an Andean trinity of a father, the administrator of justice, and two sons: the elder is the source of charity; the younger the provider of health, food, and rain ([1615] 1980:55).

24. Guaman Poma most emphatically denies that the Andean natives belonged to that category of barbarians who were incapable of self-governance and therefore deserved enslavement. This classical definition, borrowed from Aristotle's *Politics* and cited by Las Casas, refers to those who, because of their strange and awful customs and evil and perverse inclinations, turn out to be cruel and ferocious; they are not guided by reason, but rather are nearly bestial ("los que por sus extrañas y ásperas y malas costumbres, o por su mala y perversa inclinación salen crueles y feroces, . . . y no se rigen por razón . . . sino que son cuasi bestiales") ([1559] 1967, book 3, chap. 265: v. 2:641).

25. Nowhere is this more apparent than in the chapter on the Inca census. The description of the age grades of Inca society has been considered one of Guaman Poma's most significant contributions to the ethnographic record of his times; his account has been used as a principal source in constructing a single system of age-grade categories attributable to the preconquest Incas (Murra 1980:xiii–xiv; see Rowe 1958:499–522). Yet for each of the twenty descriptions of age grade that Guaman Poma offers, he returns to the text after the original redaction and adds further commentary. Almost all of these textual emendations compare the traditional Andean social order with the disarticulation caused by the imposition of the colonial regime.

26. For Las Casas, the writing of history was to be reserved for the learned, and, in his view, priests were especially well qualified: "Tampoco conviene a todo género de personas ocuparse con tal ejercicio, según sentencia de Methástenes, sino a varones escogidos, doctos, prudentes, filósofos, perspicacísimos, espirituales y dedicados al culto divino, como entonces eran y hoy son los sabios sacerdotes" ("Neither is it appropriate that all manner of persons apply themselves to such an occupation, according to the judgment of Methastenes, but rather only select men of respectability—learned, prudent, philosophical, extremely perspicacious, spiritual, and devoted to divine religion—such as were then and are today the sage ministers of God") ([1559] 1951: v. 1:6).

2. Searching for a Heroic Conception

1. Cabrera de Córdoba reminds his readers that historiography uses esthetic techniques and has esthetic as well as historiographic goals, all for the purpose of impressing on the reader the truth that the historian seeks to reveal and communicate. In his *De historia, para entenderla y escrivirla*, he notes such principles: "Engáñanse los que piensan ser historia sin artificio; tiene su dotrina leyes, por los claríssimos maestros con prudencia confirmadas" ("Those who think that history [writing] is without artifice deceive themselves; its doctrine has rules ["leyes"], which are confirmed by the prudent judgment of the greatest masters") (1611:f 15 r); "[La historia] aparta de vicios los ánimos, inflamalos a la virtud: . . . aguza el ingenio, aclara el entendimiento, ennobleze la memoria, delecta la fantasia: da contento, o dolor, al oyente, conforme lo que escriue a diuersos fines" ("[The genre of history] separates the mind from vices, kindles it to virtue: . . . sharpens intelligence, clarifies the faculty of understanding, ennobles that of memory, delights the fantasy: it offers contentment or concern to the hearer, accordingly as one writes for diverse ends") (ibid.:f 19 r–v).

His descriptions of the nine "integral parts" of history include many used in oratory and fiction: "exordios, descripciones, digresiones, oraciones, elogios, discursos, juizio, pronósticos, sentencias" ("exordiums, descriptions, digressions, speeches, panegyrics, discourses, judgment, predictions, maxims") (ibid.:f 62 v). On these, only the discourse is the constituent that admits the use of hypothetical materials:

Solo en esta parte usa de exemplos el historico, util comemoracion de alguna cosa hecha, *o como hecha*, para persuadir buen argumento con inducion inperfecta. . . . Refierense a los exemplos, las parabolas, apologos, y fabulas, similes y proverbios, impropiamente llamados exemplos. (Ibid.:f 74 r; emphasis mine)

(Only in this part does the historian use examples, as useful commemoration of some deed, either accomplished *or possible*, to persuade to good effect with faulty inducement. . . . These refer to examples, parables, apologues, and fables, comparisons and proverbs, improperly called examples.)

2. See chapter 1, notes 2 and 25.

3. Contrary to our expectations about sixteenth-century historiography, López de Gómara's opinion reveals that biography was not considered an obsolete form. If no new, important collections of biographies were written in that century, it should be noted that the great biographical collections of the late fifteenth century, Pérez de Guzmán's *Generaciones y semblanzas* ([1450] 1924) and Hernando del Pulgar's *Claros varones de Castilla* ([1486] 1923), were widely read and reedited often during the sixteenth century. In fact, the biography was a historiographic genre of continued vitality as the seventeenth century showed considerable interest in the moralistic literature of exempla of the Middle Ages (Maravall 1972:160–161). Nevertheless, among historians themselves, writing the history of public deeds held a higher priority.

4. The importance of medieval historiography to colonial Spanish American literature has been noted in at least one other work, Rodríguez Freyle's *El carnero* ([1636] 1976). Enrique Pupo-Walker (1982:131) suggests that the interpolated narration, adopting the historical frame and the formulas of the exemplum that the American chronicle inherited from medieval Castilian historiography, is an integral element of a rhetoric of persuasion that, in turn, is a distinctive trait of the *crónicas de Indias*.

5. On the combination of positive physical and temperamental features, we find examples in the biographies of Viracocha Inca ("Gentil hombre, blanco de cuerpo y rrostro y tenía unas pocas de barbas y tenía buen corasón"/"Refined man, white in body and face, and he had some whiskers and a good heart" [(1615) 1980:107]), and in Huayna Capac ("Y de la cara hermoso y gentil hombre, blanco, muy onrrado, amigo de todos"/"And of handsome face and a refined man, white, very honorable, friend to all" [ibid.:113]). On the contrary, Lloque Yupanqui Inca has a less felicitous combination of physical traits. "Y tenía las narises corcobados y los ojos grandes y labio y boca pequeñas y prieto de cuerpo y feo y mal ynclinado y mizerable. Y ací no hizo nada y era para poco y sus bazallos huýan de uelle la cara" ("And he had a hooked nose and large eyes and small lips and mouth, and he was dark of body and ugly and bad-spirited and a wretch. And thus he did nothing and he was good for little and his vassals fled from the sight of his face") (ibid.:97). These reveal his bad character. The prince Huascar Inca, who facilitated the fall of the Inca empire because of the civil war in which he was engaged at the time of Pizarro's arrival, is also portrayed as physically ugly and of bad character: "Y tenía su rrostro morenete y largo, sancudo y feo y de malas entrañas. . . . El dicho Uascar Ynga tenía mal corasón y malas entrañas . . . por donde de la soberbia ganó Uascar tanto pleyto y batalla y muerte" ("And he had a dark face and long, he was ungainly and ugly and of a bad nature. . . . The said Huascar Inca was mean-hearted and bad-spirited . . . because of which his sinful pride earned him so much conflict and battle and death") (ibid.:116–117).

6. The prologue thus placed could clarify the uses to which the text should be put. The statement of Albornoz's rationale follows:

Todos los que por escriptura publican algún fructo de su ingenio, suelen al principio de ella proponer el Prólogo, en que dan cuenta a el Lector de lo que más notable les parece, a fin de atraherle a que la lea. Mas yo dudoso si alguna cosa hai en mi obra que merezca ser leída, tuve por mejor, que el Lector a su riesgo se pusiesse en leerla, que no siendo por mi Prologo engañado, y en recompensa de el tiempo que en leerla havra (no se si diga) perdido, proponerle al fin el Prologo (que havia de estar al principio) para que el sea juez de mi lectura, si ella ha cumplido lo que prometio el Prologo, y no sea el Prologo su engañador, para prometerle lo que la lectura no puede cumplir, y juntamente con esto declarar el uso que de esta escriptura puede tener el Lector, que al principal servicio que le puedo hazer, aclarándoles mis motivos, para que entienda el provecho que de ella puede sacar. (Cited in Porqueras Mayo 1957:130)

(All those who, by means of writing, publish some fruits of their talent, usually place at the beginning of it the Prologue, in which they give an account to the Reader of that which seems to them most notable, with the end of attracting him to read it. But I—doubtful whether something in my work deserves to be read—took it as better that the Reader at his own risk set to reading it, that not being by my Prologue deceived, and in compensation for the time taken (not to say lost) in reading it, place the prologue (which should be at the beginning) at the end, in order that it be the judge of my text, to see if it has achieved that which the Prologue promised, and not that the Prologue be its deceiver, promising him what the text cannot fulfill, and at the same time, declare the use of which the Reader may make of this writing, of the principal service that I can do him, making clear to him my motives, in order that he understand the benefit which one can derive from it.)

7. For example, Gonzalo Fernández de Oviedo, to whom Guaman Poma refers as "el capitán Gonzalo Pizarro de Obedo y Ualdés, alcayde de la fortaleza de la ysla Españoles de Santa Domingo" in his paraphrase of Oré ([1615] 1980:1088; cf. Oré 1598:f 37 r), declares that the first unit of his *Historia general y natural de las Indias* would serve as the introduction: "Comiença el primer libro deste volumen. El cual consiste en el proemio o introdución desta primera parte de la *General y natural historia de las Indias*" ([1535] 1959: v. 1:7).

8. Many of Guaman Poma's chapters begin with *primer capítulo* as title; see pp. 79, 120, 289, 300, 303, 317, 330, 520, 575, 675, 689, 806, 923, 1004, 1005, 1140.

9. With regard to the emphasis on the exemplary value of the biographies, Guaman Poma provides an exception that serves to prove the rule. Although he paints the Incas, *coyas*, and even the viceroys as moral types vis-à-vis a given Christian cultural paradigm, he has one other series of portrait/descriptions—the four lords and ladies of the subdivisions of the kingdom—which serve as social-political archetypes of Andean society ([1615] 1980:167–182). The particular verbal descriptions of these classes indicate that Guaman Poma constructs these figures not as historical examples but as cultural archetypes. As the use of third-person plural verbs indicates, these portraits represent castes, not individuals. The absence of a prologue in this chapter further suggests that these figures are to be seen not as historical personages but as representatives of the permanent categories and constituent universals that make up the Andean social system (see Ossio 1973:176–181).

10. The pessimistic concept of man and his world lay behind the upsurge in moralist literature at the turn of the seventeenth century. The denunciation of humanity's egotism, depravity, and propensity to do ill was perhaps never so widely spread abroad as at that time (Maravall 1975:327). In practice, that literature shifted away from a view of this life as mere preparation for the next, to embrace the pressing need to reform the conduct of temporal affairs. Leaving aside speculation on ultimate truths, it turned to the normative ethics required to live a just life: "The greater attention given to practical wisdom in part corresponds to a wider acceptance of man as a political animal, and consequently of the dignity of an active life in society" (Hafter 1966:74–75).

11. Baroque culture placed great emphasis on individual experience (Warnke 1972:41). Throughout Europe in the sixteenth and seventeenth centuries, there were continual reeditions of the medieval collections of exempla (Maravall 1972: 160); exemplary literature continued to flourish among the Spanish writers and orators from the period of Quevedo, who wrote his *Política de Dios* during the reign of Guaman Poma's King Philip III (1598–1621), through the life of Gracián (Hafter 1966:10). The latter held Don Juan Manuel's *El Conde Lucanor* in high esteem and cited it frequently (Maravall 1972:160, 162). In *El pasagero*, a dialogue containing "useful advice" ("advertencias utilisimas a la vida humana"), Suárez de Figueroa confirms the unconditional power of the example: "Mueven los ejemplos con singular eficacia, siendo instrumentos bastantísimos para enfrenar las mas desenfrenadas costumbres" ("Examples move the reader with singular efficacy, being very sufficient means by which to restrain the most unbridled customs") ([1617] 1913:359). The example was particularly favored if it was historical (Maravall 1972:162), although historians themselves often became skeptical of the value of past examples (Hafter 1966:12–13).

12. *Admiratio*, or admiration, is the effect of literature on its readers that is responsible for directing them to the precepts of moral philosophy: "Seventeenth-century writers aimed to startle and impress their readers not only because this was pleasant, but in order to engage their attention and put them in a receptive frame of mind in which a moral lesson could be driven home, a universal truth revealed" (Riley 1962:91).

13. The original text reads,

Otras ay que sobre vna verdad fabrican mil ficiones, tales son las trágicas y épicas, las quales siempre, o casi siempre, se fundan en alguna historia, mas de forma que la historia es poca en respeto y comparación de la fábula; y assí de la mayor parte toma la denominación la obra que de la vna y otra se haze. Fadrique añadió: Por esso cuentan a Lucano entre los históricos, el qual, aunque tiene fábulas, son pocas en respeto de las historias.

14. According to López Pinciano, "Assí que los poemas que sobre historia toman su fundamento son como vna tela cuya vrdimbre es la historia, y la trama es la imitación y fábula. Este hilo de trama va con la historia texiendo su tela." ([1596] 1953:v. 2:98).

15. "Torno, pues, a mi lugar y digo que, quanto a este punto, tiene más perfección la épica fundada en historia que no en ficción pura" (ibid.:v. 3:167). There was little consensus on this issue at the time. The polemic over whether Tasso or Ariosto was the superior epic poet raged in Italy in the last decades of the sixteenth century. Throughout the debate, the issues at the bottom of many disagreements were precisely the role of history and the marvelous, and the importance of verisimilitude (Weinberg 1961:v. 2:991, 1073).

16. To reform society through literature was the moral end of poetry, the novel, and the theater. Maravall observes that every baroque writer took human conduct

as a central issue: "Every baroque writer puts forth as central the problem of moral conduct, and to attract readers to the system of relations that he or she considers fundamental to society, the author claims that in following it lies achievement, 'success,' or happiness" (1975:140).

17. Allegory—that concert of metaphors ("junta de metáphoras") (López Pinciano [1596] 1953:v. 2:144) that presents moral doctrine in a fabulous narration—is frequently found in the epic. As in the tales of Aesop, this allegory consists of maxims that portray the qualities of moral virtue. The *Iliad* and *Odyssey* of Homer and the *Aeneid* are full of such allegories and moral teachings:

Poco ay que entender si por alegoría ente[n]déys no la que en palabras, sino la que en sentencias está sembrada. ¿Vos no acordáys del apólogo y las fábulas de Esopo, y que, por debaxo de aquellas narraciones fabulosas, están otras sentencias y ánimas, las quales algunos dizen moralidades? Esta, pues, es la alegoría que en la épica se halla muy ordinariamente; de manera que la *Ilíada* y *Odysea* de Homero y la *Eneyda* están llenas destas alegorías y ánimas intrínsecas. (Ibid.:v. 3:175)

3. From Story to Sermon

1. Compare, respectively, Guaman Poma ([1615] 1980:1, 50, 109, 367, 954, 956) and Granada ([1566] 1945, tratados 1–7:v. 2:205, 301, 220–221, 219, 399, 206–207). Each of these cases refers to topics such as the glories of heaven and the sufferings of hell, and citations of biblical prophets such as Jeremiah, David, Habakkuk, and St. John the Baptist. Guaman Poma copies, nearly word for word, from Fray Luis's text.

2. In this case, as in his discussion of Andean racial origins, he uses the term "*español*" to refer generically to the civilizations of the Judeo-Christian biblical tradition.

3. Fray Luis was very much a theologian of his times, especially on issues concerning the nature of humanity. Grounded on the ancient faith of St. Basil and St. Ambrose and on the medieval thought of Albertus Magnus and Thomas Aquinas, Fray Luis was sensitive to news of the discoveries in the New World. His Scholastic anthropology was elaborated with an awareness of the expanding horizons of human experience (Laín Entralgo 1946:28).

4. See chapter 1, note 22, for Fray Luis's definition of natural reason.

5. My certainty that Guaman Poma copied the prayer from the *Memorial* is due to the fact that the prayer appears on the same page as the psalm of David that Guaman Poma quotes on the first page of his own book: "Como el profeta rrey Dauid nos dize en el pezalmo, *Domine Deus salutis meae*, donde nos pone grandes miedos y desanparos de Dios y grandes castigos que nos a de enbiar cada día" ("As the prophet King David tells us in the Psalm, 'Lord God of my salvation,' where he places before us great dread and fear of our abandonment by God and great punishments which are to be sent us each day") ([1615] 1980:1). His source is Fray Luis ([1566] 1945, tratado 5, chap. 2:v. 2:301): "Y como aun mas claro lo representa David en todo aquel salmo que comienza '*Domine Deus salutis meae*,'

donde el sancto Profeta nos propone grandes miedos, y temores, y desamparos de Dios."

6. The traditional Quechua prayer, which Guaman Poma also sets into his own narrative ([1615] 1980:54), is recorded in Oré:

Al qual ["*Pachacamac*, o *Pacha yachachic*, que significa hazedor del vniverso"] hazia vna elegante oracion en la lengua, cuya declaracion y romance es este: "hazedor, que estas desde los cimientos y principio del mundo, hasta en los fines del, poderoso, rico misericordioso, que diste ser y valor a los hombres, . . . a saluos, sin peligro y en pas. Adonde estas? Por ventura en lo alto del cielo, o abaxo, o en las nuues y nublados o en los abysmos? Oyeme y respondeme, y concedeme lo que pido, danos perpetua vida para siempre, ten nos de tu mano, y esta ofrenda recibela ado quiera que estuuieres, o hazedor." (1598:f 40 r–v)

(To which they made an elegant prayer in the language, whose interpretation in Spanish is as follows: "Creator, who exists from the time of the foundations and beginning of the world, to the ends of it, powerful, rich, merciful, who gave being and value to men, . . . without injury, without danger and in peace. Where are you? Perchance in the heights of the heavens, or below, or in the nebula and clouds, or in the abyss? Hear me and answer me, and concede to me what I ask. Give us perpetual life, take us by your hand, and receive this offering wherever you might be, o maker.")

A version of this prayer had already been transcribed by Cristóbal de Molina *el cuzqueño*, in his *Ritos y fábulas de los Incas* ([1575] 1959:55), and Fray Martín de Murúa would later reproduce another variation of it in his *Historia general del Perú, origen y descendencia de los Incas* ([1611] 1962–64:v. 1:37–38).

7. The first weapon of the preacher is the rhetoric of threat. In the *Memorial de la vida cristiana*, Fray Luis opens the "capítulo primero" of the first book by putting forth his reasons for engaging in talk of divine punishment: the reform of rebellious hearts can best be achieved by placing before them the spectacle of punishment and suffering for a psychological reason; humanity is always more moved by the threat of affliction than by the promise of health, more affected by the prospect of doom than by that of prosperity ([1566] 1945, tratado 1, chap. 1:v. 2:205).

8. In communicating Scholastic principles of the just war, Las Casas customarily used religious language. He converted the legal question into a moral issue, using the language of Christian morality to express his convictions about legal theory. The backbone of Las Casas's outlook was the strict application of the Christian norms of restitution for that which had been unjustly acquired (Lohmann Villena 1966:21). The Dominican view on the matter of restitution was well known in Peru, and Guaman Poma cites and commends the act of restitution made by the Dominican archbishop of Lima, Jerónimo de Loaysa, at the time of his death in 1575 (see Guaman Poma [1615] 1980:477, 712). Loaysa's exemplary deed was one among many like it, for the archbishop had persuaded many other *limeños* to

perform similar acts of penitence and restitution (Lohmann Villena 1966:38-77).

9. This work was originally written by Fray Luis in Latin and published in Lisbon in 1576. Although it is unlikely that Guaman Poma would have had access to the Spanish translation, its theoretical precepts are useful for elucidating the rhetorical practice of Fray Luis in his devotional works and of Guaman Poma in the *Nueva corónica y buen gobierno*.

10. These graphic representations could be of various types, such as emblems and *empresas* (Gállego 1972:24). *Emblemas* supposedly had their origin in the wisdom of the ancients; their object was the common good, and their moral teaching was not the exclusive property of individuals but was available to the whole of society (ibid.:21, 24). *Empresas*, however, were the patrimony of a single individual or family; because they relied on personal taste and required the recognition of esoteric signs, they typically contained secret messages decipherable only by a select few (ibid.). The graphics employed as visual aids in sermons would obviously be closer in spirit to the *emblema* than to the esoteric *empresa*.

11. Three bilingual religious works had been published in 1584 and 1585. The first, called *Doctrina christiana y catecismo para instrucción de los indios y de las demás personas*, consisted of a *cartilla*, or exposition of Christian doctrine, and two catechisms: one short, "para los rudos y ocupados" (f 13 r), and the other, more extensive, in the form of a dialogue, "para los que son mas capaces" (ibid.:f 25 r). The second publication was called *Tercero catecismo y exposición de la doctrina christiana por sermones*; it consisted of a series of thirty-one sermons that contained the catechism and much discussion of Christian doctrine as related to Andean ritual practices. The trilingual *Symbolo* (Oré 1598) ("un manual Indiano, y vn Sermonario y Symbolo y Arte en la lengua Quichua y Aymara con su declaración en romance" according to Pedro de Oré), consisted of *canticos*, which were similar to sermons.

It is worth noting that Guaman Poma also produced explicitly religious materials in his own work. The chapter on "Yndios" in the *Buen gobierno* gives instructions for the schedule and manner of religious observances and includes a long series of Christian prayers in Quechua ([1615] 1980:840-851). He likely copies many of these prayers from the works in question; he gives the *Salve Regina*, for example, in a Quechua version (ibid.:849) that is identical to the one presented in the *Doctrina christiana y catecismo para instrucción de los Indios* (1584:f 3 v).

12. *Viracocha* meant Spaniard in the Spanish-Quechua parlance of Guaman Poma's day (see [1615] 1980:49, 925). Literally, the term means "laguna de grasa" ("lagoon of grease"), with grease symbolizing powers of creation, and also of government. Thus, the *viracochas* were those in command. After 1532, the word was applied to the Europeans, and in some Andean communities today it retains the meaning of "*patrón*" ("master, protector") (see ibid.:v. 3:1107).

13. I have found some eighty references to "*soberbia*" in the *Nueva corónica y buen gobierno*. The term is consistently applied to Guaman Poma's descriptions of the arrogant abuse of the Andeans by the Spanish colonists. As he thus describes political crimes in the language of ecclesiastical rhetoric, he also describes Huascar

Inca's downfall as the result of prideful *soberbia* (ibid.:117; see also p. 388): "Por la soberbia ganó Uascar tanto pleyto y batalla y muerte" ("Because of pride, Huascar brought upon himself so much conflict and strife and death").

14. In classical rhetoric, persuasion was considered a "complex human reaction triggered by a rational belief in the truth of the orator's thesis, by an emotional acceptance of the thesis as in some way pleasurable, and by an ethical acceptance of the orator's character as that of a man of good sense, good morals, and good will" (Howell 1975:55). In Guaman Poma's own time, Suárez de Figueroa emphasized that the preacher must be of a mature age, for thus would he be able to communicate judgment, prudence, and reason:

Un moso en el trono de un púlpito disminuye grandemente la devoción, siendo en cuanto dice (a lo menos con la presencia) poco eficaz para la reprehensión, poco atractivo para la obediencia. ([1617] 1913:126)

(A boy on the throne of a pulpit greatly diminishes devotion, being, with regard to what he says [at least by his presence] hardly effective for the purpose of reprimand, hardly attractive for that of obedience.)

Yet most important for the preacher is his piety. Citing Menander, Fray Luis de Granada reminds the reader, "Quien persuade son las costumbres del orador, y no la oración" ("What persuades is the moral comportment of the orator, not the oration") ([1576] 1945, book 1, chap. 2:v. 3:494).

15. The full text of this "prologue" follows:

Nos espantéys, mugeres. El primer pecado que acometió fue muger. La Eua pecó con la mansana, quebró el mandamiento de Dios. Y así el primer ydúlatra comensastes, muger, y ciruistes a los demonios. Todo ello es cosa de burla y mentira. Deja todo y tene deboción a la Sanctícima Trinidad, Dios Padre, Dios Hijo, Dios Espíritu Sancto, un solo Dios, y a su Madre de Dios, Santa María cienpre Uirgen. Que ella os faboreserá y rrogará por bosotras del cielo para que gozemos y nos ajuntemos en el cielo y en este mundo, para que no nos tiente Satanás.

Armaos con la crus y rreza el Padrenuestro y el Auemaría y acordándoos de la pación de Nuestro Señor Jesucristo, digamos el Credo, para que seamos con la Santícima Trinidad y con Jesucristo y con su Madre Santa María y con sus sanctos y santas ángeles de la corte del cielo. Para esto armémonos con la señal de la Sancta Crus. De nuestros enemigos líbranos, Señor, de todo mal del mundo, de la carne y del demonio.

(Do not wonder, women. The first sin committed was committed by a woman. Eve sinned with the apple; she broke the commandment of God. And thus, you began the first idolatry, woman, and served the devil. All this is a matter of folly and lies. Leave everything and devote yourselves to the Holy Trinity, God the Father, God the Son, God the Holy Spirit, one God only, and the Mother of God, St. Mary ever virgin. May she favor you and implore in heaven on your behalf, so that we may re-joice and gather in heaven and in this world, so that Satan not tempt us.

Arm yourselves with the Cross and pray the Our Father and the Ave Maria and, remembering the passion of our Lord Jesus Christ, let us recite the Creed, so that we may be with the Holy Trinity, and with Jesus Christ and his mother, St. Mary, and all the holy angels in the court of heaven. For this reason, let us arm ourselves with the sign of the Holy Cross. Free us, Lord, from our enemies, from all the evils of the world, the flesh, and the devil.)

The following discussion reiterates one part of an argument about narrational point of view that I made in *Dispositio* (1979b:43-44).

4. Icons in Space: The Silent Orator

1. See Guaman Poma ([1615] 1980:598, 608, 628, 632, 634, 639, 650, 687, 688, 699, 700, 701, 702, 789, 811, 860, 863, 893, 910, 934, 1132, 1168).

2. Noting that the king is partial to the visual arts, Guaman Poma expresses the hope that the variety and originality of the drawings will lighten the reading of his burdensome prose:

Pasé trauajo para sacar con el deseo de presentar a vuestra Magestad este dicho libro . . . escrito y debojado de mi mano y engenio para que la varidad de ellas y de las pinturas y la enbinción y dibuxo a que vuestra Magestad es enclinado haga fázil aquel peso y molestia de una letura falta de enbinción y de aquel ornamento y polido ystilo que en los grandes engeniosos se hallan. (Ibid.:10)

(It gave me much toil to fulfill my desire of presenting to your Majesty this said book . . . written and drawn by my own hand and talent so that the variety of the pictures and the invention and artistic creation to which your Majesty is inclined might make less heavy the burden and annoyance of reading a work lacking genius and that ornament and polished style that is found in great and talented writers.)

However, the historical role of Philip III in supporting the arts is dubious; his name is conspicuously absent, for example, from the list of monarchs cited by Calderón de la Barca in his protocol on behalf of the painters of Madrid (1677). There, Cal-derón recalls the Spanish kings who had supported the arts since and including the reign of Fernando el Católico, and the name of Philip III is not mentioned (Curtius 1936:94). Nevertheless, the court of Philip III was noted for its artistic interests. Francisco de Sandoval y Rojas, the duke of Lerma, was the court minion who ef-fectively ruled the kingdom from the time of Philip's ascent to the throne at the age of twenty-one, and he was a generous patron of the arts. His energetic patronage system was probably better than any that the indolent and indecisive Philip might have devised (Volk 1977:7). The transfer of the court from Madrid to Valladolid in 1601, where it remained until 1606, brought about a great flourishing of the arts with the decoration of the royal palace at Valladolid and the ducal lodgings at

Lerma. The subsequent restoration (1606–1611) of El Pardo Palace outside Madrid continued the great flurry of activity for which Philip III—in spite of himself—came to be known (ibid.:9, 11).

3. In this respect, the visual text has an advantage over the verbal utterance. Guaman Poma's combination of Spanish and Quechua phrases into a single statement makes them all but unintelligible, as when, for example, he attempts to interpret the history of the world in ten historical ages ([1615] 1980:925). In contrast, a pictorial construct containing native Andean and conventional European icons can create syntactically complete statements intelligible to virtually any viewer, even when certain symbolic values remain hidden.

4. Pacheco was of the opinion that the most praiseworthy achievement of the artist was the presentation of ingenious moral observations with which he embellished his work: "En un pintor lo que más haya que elogiar son las ingeniosas moralidades de que haya esmaltado su obra" ([1638] 1956:v. 2:146; see also idem, v. 1:212–236; Volk 1977:393–397).

5. Ignatius of Loyola's *Spiritual Exercises* is credited with richly enhancing the importance of optical sensibility (Gállego 1972:93). The visual image became the abiding material of the *Exercises*, and the figurative representations engendered an entire literature of illustrations (Barthes [1971] 1976:66–67).

6. See Adorno (1974a); López-Baralt (1980).

7. See chapter 1, note 11, for the Quechua distinctions of witness and hearsay or nonwitness validation.

8. Guaman Poma opens the chapter on church inspectors with a portrait of Cristóbal de Albornoz, whom he calls "llano santo hombre, brabo jues" ("honest, holy man, fearless judge"), and whom he cites as the inspector he accompanied on an extirpation-of-idolatries campaign that probably took place in Lucanas in the 1570s ([1615] 1980:689; see Duviols 1967). Alongside this distinguished portrait of Albornoz administering one of his exemplary punishments is Guaman Poma's criticism of these inspectors (ibid.:690). In fact, the drawings of this entire chapter paint a positive picture of the inspectors while the prose text tells nothing but the dark underside of their activities.

The "primer capítulo" of the *corregidores'* chapter similarly opens with a picture of the *corregidor* tranquilly dictating to his secretary, dispensing his duties in proper fashion; yet the accompanying prose text tells us,

Y como biuen apsolutamente con poco temor de la justicia y de Dios en todo el rreyno, y sacan treynta mil pesos del corregimiento y salen rricos, haziendo daño a los yndios pobres y a los principales, menospreciando y quitándole sus oficios y cargos en este rreyno. (Ibid.:491–492)

(And how they live absolutely with little fear of justice or of God in all the kingdom, and they extract thirty thousand pesos from the municipality and come out rich, abusing the wretched Indians and their lords, scorning them and taking away their occupations, privileges, and duties in this kingdom.)

The chapter on the *encomenderos* also commences by creating a dichotomy between a picture of "Cristiano comendero de indios deste rreyno" and a verbal account that stresses the great harm that they do to the native population (ibid.:562–563).

9. Both in the chapters devoted to the "yndios prencipales," that is, the ethnic lords, and to the "yndios comunes," the pictures display an exemplary Christian devotion that is contradicted by the accompanying descriptions of vicious and corrupt behavior. While he shows Andean artisans devotedly painting a life-size crucifix, for example, he tells how such native artists often fall prey to drunkenness and he suggests a series of corrective measures to be undertaken against them (ibid.:687–688). When he pictures a devout Andean woman worshipping at an image of Golgatha symbolically materialized on the floor in front of her, he describes the devotion of such women but adds that they often become promiscuous and engage in prostitution: "Y así salen putas aprouadas, mejor que sus amas haraganes, mentirosas en este rreyno" ("And thus they turn out to be admitted whores, more accomplished than their slothful mistresses, the deceitful ones of this kingdom") (ibid.:837–838).

10. For example, Guaman Poma never draws Manco Inca's military successes in the siege of Cuzco during the conquest. While telling how Manco brought the Spaniards to their knees ("Los dichos soldados cristianos pedía misericordia; hincado de rrodillas, llamaua a Dios con lágrimas a boses y a la uirgen María y a sus santos" / "The said soldiers begged for mercy; on bended knee, they cried out loud to God, with tears to the Virgin Mary and all the saints"), he simply portrays Manco Inca seated on his throne surrounded by a multitude of Andeans, no doubt to commemorate the "cien mil millones de yndios a que abría llegado deste rreyno" ("hundred thousand millions of Indians who had arrived and come together from all over the kingdom") (ibid.:401).

11. Only once does Guaman Poma portray Andean warriors occupying a position superior to that of the Spanish conquistadores; this is the drawing in which the *caciques* guard the captured rebel, Hernández Girón (plate 2).

12. The following discussion elaborates and refines arguments I made about Guaman Poma's visual signification in *The Indian Historian* (1979c) and *Studies in the Anthropology of Visual Communication* (1979d). Simultaneous with my essays was Mercedes López-Baralt's "La persistencia de las estructuras simbólicas andinas en los dibujos de Guamán Poma de Ayala," in the *Journal of Latin American Lore* (1979c). Happily, we arrived at similar conclusions about the importance of spatial meaning in Guaman Poma's pictures. I have incorporated into my discussion here López-Baralt's references to the Coricancha drawing and El Inca Garcilaso's description of imperial Cuzco.

13. Of the 134 pictures that cannot be analyzed for relational or directional orientation, 82 contain only one figure on the perceptual field, and 37 are bird's-eye views of colonial cities.

14. Levin calls this convergence of equivalences "coupling": "When such equivalences [of a phonic] and/or semantic nature exist between the word units,

and when the units thus equivalent are set in equivalent positions in the syntagms, we have poetic coupling, and it is this type of coupling which serves to fuse form and meaning in a poem" (1962:41). In an analogous manner in the visual text, iconic signs coupled with positional signs mutually create and reinforce pictorical meaning.

15. In Guaman Poma's book, Pizarro is a less-favored character than Almagro; it was, after all, Pizarro who was responsible for Atahualpa's execution when Almagro and others opposed it ([1615] 1980:393). Guaman Poma also verbally condemns Fray Vicente de Valverde for his cruel attempt at evangelization as well as for his undue panic in the confrontation with Atahualpa. Guaman Poma registers his disapproval by placing the Dominican to the conquistadores' left. Felipillo, called by Guaman Poma the betrayer of his race, occupies the most undesirable (the leftmost) position of all.

16. See chapter 1, note 12, for a discussion of the origin of this particular devotion.

17. See chapter 1, pp. 13–18, for a discussion of Guaman Poma's treatment of the Gonzalo Pizarro uprising.

18. Guaman Poma uses this topos of European literature to describe how the traditional social hierarchy has been disordered and inverted by the presence of the Spaniards (see ibid.:222, 411, 450, 544, 618, 776, 1136, 1138). Curtius points out the antique origin of this medieval topic of "stringing together impossibilities" and associates it with a critical mood, producing censure and denunciation of the times ([1948] 1963:94–98). According to Maravall, the world-upside-down was one of the great topics revitalized in the baroque period, and he associates it with the marginal culture of the dispossessed, that is, with popular counterculture. For Spain, Maravall sees the topos as the product of a society in transition, in which the alterations in social function and position of various groups created a mood of instability. Citing authors from Tirso and Suárez de Figueroa to Quevedo and Gracián who exploit the theme, he indicates how it was converted into a formula of serious social protest (1975:313–315). It is precisely in this manner that Guaman Poma articulates his vision of a "mundo al rreués." As I shall argue in chapter 5, this commonplace sums up Guaman Poma's loss of faith in the ability of colonized Peruvian society to achieve justice and social harmony. His assessment speaks to the hopelessly inverted order of things, which, he fears, cannot be righted.

5. Mediating among Many Worlds

1. On another occasion (1981a), I undertook a related discussion on how Guaman Poma sets up a model of culture versus barbarity in his pictorial text. Using as a point of departure Juri Lotman's theory of cultural modeling, I examined Guaman Poma's employment of various codes of pictorial representation (Christian iconography, background representation, and vestimentary codes). These visual signifiers separate Andean and European cultural spaces into mutually exclusive categories, with the result that the artist reverses the Europeans' equation and identifies Andean culture with the signs of civilization and the European, with those of barbarity.

2. López Pinciano in the *Philosophía antigua poética* ([1596] 1953:v. 3:55), defines allegory as follows:

Sigue en orden la alegoría, la qual es junta de metáphoras, y de la qual sea exemplo Cicerón, que dixo de Celio, orador, que tenía mejor siniestra que diestra, porque sabía mejor acusar que defender.

(In this order follows allegory, which is a gathering of metaphors, and of which Cicero might be an example, who said of Caelius the orator, that he had a better left hand than a right, because he knew better how to accuse than to defend.)

3. About such effects, López Pinciano remarks (ibid.:v. 2:95),

Si alguna vez por la alegoría dexaron la imitación, lo hizieron como philósophos y no como poetas, como lo hizo Esopo con otros que han escrito apólogos, cuyas narraciones son disparates y frívolas, pero las alegorías muy útiles y necesarias.

(If some time they abandoned imitation because of allegory, they did so as philosophers and not as poets, as Aesop did it, like others who have written apologues, whose narrations are nonsense and frivolous, but the allegories, very profitable and true.)

4. All but one of this series of nine sermons in Quechua are satirical. Two other examples, translated to Spanish by Jorge Urioste, follow: "Hijos míos, no me hagan enojar. Si me enojo, soy un puma; pero si no me enojo, soy como un caballo, el cabestro que extira una llama" ("My sons, don't make me angry. If I get angry, I am a mountain lion; but if I don't get angry, I am like a horse, the halter that leads the llama") ([1615] 1980:624). Guaman Poma attributes the "sermon" that follows to a "creole priest from Huamanga":

¡Hipócritas! Ustedes han mandado cartas al obispo, diciendo: "Este padre no es bueno; expúlselo. Este otro padre es muy bueno." Los judíos defamaban; ustedes me han defamado igualmente. Arrogantes, lascivos, hipócritas. ¡Oíganme bien! (Ibid.)

(Hypocrites! You have sent letters to the bishop, saying: "This father is no good; expel him. This other priest is very good." The Jews were defamers; you have defamed me. Arrogant, lascivious, hypocrites! Heed what I say!)

5. This discussion of narrational viewpoint first appeared in *Dispositio, Revista Hispánica de Semiótica Literaria* (Adorno 1979b:28–41).

Bibliography

Abrams, Morris H. [1941] 1971. *A Glossary of Literary Terms*. 3d ed. New York: Holt, Rinehart & Winston.

Acosta, Antonio. 1982. "Religiosos, doctrinas y excedente económico indígena en el Perú a comienzos del siglo XVII." *Histórica* 6, no. 1:1–34.

Acosta, José de. [1588] 1954. *De procuranda indorum salute o predicación del evangelio en las Indias*. In *Obras del P. José de Acosta*, edited by Francisco Mateos. Biblioteca de Autores Españoles, vol. 73. Madrid: Atlas.

————. [1590] 1962. *Historia natural y moral de las Indias*. 2d ed., edited by Edmundo O'Gorman. Mexico City: Fondo de Cultura Económica.

Adorno, Rolena. 1974a. "*The Nueva Corónica y Buen Gobierno* of Don Felipe Guaman Poma de Ayala: A Lost Chapter in the History of Latin American Letters." Ph.D. diss., Cornell University.

————. 1974b. "Racial Scorn and Critical Contempt." *Diacritics* 4, no. 4:2–7.

————. 1978a. "Felipe Guaman Poma de Ayala: An Andean View of the Peruvian Viceroyalty, 1565–1615." *Journal de la Société des Américanistes* 65:121–143.

————. 1978b. "Las otras fuentes de Guamán Poma: sus lecturas castellanas." *Histórica* 2, no. 2:137–158.

————. 1979a. "El arte de la persuasión: el padre Las Casas y Fray Luis de Granada en la obra de Waman Puma de Ayala." *Escritura, Teoría y Crítica Literarias* 4, no. 8:167–189.

————. 1979b. "Of *Caciques, Coyas*, and Kings: The Intricacies of Point of View." *Dispositio, Revista Hispánica de Semiótica Literaria* 4, no. 10:27–47.

————. 1979c. "Icon and Idea: A Symbolic Reading of the Visual Text of Guaman Poma." *The Indian Historian* 12, no. 3:27–50.

————. 1979d. "Paradigms Lost: A Peruvian Indian Surveys Spanish Colonial Society." *Studies in the Anthropology of Visual Communication* 5, no. 2:78–96.

————. 1979–80. "The *Nueva Corónica y Buen Gobierno*: A New Look at the Royal Library's Peruvian Treasure." *Fund og Forskning* 24:7–28.

————. 1980. "La redacción y enmendación del autógrafo de la *Nueva Corónica y Buen Gobierno*." In Guaman Poma [1615] 1980:xxxii–xlvi.

————: 1981a. "On Pictorial Language and the Typology of Culture in a New World Chronicle." *Semiotica* 36, nos. 1-2:51-106.

————. 1981b. "Waman Puma de Ayala: 'Author and Prince.'" *Review* 28:12-16.

————. 1982. "Bartolomé de las Casas y Domingo de Santo Tomás en la obra de Felipe Waman Puma." *Revista Iberoamericana*, nos. 120-121, pp. 673-679.

————, ed. 1982. *From Oral to Written Expression: Native Andean Chronicles of the Early Colonial Period*. Foreign and Comparative Studies/Latin American Monograph Series, no. 4. Syracuse, N.Y.: Maxwell School of Citizenship and Public Affairs, Syracuse University.

Alarcos Llorach, Emilio. 1969. *Gramática estructural*. Madrid: Gredos.

Albornoz, Bartolomé de. 1573. *Arte de los contractos*. Valencia: Pedro Huete.

Arte y vocabulario en la lengua general del Perú llamada quichua, y en la lengua española. 1614. Lima: Francisco del Canto.

Bakhtin, Mikhail. [1929] 1978. "Discourse Typology in Prose." In *Readings in Russian Poetics*, edited by Ladislav Matejka and Krystyna Pomorska, pp. 176-196. Ann Arbor: University of Michigan.

————. [1965] 1968. *Rabelais and His World*, translated by Helene Iswolsky, foreword by Krystyna Pomorska. Cambridge, Mass.: MIT Press.

Barthes, Roland [1957] 1972. *Mythologies*, translated by Annette Lavers. New York: Hill & Wang.

————. [1964] 1972. *Critical Essays*, translated by Richard Howard. Evanston, Ill.: Northwestern University.

————. [1967] 1970. "Historical Discourse," translated by Peter Wexler. In *Introduction to Structuralism*, edited by Michael Lane, pp. 145-155. New York: Basic Books.

————. [1971] 1976. *Sade/Fourier/Loyola*, translated by Richard Miller. New York: Hill & Wang.

Beaujour, Michel. 1977. "For a Science of Literature." *Punto de Contacto/Point of Contact* 1, no. 4:4-11.

Benveniste, Emile. [1966] 1971. *Problems in General Linguistics*, translated by Mary Elizabeth Meek. Coral Gables, Fl.: University of Miami.

Berthoff, Warner. 1971. *Fiction and Events: Essays in Criticism and Literary History*, pp. 30-55. New York: E. P. Dutton.

Booth, Wayne C. 1974. *A Rhetoric of Irony*. Chicago: University of Chicago.

————. 1983. "A New Strategy for Establishing a Truly Democratic Criticism." *Daedalus* 112, no. 1:193-214.

Braudel, Fernand. [1949] 1976. *The Mediterranean and the Mediterranean World in the Age of Philip II*, vol. 2, translated by Siân Reynolds. New York: Harper & Row.

Bravo, María Concepción. 1983. "Polo de Ondegardo y Guaman Poma, dos mentalidades ante un problema: la condición del indígena en el Perú del siglo XVI." In *Homenaje a Gonzalo Fernández de Oviedo, cronista de Indias, América y la España del siglo XVI*. Vol 2, edited by Francisco de Solano and Fermín del Pino, pp. 275-289. Madrid: Consejo Superior de Investigaciones Científicas, Instituto "Gonzalo Fernández de Oviedo."

Bull, William E. 1960. *Time, Tense, and the Verb: A Study in Theoretical and Applied Linguistics, with Particular Attention to Spanish.* University of California Publications in Linguistics, vol. 19. Berkeley & Los Angeles: University of California Press.

Burnham, Jack, assisted by Charles Harper and Judith B. Burnham. 1971. *The Structure of Art.* New York: George Braziller.

Bustíos Gálvez, Luis. 1956–66. *La nueva corónica y buen gobierno, escrita por Don Felipe Guamán Poma de Ayala: Edición e interpretación.* 3 vols. Lima: Talleres de Servicio de Prensa, Propaganda y Publicaciones Militares.

Cabello Valboa, Miguel. [1586] 1951. *Miscelánea antártica: una historia del Perú antiguo.* Lima: Instituto de Etnología, Universidad Nacional Mayor de San Marcos.

Cabrera de Córdoba, Luis. 1611. *De historia, para entenderla y escrivirla.* Madrid: Luis Sánchez.

Calancha, Antonio de la. 1639–53. *Corónica moralizada del orden de San Agustín en el Perú con sucesos egenplares vistos en esta monarqvia.* Barcelona: P. Lacavalleria.

Calderón de la Barca, Pedro. 1677. "Don Pedro Calderón de la Barca, en favor de los profesores de la Pintura." In Curtius 1936.

Carro, Venancio. 1944. *La teología y los teólogos-juristas españoles ante la conquista de América.* 2 vols. Madrid: Consejo Superior de Investigaciones Científicas.

————. 1966. "Los postulados teológicos-jurídicos de Bartolomé de las Casas: sus aciertos, sus olvidos y sus fallas, ante los maestros Francisco de Vitoria y Domingo de Soto." In *Estudios lascasianos: IV centenario de la muerte de Fray Bartolomé de las Casas (1566–1966)*, pp. 109–246. Publicaciones de la Escuela de Estudios Hispanoamericanos, no. 175. Seville: Facultad de Filosofía y Letras, Escuela de Estudios Hispano-Americanos, Universidad de Sevilla.

Casas, Bartolomé de las. [1559] 1967. *Apologética historia sumaria*, edited by Edmundo O'Gorman. Mexico City: Instituto de Investigaciones Históricas, Universidad Nacional Autónoma.

————. [1559] 1951. *Historia de las Indias*, edited by Agustín Millares Carlo. Introductory essay by Lewis Hanke, 2 vols. Mexico City: Fondo de Cultura Económica.

————. [1560] 1958. "Memorial del obispo fray Bartolomé de las Casas y fray Domingo de Santo Tomás." In *Obras escogidas de fray Bartolomé de las Casas*, vol. 5, edited by Juan Pérez de Tudela Bueso, pp. 465–468. Biblioteca de Autores Españoles, vol. 110. Madrid: Atlas.

————. [1564] 1958. *Tratado de las doce dudas.* In *Obras escogidas de fray Bartolomé de las Casas*, vol. 5, edited by Juan Pérez de Tudela Bueso, pp. 478–536. Biblioteca de Autores Españoles, vol. 110. Madrid: Atlas.

Castro-Klarén, Sara. 1981. "Huamán Poma y el espacio de la pureza." *Revista Iberoamericana*, nos. 114–115, pp. 45–67.

Cervantes Saavedra, Miguel de. [1605] 1962. *El ingenioso hidalgo Don Quijote de la Mancha.* 1st part. 7th ed., edited by Francisco Rodríguez Marín. Madrid: Espasa-Calpe.

Chang-Rodríguez, Raquel. 1980. "A Forgotten Indian Chronicle of Peru: Titu Cusi Yupanqui's *Relación de la conquista del Perú.*" *Latin American Indian Literatures* 4:87–95.

————. 1982a. "Coloniaje y conciencia nacional: Garcilaso de la Vega Inca y Felipe Guamán Poma de Ayala." *Caravelle*, no. 38, pp. 29–43.

————. 1982b. "Sobre los cronistas indígenas del Perú y los comienzos de una escritura hispanoamericana." *Revista Iberoamericana*, nos. 120–121, pp. 533–548.

————. 1982c. "Writing as Resistance: Peruvian History and the *Relación* of Titu Cusi Yupanqui." In *From Oral to Written Expression: Native Andean Chronicles of the Early Colonial Period*, edited by Rolena Adorno, pp. 41–64. Syracuse, N.Y.: Maxwell School of Citizenship and Public Affairs, Syracuse University.

Chevalier, François. 1944. "El códice ilustrado de Poma de Ayala." *Revista de Indias* 5, no. 17:525–534.

Condarco Morales, Ramiro. 1967. *Protohistoria andina propedéutica*, pp. 288–309. Oruro, Bolivia: Universidad Técnica.

Covarrubias Horozco, Sebastián de. [1611] 1943. *Tesoro de la lengua castellana o española*, edited by Martín de Riquer. Barcelona: S. A. Horta.

Cros, Edmond. 1971. *Mateo Alemán: Introducción a su vida y a su obra.* Salamanca: Anaya.

Curtius, Ernst Robert. 1936. "Calderón und die Malerei." *Romanische Forschungen* 50:89–136.

————. [1948] 1963. *European Literature and the Latin Middle Ages*, translated by Willard R. Trask. New York: Harper & Row.

de Man, Paul. 1979. "Semiology and Rhetoric." In *Textual Strategies: Perspectives in Post-Structuralist Criticism*, edited by Josué Harari, pp. 121–140. Ithaca, N.Y.: Cornell University.

Diccionario de autoridades. [1726-37] 1964. Facsimile ed. 3 vols. Madrid: Gredos.

Doctrina christiana y catecismo para instrucción de los indios y de las demás personas. 1584. Lima: Antonio Ricardo.

Domingo de Santo Tomás. [1560] 1951a. *Grammática o arte de la lengua general de los indios de los reynos del Perú.* Lima: Instituto de Historia, Universidad Nacional de San Marcos.

————. [1560] 1951b. *Lexicón y vocabulario de la lengua general del Perú.* Lima: Instituto de Historia, Universidad Nacional de San Marcos.

Domínguez Bordona, J. 1924. "Introducción." In Fernán Pérez de Guzmán, *Generaciones y semblanzas*, edited by J. Domínguez Bordona, pp. vii–xxxvi. Madrid: La Lectura.

Duviols, Pierre. 1967. "Un inédit de Cristóbal de Albornoz: la instrucción para descubrir todas las *guacas* del Pirú y sus *camayos* y haziendas." *Journal de la Société des Américanistes* 56:7–39.

————. 1980. "Periodización y política: la historia pre-hispánica del Perú según Guaman Poma de Ayala." *Bulletin de l'Institut Français d'Etudes Andines* 9, nos. 3-4:1–18.

————. 1980–81. "Religions et Société de l'Amérique du Sud (région andine)." *Annuaire de l'Ecole Pratique des Hautes Etudes 5^{em} section* 89:109–114.

Espinosa Soriano, Waldemar. 1971–72. "Los huancas aliados de la conquista: tres informaciones inéditas sobre la participación indígena en la conquista del Perú: 1558, 1560 y 1561." *Anales científicos de la Universidad del Centro* 1:9–407.

Esteve Barba, Francisco. 1964. *Historiografía indiana*. Madrid: Gredos.

Feinberg, Leonard. 1967. *Introduction to Satire*. Ames: Iowa State University.

Fernández, Diego [1571] 1963. *Primera y segunda parte de la historia del Perú*. In *Crónicas del Perú*, vols. 1, 2, edited by Juan Pérez de Tudela Bueso. Biblioteca de Autores Españoles, vols. 164, 165. Madrid: Atlas.

Fernández de Oviedo y Valdés, Gonzalo. [1535] 1959. *Historia general y natural de las Indias*, vols. 1–5, edited by Juan Pérez de Tudela Bueso. Biblioteca de Autores Españoles, vols. 117–121. Madrid: Atlas.

Fish, Stanley. 1972. *Self-Consuming Artifacts: The Experience of Seventeenth-Century Literature*. Berkeley & Los Angeles: University of California Press.

————. 1983. "Short People Got No Reason to Live: Reading Irony." *Daedalus* 112, no. 1:175–191.

Frye, Northrop. [1957] 1973. *The Anatomy of Criticism*. Princeton: Princeton University Press.

————. 1962. "The Nature of Satire." In *Satire: Theory and Practice*, edited by Charles A. Allen and George D. Stephens, pp. 15–30. Belmont, Cal.: Wadsworth.

————. 1964. *The Educated Imagination*. Bloomington: Indiana University Press.

Fueter, Eduard. 1911. *Geschichte der neueren Historiographie*. Munich: R. Olderbourg.

Gállego, Julián. 1972. *Visión y símbolos en la pintura española del Siglo de Oro*. Madrid: Aguilar.

Garcilaso de la Vega, El Inca. [1609] 1963. *Los commentarios reales de los Incas, Primera parte*. In *Obras completas del Inca Garcilaso de la Vega*, vol. 2, edited by Carmelo Sáenz de Santa María. Biblioteca de Autores Españoles, vol. 133. Madrid: Atlas.

————. [1609] 1966. *Royal Commentaries of the Incas and General History of Peru, Part One*, translated by Harold V. Livermore; foreword by Arnold J. Toynbee. Austin: University of Texas Press.

Genette, Gérard. [1966] 1970. *Figuras: retórica y estructuralismo*, translated by Nora Rosenfeld and María Cristina Mata. Córdoba, Argentina: Nagelkop.

González Echevarría, Roberto. 1976. *Relecturas: estudios de literatura cubana*. Caracas: Monte Avila.

————. 1980. "The Life and Adventures of Cipión: Cervantes and the Picaresque." *Diacritics* 10:15–26.

Granada, Luis de. [1566] 1945. *Memorial de la vida cristiana*. In *Obras de fray Luis de Granada*, vol. 2, prologue by José Joaquín de Mora, pp. 203–411. Biblioteca de Autores Españoles, vol. 8. Madrid: Atlas.

————. [1576] 1945. *Los seis libros de la retórica eclesiástica, o de la manera de predicar*. In *Obras de fray Luis de Granada*, vol. 3, edited by Buenaventura Carlos Aribau, pp. 488–642. Biblioteca de Autores Españoles, vol. 11. Madrid: Atlas.

————. [1582] 1944. *Introducción del símbolo de la fe*. In *Obras de fray Luis de Granada*, vol. 1, edited by Buenaventura Carlos Aribau, pp. 181–733. Biblioteca de Autores Españoles, vol. 6. Madrid: Atlas.

Grant, Helen. 1972. "El mundo al revés." In *Hispanic Studies in Honour of Joseph Manson*, edited by Dorothy M. Atkinson and Anthony H. Clarke, pp. 119–137. Oxford: Dolphin.

Gray, Hannah. 1968. "Renaissance Humanism: The Pursuit of Eloquence." In *Renaissance Essays from the Journal of the History of Ideas*, edited by Paul O. Kristeller and Philip Weiner, pp. 199–216. New York: Harper & Row.

Guaman Poma de Ayala, Felipe. [1615] 1936. *Nueva corónica y buen gobierno*. (*Codex péruvien illustré*.) Travaux et Mémoires de L'Institut d'Ethnologie, vol. 23. Rpt. Paris: L'Institut d'Ethnologie, 1968.

————. [1615] 1944. *Primer nueva corónica y buen gobierno*, edited by Arturo Posnansky. La Paz: Instituto "Tihuanacu" de Antropología, Etnografía y Prehistoria.

————. [1615] 1980. *El primer nueva corónica y buen gobierno*, critical edition by John V. Murra and Rolena Adorno; translation and textual analysis of Quechua by Jorge L. Urioste. 3 vols. Mexico City: Siglo Veintiuno.

————. [1615] 1980a. *Nueva corónica y buen gobierno*, edited by Franklin Pease. 2 vols. Caracas: Biblioteca Ayacucho.

Hafter, Monroe Z. 1966. *Gracián and Perfection: Spanish Moralists of the Seventeenth Century*. Cambridge: Harvard University Press.

Hamburger, Käte. 1973. *The Logic of Literature*. 2d ed., translated by Marilynn J. Rose. Bloomington: Indiana University Press.

Hanke, Lewis. [1959] 1975. *Aristotle and the American Indians: A Study of Race Prejudice in the Modern World*. Bloomington: Indiana University Press.

Harrison, Regina. 1981. "The Quechua Oral Tradition: From Waman Puma to Contemporary Ecuador." *Review* 28:19–22.

————. 1982. "Modes of Discourse: The *Relación de antigüedades deste reyno del Pirú* by Joan de Santacruz Pachacuti Yamqui Salcamaygua." In *From Oral to Written Expression: Native Andean Chronicles of the Early Colonial Period*, edited by Rolena Adorno, pp. 65–100. Syracuse, N.Y.: Maxwell School of Citizenship and Public Affairs, Syracuse University.

Hodgart, Matthew. 1969. *Satire*. London: Weidenfeld & Nicolson.

Höffner, Joseph [1947] 1957. *La ética colonial española del Siglo de Oro: cristianismo y dignidad humana*, prologue by Antonio Truyol Serra; translated by Francisco de Asís Caballero. Madrid: Cultura Hispánica.

Howell, Wilbur Samuel. 1975. *Poetics, Rhetoric, and Logic: Studies in the Basic Disciplines of Criticism*. Ithaca, N.Y.: Cornell University Press.

Isbell, Billie Jean. 1976. "La otra mitad esencial: un estudio de complementariedad sexual andina." *Estudios Andinos* 5, no. 1:37–56.

Jakobson, Roman. 1960. "Linguistics and Poetics." In *Style in Language*, edited by Thomas Sebeok, pp. 350–377. Cambridge: MIT Press.

Jerónimo de San José. [1651] 1957. *Genio de la historia*, edited by Fray Higinio de Santa Teresa. Victoria, Spain: del Carmen.

Jiménez de la Espada, Marcos, ed. 1965. *Relaciones geográficas de Indias: Perú* [1586], vols. 1, 2, 3, edited by José Urbano Martínez Carreras. Biblioteca de Autores Españoles, vols. 183, 184, 185. Madrid: Atlas.

Knox, Norman. 1961. *The Word Irony and its Context, 1500–1755*. Durham, N.C.: Duke University Press.

Krieger, Murray. 1974. "Fiction and Historical Reality: The Hourglass and the Sands of Time." In *Literature and History*, edited by Ralph Cohen and Murray Krieger, pp. 43–77. Los Angeles: Clark Memorial Library.

Laín Entralgo, Pedro. 1946. *La antropología en la obra de fray Luis de Granada*. Madrid: Consejo Superior de Investigaciones Científicas.

Leonard, Irving. 1940. "Don Quijote and the Book Trade in Lima, 1616." *Hispanic Review* 8:285–304.

―――. 1941. "On the Cuzco Book Trade, 1606." *Hispanic Review* 9:359–375.

―――. 1942. "Best Sellers of the Lima Book Trade." *Hispanic American Historical Review* 22:5–33.

―――. [1959] 1966. *Baroque Times in Old Mexico: Seventeenth-Century Persons, Places and Practices*. Ann Arbor: University of Michigan Press.

Levin, Samuel R. 1962. *Linguistic Structures in Poetry*. Janua Linguarum, no. 23. The Hague: Mouton.

Lohmann Villena, Guillermo. 1945. "Una carta inédita de Huamán Poma de Ayala." *Revista de Indias* 20:325–327.

―――. 1966. "La restitución por conquistadores y encomenderos: un aspecto de la incidencia lascasiana en el Perú." In *Estudios lascasianos: IV centenario de la muerte de Fray Bartolomé de las Casas (1566–1966)*, pp. 21–89. Publicaciones de la Escuela de Estudios Hispanoamericanos, no. 175. Seville: Facultad de Filosofía y Letras, Escuela de Estudios Hispano-Americanos, Universidad de Sevilla.

López-Baralt, Mercedes. 1979a. "La Contrarreforma y el arte de Guamán Poma: notas sobre una política de comunicación visual." *Histórica* 3, no. 1:81–95.

―――. 1979b. "Guamán Poma de Ayala y el arte de la memoria en una crónica ilustrada del siglo XVII." *Cuadernos Americanos* 38, no. 3:119–151.

―――. 1979c. "La persistencia de las estructuras simbólicas andinas en los dibujos de Guamán Poma de Ayala." *Journal of Latin American Lore* 5, no. 1:83–116.

―――. 1980. "La *Crónica de Indias* como texto cultural: policulturalidad y articulación de códigos semióticos multiples en el arte de reinar de Guamán Poma de Ayala." Ph.D. diss., Cornell University.

―――. 1982. "La *Crónica de Indias* como texto cultural: articulación de los códigos icónico y lingüístico en los dibujos de la 'Nueua corónica' de Guamán Poma." *Revista Iberoamericana*, nos. 120–122, pp. 461–531.

López de Gómara, Francisco. [1545] 1853. *Crónica de los Barbarrojas*. In *Memorial histórico español*, vol. 6, pp. 327–439. Madrid: Real Academia de la Historia.

―――. [1552] 1946. *Hispania Victrix, primera y segunda partes de la historia general de las Indias*. In *Historiadores primitivos de Indias*, vol. 1, pp. 155–455. Madrid: Atlas.

López Pinciano, Alonso. [1596] 1953. *Philosophía antigua poética*, edited by

Alfredo Carballo Picazo. Madrid: Instituto "Miguel de Cervantes," Consejo Superior de Investigaciones Científicas.

López y Sebastián, Lorenzo Eladio. 1983. "La iconografía imaginaria de las ciudades andinas en la 'Nueva Corónica y Buen Gobierno' de Felipe Guaman Poma de Ayala." In *Homenaje a Gonzalo Fernández de Oviedo, cronista de Indias, América y la España del siglo XVI.* Vol. 2, edited by Francisco de Solano and Fermín del Pino, pp. 213–230. Madrid: Instituto "Gonzalo Fernández de Oviedo," Consejo Superior de Investigaciones Científicas.

Lotman, Juri M. 1975a. "The Discrete Text and the Iconic Text: Remarks on the Structure of Narrative." *New Literary History* 4, no. 2:333–338.

———. 1975b. "On the metalanguage of a typological description of culture." *Semiotica* 14, no. 2:97–123.

Lyell, James P. R. [1926] 1976. *Early Book Illustration in Spain*, introduction by Konrad Haebler. New York: Hacker Art Books.

Maravall, José Antonio. 1960. *Velázquez y el espíritu de la modernidad.* Madrid: Gredos.

———. 1972. *Teatro y literatura en la sociedad barroca.* Madrid: Seminarios y Ediciones.

———. 1975. *La cultura del barroco: análisis de una estructura histórica.* Barcelona: Ariel.

Mazzeo, Joseph Anthony. 1964. *Renaissance and Seventeenth-Century Studies.* New York: Columbia University Press.

Means, Philip Ainsworth. 1928. *Biblioteca andina, Part one.* Connecticut Academy of Arts and Sciences, vol. 29. New Haven.

Medina, José Toribio. [1904–07] 1965. *La imprenta en Lima (1584–1824).* Vol. 1. Amsterdam: N. Israel.

Mendizábal Losack, Emilio. 1961. "Don Phelipe Guamán Poma de Ayala, Señor y Príncipe, último *quellqacamayoc.*" *Revista del Museo Nacional* 30:228–330.

Menéndez Pidal, Ramón. [1958] 1966. *El padre Las Casas y Vitoria con otros temas de los siglos XVI y XVII.* 2d ed. Madrid: Espasa-Calpe.

Menéndez y Pelayo, Marcelino. 1940. *Historia de las ideas estéticas en España.* Vol. 2, edited by Enrique Sánchez Reyes. Santander: Aldus.

Mignolo, Walter. 1981. "El metatexto historiográfico y la historiografía indiana." *Modern Language Notes* 96:358–402.

———. 1982. "Cartas, crónicas y relaciones del descubrimiento y la conquista." In *Historia de la literatura hispanoamericana, época colonial.* Vol. 1, edited by Luis Iñigo Madrigal, pp. 57–116. Madrid: Cátedra.

Molina, Cristóbal de. [1575] 1959. *Ritos y fábulas de los Incas.* Buenos Aires: Futuro.

Montero Díaz, Santiago. 1948. "La doctrina de la historia en los tratadistas del Siglo de Oro." In *De historia: para entenderla y escrivirla,* by Luis Cabrera de Córdoba, pp. xi–lvi. Madrid: Instituto de Estudios Políticos.

Montesinos, Fernando. [1664] 1882. *Memorias antiguas historiales y políticas del Perú.* Colección de Libros Raros y Curiosos, vol. 16. Madrid: Imprenta de M. Ginesta.

Muecke, D. C. 1969. *The Compass of Irony*. London: Methuen.

Murra, John V. 1961. "Guaman Poma de Ayala. A Seventeenth-Century Indian's Account of Andean Civilization." *Natural History* 70, no. 7:35–47; no. 8:52–63.

————. 1962. "Cloth and its Functions in the Inca State." *American Anthropologist* 64:710–728.

————. 1970. "Current Research and Prospects in Andean Ethnohistory." *Latin American Research Review* 5, no. 1:3–36.

————. 1980. "Waman Puma, etnógrafo del mundo andino." In *El primer nueva corónica y buen gobierno* [1615], Felipe Guaman Poma de Ayala, pp. xiii–xix. Mexico City: Siglo Veintiuno, 1980.

Murúa, Martín de. [1590] 1946. *Historia del origen y genealogía real de los reyes Incas del Perú*, edited by Constantino Bayle. Madrid: Instituto Santo Toribio de Mogrovejo, Consejo Superior de Investigaciones Científicas.

————. [1611] 1962–64. *Historia general del Perú, origen y descendencia de los Incas*. 2 vols. Introduction and notes by Manuel Ballesteros-Gaibrois, prologue by Duque de Wellington y Ciudad Rodrigo. Madrid: Instituto Gonzalo Fernández de Oviedo, Consejo Superior de Investigaciones Científicas.

Nelson, William. 1973. *Fact or Fiction: The Dilemma of the Renaissance Storyteller*. Cambridge: Harvard University Press.

Noreña, Carlos G. 1975. *Studies in Spanish Renaissance Thought*. The Hague: Martinus Nijhoff.

Oré, Luis Jerónimo de. 1598. *Symbolo catholico indiano*. Lima: Antonio Ricardo.

Ortega, Julio. 1978. *La cultura peruana*. Mexico City: Fondo de Cultura Económica.

————. 1980a. "La crónica de Guamán Poma: historia y ficción." *Socialismo y Participación* 10:111–115.

————. 1980b. "Guamán Poma de Ayala y la producción del texto." *Cuadernos Hispanoamericanos* 360:1–12.

————. 1981. "History and Fiction: A Model of Narrative," translated by Rolena Adorno. In *The Plaza of Encounters*, edited by Julio Ortega and Ewing Campbell, pp. 86–93. Austin, Tex.: Latitudes Press.

Ossio, Juan M. 1970. "The Idea of History in Felipe Guamán Poma de Ayala." B. Litt. thesis, Oxford University.

————. 1973. "Guamán Poma: *Nueva Corónica* y carta al rey: Un intento de aproximación a las categorías del mundo andino." In *Ideología mesiánica del mundo andino*, edited by Juan M. Ossio, pp. 155–213. Lima: Biblioteca de Antropología, Ignacio Prado Pastor.

————. 1976–77. "Guamán Poma y la historiografía indianista de los siglos XVI y XVII: historia y cultura." *Revista del Museo Nacional de Historia* 10:181–206.

————. 1977. "Myth and History: The Seventeenth-Century Chronicle of Guaman Poma de Ayala." In *Text and Context: The Social Anthropology of Tradition*, edited by Ravindra K. Jain, pp. 51–93. Philadelphia: Institute for the Study of Human Issues.

Ots Capdequí, J. M. [1941] 1975. *El estado español en las Indias*. Mexico City: Fondo de Cultura Económica.

Pachacuti Yamqui Salcamayhua, Juan de Santacruz. [1613] 1879. *Relación de anti-*

güedades deste reyno del Pirú. In *Tres relaciones de antigüedades peruanas*, edited by Marcos Jiménez de la Espada, pp. 229–328. Madrid: Ministerio de Fomento.

————. [1613] 1968. *Relación de antigüedades deste reyno del Perú*. In *Crónicas peruanas de interés indígena*, edited by Francisco Esteve Barba. Biblioteca de Autores Españoles, vol. 209, pp. 281–319. Madrid: Atlas.

Pacheco, Francisco. [1638] 1956. *Arte de la pintura: su antigüedad y grandezas*. 2 vols. Edited by F. J. Sánchez Cantón. Madrid: Instituto de Valencia de Don Juan.

Padilla Bendezú, Abraham. 1979. *Huamán Poma: el indio cronista dibujante*. Mexico City: Fondo de Cultura Económica.

Pagden, Anthony. 1982. *The Fall of Natural Man*. Cambridge: At the University Press.

Paz, Octavio. [1961] 1966. *Puertas al campo*, pp. 11–19. Mexico City: Universidad Nacional Autónoma.

Pease G. Y., Franklin. 1980. "Prólogo." In Felipe Guamán Poma de Ayala, *Nueva corónica y buen gobierno*. 2 vols. Edited by Franklin Pease, pp. ix–lxxxix. Caracas: Biblioteca Ayacucho.

Pérez de Guzmán, Fernán. [1450] 1924. *Generaciones y semblanzas*, edited by J. Domínguez Bordona. Madrid: La Lectura.

Porqueras Mayo, Antonio. 1957. *El prólogo como género literario: su estudio en el Siglo de Oro español*. Madrid: Consejo Superior de Investigaciones Científicas.

Porras Barrenechea, Raúl. 1948. *El cronista indio Felipe Huamán Poma de Ayala*. Lima: Lumen.

————. 1962. *Los cronistas del Perú (1528–1650)*. Lima: Sanmartí.

Pulgar, Hernando del. [1486] 1923. *Claros varones de Castilla*, edited by J. Domínguez Bordona. Madrid: La Lectura.

Pupo-Walker, Enrique. 1982. *La vocación literaria del pensamiento histórico en América. Desarrollo de la prosa de ficción: siglos XVI, XVII, XVIII y XIX*. Madrid: Gredos.

Riley, Edward C. 1962. *Cervantes' Theory of the Novel*. Oxford: Oxford University Press.

Roaten, Darnell H., and F. Sánchez y Escribano. 1952. *Wölfflin's Principles in Spanish Drama: 1500–1700*. New York: Hispanic Institute.

Rodríguez de Almela, Diego. [1487] 1793. *Valerio de las historias de la Sagrada Escritura y de los hechos en España*, edited by Juan Antonio Moreno. Madrid: Don Blas Román.

Rodríguez Freyle, Juan. [1636] 1976. *El carnero: conquista y descubrimiento del nuevo reino de Granada*, edited by Miguel Aguilera. Medellín, Colombia: Bedout.

Romero, José Luis. 1944. "Sobre la biografía española del siglo XV y los ideales de la vida." *Cuadernos de Historia de España* 1–2:115–138.

Rowe, John Howland. 1958. "The Age Grades of the Inca Census." In *Miscellanea Paul Rivet, octogenario dicata*. Vol. 2, pp. 499–522. XXX Congreso Internacional de Americanistas. Publicaciones del Instituto de Historia, 1st series, no. 50. Mexico City: Universidad Nacional Autónoma de México.

Ruano, Eloy Benito. 1952. "La historiografía en la alta edad media española." *Cuadernos de Historia de España* 17:50–104.

Salomon, Frank. 1982. "Chronicles of the Impossible: Notes on Three Peruvian Indigenous Historians." In *From Oral to Written Expression: Native Andean Chronicles of the Early Colonial Period*, edited by Rolena Adorno, pp. 9–39. Syracuse, N.Y.: Maxwell School of Citizenship and Public Affairs, Syracuse University.

Sánchez Alonso, Benito. 1947. *Historia de la historiografía española: ensayo de un examen de conjunto.* Vol. 1. 2d ed. Madrid: Consejo Superior de Investigaciones Científicas.

Schapiro, Meyer. 1969. "On Some Problems in the Semiotics of Visual Art: Field and Vehicle in Image-Signs." *Semiotica* 1:223–242.

———. 1973. "Words and Pictures: On the Literal and the Symbolic in the Illustration of a Text." In *Approaches to Semiotics*, no. 11, edited by Thomas Sebeok. The Hague: Mouton.

Shepard, Sanford. 1962. *El Pinciano y las teorías literarias del Siglo de Oro.* Madrid: Gredos.

Stern, Steve J. 1978. "Algunas consideraciones sobre la personalidad histórica de don Felipe Guamán Poma de Ayala." *Histórica* 2, no. 2:225–228.

———. 1982. *Peru's Indian Peoples and the Challenge of Spanish Conquest.* Madison: University of Wisconsin Press.

Struever, Nancy S. 1970. *The Language of History in the Renaissance: Rhetoric and Historical Consciousness in Florentine Humanism.* Princeton: Princeton University Press.

Suárez de Figueroa, Cristóbal. [1617] 1913. *El pasagero: Advertencias utilísimas a la vida humana*, edited by Francisco Rodríguez Marín. Madrid: Biblioteca Renacimiento.

Téllez, Gabriel. [1621] 1913. *Los cigarrales de Toledo*, edited by Victor Said Armesto. Madrid: Biblioteca Renacimiento.

———. [1635] 1970. *La Peña de Francia.* In *Obras de Tirso de Molina*, vol. 3, edited by María del Pilar Palomo, pp. 117–174. Biblioteca de Autores Españoles, vol. 237. Madrid: Atlas.

Tello, Julio C. 1939. *Las primeras edades del Perú por Guamán Poma: ensayo de interpretación.* Spanish translation of Quechua terms by Toribio Mejía Xesspe. Lima: Museo de Antropología.

———. 1942. *Origen y desarrollo de las civilizaciones prehistóricas andinas.* In *Actas y Trabajos Científicos del XXVII Congreso Internacional de Americanistas (1939).* Vol. 1, pp. 589–720. Lima.

Tercero catecismo y exposición de la doctrina christiana por sermones. [1585] 1773. Lima: Oficina de la Calle de San Jacinto.

Titu Cusi Yupanqui, Diego de Castro. [1570] 1973. *Relación de la conquista del Perú.* Lima: Biblioteca Universitaria.

Todorov, Tzvetan. 1973. "The Notion of Literature." *New Literary History* 5:5–16.

Urioste, Jorge L. 1973. "*Chay Simire Caymi*: The Language of the Manuscript of Huarochirí." Ph.D. diss., Cornell University.

————. 1980. "Estudio analítico del Quechua en la *Nueva Corónica*." In Guaman Poma [1615] 1980:xx–xxxi.

————. 1981. "The Spanish and Quechua Voices of Waman Puma." *Review* 28: 16–19.

Uspensky, Boris. [1970] 1973. *A Poetics of Composition*, translated by Valentina Zavarin and Susan Wittig. Berkeley & Los Angeles: University of California Press.

————. [1973] 1975. " 'Left' and 'Right' in Icon Painting." *Semiotica* 13:33–39.

————. [1970] 1976. "The Language of Ancient Painting." *Dispositio, Revista Hispánica de Semiótica Literaria* 1, no. 3:219–246.

Uspensky, Boris, et al. 1973. "Theses on the Semiotic Study of Cultures." In *Structure of Texts and Semiotics of Culture*, edited by Jan Van Der Eng and Mormir Grygar, pp. 1–28. The Hague: Mouton.

Valesio, Paolo. 1978. "The Practice of Literary Semiotics." *Punto de Contacto/ Point of Contact* 2, no. 1:22–41.

Varallanos, José. 1959. *Historia de Huánuco*. Buenos Aires: Imprenta López.

————. 1979. *Guamán Poma de Ayala: cronista, precursor y libertario*. Lima: G. Herrera.

Vitoria, Francisco de. [1532] 1967. *Relectio de Indis o libertad de los indios*, edited by L. Pereña y J. M. Pérez Prendes. Madrid: Consejo Superior de Investigaciones Científicas.

Volk, Mary Crawford. 1977. *Vicencio Carducho and Seventeenth-Century Castilian Painting*. New York: Garland.

Vološinov. V. N. [1930] 1978. "Reported Speech." In *Readings in Russian Poetics*, edited by Ladislav Matejka and Krystyna Pomorska, pp. 149–175. Ann Arbor: University of Michigan Press.

Wachtel, Nathan. 1973. *Sociedad e ideología: ensayos de historia y antropología andinas*, pp. 165–228. Lima: Instituto de Estudios Andinos.

————. [1971] 1976. *Los vencidos: Los indios del Perú frente a la conquista española (1530–1570)*, translated by Antonio Escohotado. Madrid: Alianza.

————. [1971] 1977. *The Vision of the Vanquished. The Spanish Conquest of Peru through Indian Eyes: 1530–1570*, translated by Ben Reynolds and Siân Reynolds. New York: Harper & Row.

Warnke, Frank J. 1972. *Versions of Baroque: European Literature in the Seventeenth Century*. New Haven: Yale University Press.

Weinberg, Bernard. 1952. "Robortello on the *Poetics*." In *Critics and Criticism, Ancient and Modern*, edited by R. S. Crane, pp. 319–348. Chicago: University of Chicago Press.

————. 1961. *A History of Literary Criticism in the Italian Renaissance*. 2 vols. Chicago: University of Chicago Press.

Welter, Jean Thiébaut. 1927. *L'exemplum dans la littérature religieuse et didactique du Moyen-Age*. Paris: Occitania.

White, Hayden. 1973a. "Interpretation in History." *New Literary History* 4, no. 2:281–314.

————. 1973b. *Metahistory: The Historical Imagination in Nineteenth-Century Europe*. Baltimore: Johns Hopkins University Press.

————. 1976. "The Fictions of Factual Representation." In *The Literature of Fact: Selected Papers from the English Institute*, edited by Angus Fletcher, pp. 21–44. New York: Columbia University Press.

Zárate, Agustín de. [1555] 1947. *Historia del descubrimiento y conquista del Perú*. In *Historiadores primitivos de Indias*. Vol. 2. Biblioteca de Autores Españoles, vol. 26, pp. 459–574. Madrid: Atlas.

Zavala, Silvio. [1947] 1972. *La filosofía política en la conquista de América*. 2d ed. Mexico City: Fondo de Cultura Económica.

Zorrilla, Juan C. 1977. "La posesión de Chiara por los indios Chachapoyas." *Wari* (Instituto Nacional de Cultura, Filial en Ayacucho) 1:49–64.

Index

Acosta, Antonio, 66
Acosta, Padre José de, 150n. 15; as historian, 6, 24, 146n. 7; on lack of miracles in New World evangelization, 31
Adam and Eve, 100, drawing of, 101
Addressee: Andeans as, 50, 139; female Andeans as, 75–77, 160n. 15; Philip III as, 4, 7, 14, 40, 86, 87, 88, 122, 123, 131, 139, 161n. 2; Spaniards as, 51, 58, 70
Admiratio, 156n. 12
Adorno, Rolena: 25, 42, 69, 99, 116, 123, 131, 140–141, 145n. 3, 161n. 15, 162n. 6, 163n. 12, 164n. 1, 165n. 5
Alarcos Llorach, Emilio, 135, 136
Albornoz, Bartolomé de, 48, 49, 154 n. 6
Albornoz, Cristóbal de, 162n. 8
Allegory: definition of, 123, 157n. 17, 165n. 2; as moral teaching, 125, 165n. 3; pictorial, 124, 126–127; related to epic, 157n. 17
Almagro, don Diego de: 14, 29, 95–96, 123, 164n. 15; in drawing, 124
Amplification. *See* Rhetoric, ecclesiastical
Anticlericalism, 86, 105, 128–129
Apo Alanya, *cacique*, 18, drawing of, 20

Apologética historia sumaria (Fray Bartolomé de las Casas), 6, 152n. 24
Archetypes, Andean cultural, 155n. 9
Art, visual: internal viewpoint in, 132, 134; linear and inverse perspective in, 132, 134; in religious and moral persuasion, 81–83, 162n. 4; as superior to verbal art, 81–82
Arte de la pintura: su antigüedad y grandezas (Francisco Pacheco), 81
Arte de los contractos (Bartolomé de Albornoz), 48
Arte y vocabulario en la lengua general del Perú llamada quichua, y en la lengua española, 66
Atahualpa Inca, 29, 44, 88, 114; at Cajamarca, 93, 95, 164n. 15; drawing of, 96; execution of, 73
Auca Runa. *See* Pre-Incaic Andean history, epochs of
Avalos de Ayala, Luis de, 17, 87–88, 149n. 10, 151n. 18. *See also* Guaman Malqui de Ayala, Martín
Ayala, Martín de, Padre, 146n. 5

Bakhtin, Mikhail, 5, 76–77, 128, 131, 146n. 6
Barbarity: as bestial behavior, 152n. 24; definition of, 33, 152n. 24; as lack of writing system, 35

Guaman Poma

Latin American Monographs, No. 68
Institute of Latin American Studies
The University of Texas at Austin

GUAMAN POMA
Writing and Resistance in Colonial Peru

By Rolena Adorno

University of Texas Press, Austin

Second Paperback Printing, 1991

Requests for permission to reproduce material from this work should be sent to
  Permissions
  University of Texas Press
  P.O. Box 7819   Austin, Texas 78713-7819

♾ The paper used in this publication meets the minimum requirements of American National Standard for Information Sciences—Permanence of Paper for Printed Library Materials, ANSI Z39.48–1984.

This publication has been supported by the National Endowment for the Humanities, a federal agency that supports the study of such fields as history, philosophy, literature, and languages.

Library of Congress Cataloging-in-Publication Data

Adorno, Rolena.
  Guaman Poma: Writing and resistance in colonial Peru.

  (Latin American monographs/Institute of Latin American Studies, the University of Texas at Austin; no. 68)
  Bibliography: p.
  Includes index.
  1. Guaman Poma de Ayala, Felipe, fl. 1613. 2. Peru—History—To 1820—Historiography. I. Title. II. Series: Latin American monographs (University of Texas at Austin. Institute of Latin American Studies); no. 68.
F3430.6.G8A63   1986   985'.0072   85-20881
ISBN 0-292-72741-0 pbk.